The ESSENTIAL DICTIONARY of REAL ESTATE

The ESSENTIAL DICTIONARY of REAL ESTATE

LISA HOLTON

BARNES
& NOBLE
BOOKS

NEW YORK

Table of Contents

INTRODUCTION:

Every business has its own language. Yet even though buying, renting or investing in real estate are among the most common transactions people do, the language of real estate is often complicated, antiquated and frightening enough to keep people from making the best decisions with their money.

The Essential Dictionary of Real Estate can help you decipher the complexities of real estate word-by-word. It is organized as a traditional dictionary, referring to related words and concepts through italicized lettering. Alphabetization is letter-by-letter. InfoBoxes help you learn more about various concepts, and listed agencies and associations include phone numbers or websites where you can learn more.

Whether you're renting your first apartment or buying your first piece of investment property to help fund your kids' education or your retirement, this book will help make that process easier.

Barnes & Noble will be updating this dictionary over time to accommodate the fast-paced changes in the world of real estate. If you have suggestions or think we've missed any words or concepts, please e-mail us at Lisa@TheLisaCo.com

— Lisa Holton

The ESSENTIAL
DICTIONARY of
REAL ESTATE

A

abandonment: the voluntary surrendering of property rights but not transferring title to someone else.

abatement: for real estate purposes, a reduction in tax, rent, or utility rates, typically offered as an incentive by landlords or local governments.

abeyance: a lapse in succession during which title to a piece of property is not clearly established.

absentee owner: a landlord who lives elsewhere.

absolute priority rule: the idea that creditors' claims take precedence over shareholders' claims in the event of a liquidation or reorganization.

absolute title: a clear title without any liens or judgments.

absorbed: treated as an expense, rather than passing the cost on to customers. A business that is merged into another company due to an acquisition.

absorption rate: how a developer estimates the expected annual sales or new occupancy of new homes or commercial property. For example, if there are 100 new homes for sale in a given month and 10 sell while another 10 are built, that month's absorption rate is 10 percent.

abstract of judgment: a court judgment filed with the county that creates a lien against a piece of property.

abstract of title search: a historical review of public records to determine whether liens or defects of title exist on a piece of property, to determine any complications that could interfere with clear ownership transfer. Done prior to closing of title on a sale.

abutting: property adjoining or bordering another property.

accelerated amortization: by paying additional principal on a mortgage or other loan, the borrower can shorten the effective term of the loan. As an example, a $100,000, 30-year mortgage at 8 percent interest has a monthly payment of $733.76. By paying an additional $100 a month—thereby accelerating the amortization of the loan—a borrower can reduce the 30-year term of the loan to 20 years. See *additional principal payment.*

accelerated cost recovery system (ACRS): a depreciation method used for most property placed into service from 1981 to 1986. This method allowed assets to be depreciated at a faster rate than had been allowed previously. The *modified accelerated cost recovery system (MACRS)* replaced ACRS for assets placed into service after 1986.

accelerated depreciation: a bookkeeping method that allows a taxpayer to depreciate property more quickly in the early years of ownership.

acceleration clause: a loan provision that allows the lender to declare the entire loaned amount due immediately if the borrower pays late or breaks other covenants.

accession: the right of an owner to have the advantages of property ownership, which include air rights, mineral rights, water (see *riparian*) rights, and man-made improvements.

accessory apartment: a separate apartment created within a single-family home and occupied by a family member or a renter. It is advisable to check with the local zoning board to see if these units are legal before it's time to build.

access right: an owner's right to get to and from his or her property.

accommodating party: the intermediary or facilitator in a *1031* or *like-kind exchange.* This individual or entity holds the property while the exchange is being completed.

account:
(1) a record of financial transactions for an asset or individual, such as at a bank, brokerage, credit card company, or retail store.
(2) generally, an arrangement between a buyer and a seller in which payments are to be made in the future.

accountant: one who is skilled in the practice of accounting or who is in charge of public or private accounts.

accountant's letter: same as *accountant's opinion.*

accountant's opinion: a letter preceding a financial report, written and signed by an independent accountant, which describes the scope of the statement and presents an opinion on the quality of the data presented. Also called *accountant's letter.*

accounting: the systematic recording, reporting, and analysis of financial transactions of a business.

accounting equation: the fundamental balance sheet equation:

assets − liabilities = net worth.

accounting method: the method under which income and expenses are determined for tax purposes. Major accounting methods are the *cash* method and the *accrual* method.

accounting period: the 12-month period that a taxpayer uses to determine federal income tax liability. Unless a taxpayer makes a specific choice to the contrary, his or her accounting period is the calendar year.

account reconciliation: the act of confirming that the balance in one's checkbook matches the corresponding bank statement.

accounts payable: the money that a company owes to vendors for products and services purchased on credit.

accounts receivable: the money owed to a company by a customer for products and services provided on credit. Treated as a current asset on a balance sheet.

account statement: a record of transactions and their effect on account balances over a specified period of time for a given account.

accrual: the recognition of revenue when earned or expenses when incurred regardless of when cash is received or disbursed.

accrual accounting: the most commonly used accounting method, which reports income when earned and expenses when incurred, as opposed to *cash method of accounting*, which reports income when received and expenses when paid.

accrued expense: an expense that is incurred, but not yet paid for, during a given accounting period.

accumulated depreciation: the amount of depreciation expense that's been claimed to date.

acid-test ratio: same as *quick ratio.*

acknowledgment: a declaration, in writing, that a person has acted voluntarily, usually verified by an authorized official.

acquest: to acquire property through purchase.

acquiescence: accepting or complying without objection, thus implying the waiver of the right to legal action.

acquisition: the securing of ownership or controlling interest in a property or other object through either purchase or a merger.

acquisition cost: the total cost of property and the fees incurred in buying it. If the selling price of a property is $100,000 and the fees to buy it totaled $5,700, the total acquisition cost of the property is $105,700.

acquisition debt: debt incurred to acquire, construct, or improve the taxpayer's principal or secondary residence.

acre: a unit for measuring the area of land equal to160 square rods, or 43,560 square feet (4,047 square meters).

ACRS: see *accelerated cost recovery system.*

action: a procedure brought before a court, in the form of a complaint, to demand a legal right, which in real estate would be to repossess or regain certain properties.

action in personam: (*Latin*) a judicial proceeding against a person rather than against the property of that person. It would seek to have that person uphold the terms of a contract, make up for a loss, or provide a service. In common law, it seeks the payment for a debt or damages incurred.

action in rem: (*Latin*) judicial proceedings against property, literally "against the thing." While in legal theory an action in rem occurs only against property, in actuality it consists of a legal action between parties for the purpose of attaching or disposing of property owned by them.

active asset: an asset used in the daily operations of the business.

active income: for purposes of the passive loss rules, income must be divided into three categories: active income, passive income, and portfolio income. Active income is income for which the taxpayer performs services. Examples are wages, salaries, tips, bonuses, and business and partnership income when the taxpayer materially participates in the business or partnership. See *passive income* and *portfolio income*.

active participation: the involvement in real estate ownership and management on a continuing basis, as opposed to engaging a property manager or some other intermediary to handle all the work and details of owning property. Tax laws and lenders provide greater benefits when the owner actively participates in real estate property and rentals. See *sweat equity*.

Act of God: an action occurring without the intervention of man, which could include but not be limited to hurricanes, earthquakes, floods, lightning, etc.

actual notice: the confirmation that the purchaser has been shown all the relevant details of a transaction. These details include all information in the public record relating to the title; liens, surveys, access, air rights, mineral rights, water rights, etc. Actual notice is either express or implied: express notice means that the purchaser was shown all the relevant details; implied notice assumes that the purchaser's knowledge was sufficient to institute investigation and inquiry.

ADA: see *Americans with Disabilities Act*.

addendum: contractual changes or additions. Supplement or addition to a transaction agreement of any kind.

additional principal payment: a payment made in excess of the required monthly payment; therefore, reducing the principal and shortening the term of the loan. See *accelerated amortization*.

add-on-interest: the amount of interest paid on the principal of a loan for the duration of that loan.

adhesion contract: a legally enforceable contract that is offered on a take it or leave it basis, and must be accepted as is, leaving no opportunity for the purchaser to negotiate. Depending on the item, it could put the purchaser at a distinct disadvantage.

ad hoc: (*Latin*) for this; used for the purpose at hand and not considered for a wider application.

ad infinitum: (*Latin*) without end.

adjacent property: property that is close to, but not necessarily touching, another property.

adjoining owners: property owners with property touching a common property and who have a legal right to notification when a zoning variance or change to the common property is being formally considered.

adjoining property: contiguous property sharing a common border.

adjournment of closing: the postponement of closing of title until another day or place. This can occur for various reasons, such as the absence of one party, or incomplete documents.

adjudication: the formal court decision taken in an action which has been brought, reaching a final determination for all parties involved.

adjudication order: the formalized court order. Also referred to as a *decree* or *judgment*.

adjustable-rate mortgage (ARM): a mortgage loan with a periodically adjustable interest rate, reflecting the changes in a specific financial index. ARMs are typically offered with one-, three-, or five-year periods before the rate can change. Before a borrower signs, it is good to know how the interest rate will change when it does—it will usually be tied to Treasury bill rates, but not always. An *interest rate cap* limits the amount by which the interest rate can change when the lock period ends; look for this feature in considering an ARM loan. The following chart illustrates the popularity of ARMs.

adjusted balance method: a technique for calculating finance charges (such as in a bank account, charge account, or credit card account) based on the remaining account balance after adjustments are made for payments and credits during the billing period. Interest charges are usually lower under this method than under other methods, such as average daily balance and previous balance methods.

InfoBox: **FAMILY MORTGAGE ORIGINATIONS, 1990–2001**

	Total Volume (Mil $)	Refi share* (percent)	ARM share** (percent)
1990	458,404	15	28
1991	562,074	31	23
1992	893,681	47	20
1993	1,019,861	52	20
1994	768,748	24	39
1995	639,436	21	33
1996	785,233	29	27
1997	833,650	29	22
1998	1,507,000	50	12
1999	1,285,000	34	22
2000	1,024,000	19	25
2001	2,030,000	57	12

* Refi share is the share of mortgage applications that went to refinancing.

** ARM share is percent of total volume of conventional purchase loans.

Source: HUD Survey of Mortgage Lending Activity, Mortgage Bankers Association of America, Federal Housing Finance Board

adjusted basis: the base price of an asset or security that reflects any deductions taken on or improvements to the asset or security, used to compute the gain or loss when sold.

adjusted book value: the book value on a company's balance sheet after assets and liabilities are adjusted to market value. Property is typically part of this calculation.

adjusted cost basis: a tax-purpose cost measuring method that allows cost to be increased by the cost of capital improvements or reduced due to depreciation. The cost of a home would be increased by the amount paid to install a permanent improvement, such as air conditioning.

adjusted gross income: a federal tax term that refers to the difference between a taxpayer's gross income and adjustments to that income, which may include deductions for individual retirement accounts (IRA) and Keogh pension plans, which may be invested in real estate. Adjusted gross income is the basis for determining the limitations or eligibility of other components, such as miscellaneous expenses (2 percent of AGI), in calculation of taxpayer's tax liability.

adjusted price: price plus accrued interest.

adjusted sales price: the net sales price of a piece of property with the commissions and closing costs deducted from the actual sales price. For appraisal purposes: the price of a comparable piece of property with the differences between it and the property in question, accounted for. For income tax purposes: the sales price of a property reduced by the costs of improvements necessary to bring it to the condition of the comparable property.

adjusted tax basis: the amount used to determine profit or loss from a sale or exchange of property. To determine an adjusted basis for an asset, start with the original cost. Add cost of improvements and assessments to the asset, and subtract deductions taken, such as depreciation and depletion. Example: A property was purchased for $300,000, and the owner made $100,000 of capital improvements. With an accumulated depreciation of $75,000, the adjusted cost basis for tax purposes would be $325,000 ($300,000 + $100,000 - $75,000). If the property was sold for $400,000, the taxable gain would be $75,000.

adjuster: the insurance company employee who settles the value of any damage done to insured property so that the insured owner may be compensated.

adjusting entry: a bookkeeping entry made at the end of an accounting period to correct the data for, and assign income and expenses to, a prior period.

adjustment: a change made in the selling price, purchase price, or payment amount.

adjustment date: the date on which the interest rate changes for an *adjustable-rate mortgage* (*ARM*).

adjustment interval: on an *adjustable-rate mortgage* loan, the adjustment interval is the time when changes in the interest rate or monthly payment are made.

adjustments in appraisal: the change in the value of one particular property based on the value of a comparable property. Adjustment in the appraisal of a comparable property will then affect the value of the original property.

administrator: a court-appointed individual who manages and distributes the estate of a person who has died without a will.

administrator's deed: the deed used by the court-appointed administrator of an estate to transfer property.

adult communities: housing projects specifically designed to meet the needs of mainly older, retired persons with no small children.

ad valorem: (*Latin*) according to value.

ad valorem tax: a tax based on the value of the item being taxed; governments and school districts raise most of their revenues from property taxes.

advance: the increase in the price or market value of real estate, or, most commonly, the money given to someone before it is earned, as in payment for services or good received prior to receipt of it.

adverse land use: the use of real estate contrary to the interests of the property owner.

adverse possession: the acquisition of title to property through possession for a certain period of time set in state law, without knowledge by the owner. Adverse possession is a statute of limitations that prevents a legal owner from claiming title to the land when the owner has done nothing to evict an adverse occupant during the statutory period.

adverse use: the use and access of a certain property without the consent of the owner.

advocacy role: representing the best interests of a client.

aerial photos: photographs of land areas and buildings taken by cameras mounted in airplanes or satellites. Developers, builders, civil engineers, geologists, geographers, and archaeologists use aerial photographs.

aesthetic value: the enhancement of a property's value by appearance or favored location.

affidavit of title: the document in which the seller identifies himself/herself and swears to his/her marital status and that he/she is in possession of the property and certifies that, since the date of the examination of title, there have been no judgments, divorces, unrecorded deeds, unpaid repairs, bankruptcies, or defects in title which are known to him/her.

affidavits: legal documents that prove that the signer understands various important parts of an agreement. A homebuyer will sign a variety of affidavits at *closing.* They include affidavits of occupancy, which state that the signer will use the property as a principal residence. A buyer and seller may have to sign an affidavit stating that all of the improvements to the property required in the sales contract were completed before closing. Lenders can answer questions about these documents before closing.

affirm: to confirm, ratify, verify, and accept a transaction.

affirmation: an alternative to an oath, which can be used by people whose religious beliefs will not allow an oath.

affirmative lending: an effort by banks to make loans and loan assistance more available to particular communities, mainly minorities. It is based on the *Community Reinvestment Act,* and is intended to increase the availability of loan dollars in poorly served neighborhoods.

affordability analysis: a detailed analysis of a borrower's ability to afford the purchase of a home. An affordability analysis takes into consideration income, liabilities, and available funds. It also considers the borrower's ability to pay for a particular type of mortgage and the closing costs associated with it.

affordable housing: the public and private sector movement to help low- and moderate-income people buy homes.

afforestation: creating a forest cover on land area not previously covered with trees, to preserve the ecology and increase the aesthetic value of the land.

A-frame: the outer shape of a structure that has steeply sloped roofs and is in the shape of an "A," hence the name. It is a design more common in vacation homes than primary residences. (*see Appendix A*)

after-completion costs: the expenditures incurred after the completion of a building.

after-tax cash flow: the cash flow (from income-producing property), which is reduced by income taxes resulting from the property's income.

after-tax equity yield: the net return rate, after deduction of interest costs and taxes, on an equity investment in real estate.

after-tax rate of return: the *rate of return* on investment once income taxes are deducted.

age-life depreciation: the depreciation method based on the projected useful life of the property, allowing for normal wear and tear.

agency: the relationship between two people or entities where one is a principal and the other is an agent representing the principal in activities with other parties, such as a real estate agent buying or selling for a client.

agency closing: the use of a *title company* or another firm to complete a loan.

agency disclosure: a law requiring real estate agents to disclose whether they represent the buyer or seller. Laws vary in different states.

agent: a person empowered to act on behalf of another in dealings with third parties.

AGI: see *adjusted gross income*.

agreed boundary: a compromise reached by two property owners to resolve a dispute over borders.

agreement of sale: a document detailing the terms and sale price of a transaction, along with a description of the property and any time limits. A contract obligates the buyer to buy and the seller to sell, and is normally accompanied by a deposit from the buyer.

agricultural property: a property zoned for use in farming, including the raising of crops and livestock.

agricultural use value: the determination of value of agricultural land by taking into consideration the amount of arable land (property not disrupted by trees or overgrowth or untillable terrain), its proximity to an adequate water supply, and the climatic location.

AIA: see *American Institute of Architects*.

air rights: the rights to use the open air space above property. Sometimes used to allow construction of billboards or other signage. Air rights may also allow—or prevent—the construction of entire buildings, such as when a development is constructed over an existing highway.

a la carte real estate service: transactions rendered one at a time instead of a commission-based, full-service relationship.

alienation clause: a mortgage provision requiring that the balance of that loan be repaid in full if the property is sold or transferred.

allegation: a charge, claim, accusation, or statement of a party to an action against a respondent. The allegation establishes the circumstances to be proved in a formal action before the court.

all-inclusive trust deed: a *mortgage (trust deed)* that encompasses all existing mortgages and is subordinate to them.

allocation method: an approach used to allocate the price that is paid for two or more properties and is based on their fair market value rather than appraised value.

allodium: a piece of property that is owned outright with nothing due to another party.

allotment: the allocation of real estate made on an equitable basis to prospective buyers. See *apportionment*.

allowable span: the maximum allowable distance between structural supports.

allowance: an amount of money offered by builders of new homes, to be applied toward the cost of items subject to customer selection, such as lighting fixtures or carpeting.

allowance for depreciation: an accumulated expense that writes off the cost of a fixed asset over its expected useful life.

allowance for vacancy and income loss: when valuing income-producing property, the allowance must be made for the income lost from unoccupied premises.

ALTA title policy: American Land Title Association policy. See *American Land Title Association*.

alteration: a change or modification to a building or structure.

alternative documentation: a method of documenting a loan file that relies on information the borrower is likely to be able to provide instead of waiting on verification sent to third parties for confirmation of statements made in the application.

alternative minimum tax (AMT): a tax designed to prevent taxpayers from escaping a fair share of tax liability by use of certain tax breaks. A taxpayer is subject to this tax if he or she has certain minimum tax adjustments or tax preference items and his or her alternative minimum taxable income exceeds the exemption allowed for his or her filing status and income level. The AMT allows a deduction for interest on mortgage borrowings used to buy, build or improve your home. If you borrowed against your home for some other purpose, the interest deduction isn't allowed under the alternative minimum tax. For more information, go to www.irs.gov.

alternative mortgage: a loan other than a standard fixed-rate mortgage. An alternative mortgage may vary in interest rate, maximum loan amount, or loan-to-value ratio.

amenity: a feature of real property that enhances its attractiveness and increases the occupant's or user's satisfaction even though that feature is not essential to the property's use. Natural amenities include a pleasant or desirable location near water, upgraded landscaping, or scenic views. Human-made amenities include swimming pools, tennis courts, community buildings, and other recreational facilities.

American Institute of Architects (AIA): a professional society of architects founded in 1857 and located in Washington, D.C., with 301 local groups in all 50 states and over 54,000 members; it promotes excellence and professionalism in the field. Phone: 800-242-3837, Web: www.aia.org.

American Land Title Association (ALTA): an organization located in Washington, D.C., with over 2,400 members in 40 states. It was founded in 1906 and fosters uniformity and quality in title abstracts and insurance policies. Its publications are the monthly *Capital Comment*, the bi-monthly *Title News*, and the annual *Directory of Members*. Phone: 800-787-2582, Web: www.alta.org.

American Motel Hotel Brokers (AMHB) Network: an association of real estate brokers who specialize in the sale and purchase of lodging institutions. Phone: 602-230-9244,
Web: www.amhbnetwork.com.

American Planning Association (APA): a non-profit public interest and research organization founded in 1978 to encourage the best techniques and decisions for the planned development of communities and regions. Main offices located in Washington, D.C., and Chicago, IL, it has 30,000 members, with 45 regional groups in the U.S. Phone: 312-431-9100, Web: www.planning.org.

American Society for Testing Materials (ASTM): a non-profit organization of a variety of qualified professionals who decide the level of quality that must be used in building materials for a particular job. A standard is proposed and these professionals either approve it or suggest changes. There is a vote to decide on approval, and then the standard is published and manufacturers are expected to comply. If they do not, they are not given an ASTM number and cannot be used for jobs that require ASTM-approved products. Phone: 610-832-9585, Web: www.astm.org.

American Society of Appraisers (ASA): a society primarily concerned with the advancement of the appraisal profession, including teaching, certifying, and testing. It was founded in 1952 and has 6,000 members. Phone: 703-478-2228,
Web: www.appraisers.org.

American Society of Farm Managers and Rural Appraisers: a society that focuses solely on appraisal of farm and rural properties. Phone: 303-758-3513, Web: www.asfmra.org.

American Society of Home Inspectors (ASHI): a professional association of independent home inspectors. These members must meet the group's education and performance requirements. Phone: 800-743-2744, Web: www.ashi.com.

Americans With Disabilities Act (ADA): a law that makes it illegal to discriminate against a person with a disability, in housing, public accommodations, transportation, employment, government services, and telecommunications. Part of a broad series of laws requiring commercial and residential builders to make construction accommodations for the disabled.

amortizable expenses: certain capital expenses that can be deducted over a fixed period of time. They include start-up expenses, qualified forestation or reforestation costs, goodwill, going-concern value, covenants not to compete, franchises, trademarks, and trade names.

amortization: a regular payment of both principal and interest to pay off a loan. Early in the loan most of the payment is applied toward interest, with increasing amounts paid toward principal as the loan moves toward maturity.

amortization schedule: the schedule that shows the breakdown of each loan payment that consists partly of principal and partly of interest.

amortization tables: mathematical tables showing the monthly payment on a loan.

amortization term: the amount of time required to amortize the mortgage loan. The amortization term is often expressed as a number of months. For example, for a 30-year fixed-rate mortgage, the amortization term is 360 months.

amortize: the gradual elimination of a financial obligation through periodic payments.

amortized mortgage: a mortgage where the interest and principal have been fully repaid by the mortgagee.

amount realized: the amount received by a taxpayer on the sale or exchange of property. The amount received is the sum of the cash and the fair market value of any property or services plus any of the seller's liabilities assumed by the purchaser. Determining the amount realized is the starting point for arriving at realized gain or loss.

anchor bolt: a bolt embedded in concrete that fastens the building frame to the foundation.

anchor tenant: the major tenant in a shopping center that helps the center attract shoppers who benefit the other tenants as well; often a supermarket or department store.

ancillary administrator: an out-of-state or out-of-jurisdiction administrator who is appointed to probate a decedent's property when there is no executor/executrix.

ancillary tenant: in a shopping center, an ancillary tenant is one who occupies less space than an *anchor tenant*. Specialty stores are typical ancillary tenants in a shopping mall.

annexation: a legal process used by a municipality to expand its territory to include part of an adjacent unincorporated area.

annual assessments: the valuation on property for purposes of taxation, sewer charges, etc.

annual cap: the amount the interest rate of an adjustable-rate mortgage can be raised or lowered in any consecutive 12-month period.

annual debt service: the total annual interest and principal loan payments required on a loan.

annualizing: making calculations for a period of less than a year as if the period were a whole year.

annual mortgage constant: the ratio of annual mortgage payments divided by the initial principal of the mortgage; only applies to loans involving constant payment. Annual mortgage constant = annual debt service ÷ mortgage principal.

annual mortgagor statement: the statement sent to borrower, on a yearly basis, detailing principal remaining on the loan and amounts paid toward interest and taxes.

annual percentage rate (APR): the rate a borrower actually pays, including interest, points, and loan origination fees, when expressed as a percentage rate per year. On an *adjustable-rate mortgage*, assumption is made that the loan's index remains the same as its initial value.

annual percentage yield (APY): the real rate of interest on a loan: the coupon rate divided by the net proceeds of the loan. See *effective interest rate.*

annuity: fixed sums paid, at regular intervals, to an investor.

annuity due: an annuity where the payments are made at the beginning of the period, either monthly, quarterly, or yearly.

annuity factor: a calculation that shows the value of a property's income stream.

anticipated holding period: the time period one expects to own property as an investment.

anticipatory breach: a communication—usually by letter—informing the other party that the terms of their original contract will not be fulfilled.

apartment: a unit of one or more rooms within a multifamily complex of similar units.

appeals board: a government entity with the authority to overturn earlier government rules and policy on zoning and other property-related issues.

application fee: the fee paid to the lender at the time of application for a loan. It may include charges for a credit report, property appraisal, etc.

apportionment: a division or assignment based on a plan or proportion, as in prorating property expenses, such as insurance and taxes, between the buyer and seller.

apportionment clause: the contractual provision requiring *apportionment.*

appraisal: the market value of a property or home as supplied by a third party, usually a licensed professional.

appraisal approach: there are three basic methods of valuing property:

- replacement value;
- comparable sales approach—comparing properties with similar properties; and
- appraisal method—determining interest income that a property will return to the investor.

appraisal fee: the fee, charged by a licensed professional, to estimate the *market value* of a piece of real estate.

Appraisal Institute (AI): an organization whose members are professional valuers of real estate. Based in Chicago, the AI's number is (312) 335-4100, website address is www.appraisalinstitute.org.

appraisal of damage: an assessment of property loss, usually done by a professional appraiser or the insurance industry, that takes into account the quality, quantity, and age of a property.

appraisal report: a detailed written report that shows the value of a property, based on the area's recent comparable sales. It also includes a description of the property and structures, street address, zoning allowed, assessed valuation and taxes, best use for the property, and information about the appraiser.

appraised value: a professional opinion of the *market value* of a home or property.

appraiser: a licensed professional permitted to do appraisals and appear as an expert witness in a court of law regarding the evaluating process as well as testimony concerning real estate and market value.

appreciation: the increase in the value of real estate over a period of time.

approval:

(1) a confirmation of an amount able to be borrowed by an individual, based upon assessment of his ability to repay said loan. (2) alternatively, an authorization obtained from governmental authorities for a building project to proceed.

approximate compound yield: the measure of the annualized compound growth of a real estate investment.

appurtenance: an item that is outside the property itself but is considered a part of the property and adds to its enjoyment, such as a *right of way.*

appurtenant structure: a structure not belonging to a property but considered a part of it through the use of an *easement* of common interest.

APR: see annual percentage rate.

aqueduct: a large pipe made for bringing water from a distant source.

arbitration: a dispute-resolving method involving a third-party decision.

arbitrator: a neutral individual brought in to help settle a dispute in business or personal dealings.

arbor:

(1) a latticework structure holding vines or flowers.

(2) alternately, an arbor is a specially planted area filled with trees.

architect: a licensed designer of homes, buildings, and other structures.

architect's punch list: a list of design items needing to be corrected or resolved prior to finalization of a building design.

architectural fees: the fees charged by an architect for services rendered. Charges can be per square footage, hourly, or as a percentage of the projected budget.

area wall: a retaining wall, below grade, around a basement window.

areaway: a below-grade, open space, which allows light or access to a basement door or window.

ARM: see adjustable-rate mortgage.

ARM index: the index used to adjust the interest rates on *adjustable-rate mortgages*. *Treasury-bills* or *prime lending rate* are usually used for this index, which is not controlled by individual lenders.

array: a *tax assessor* term describing a certain category of properties sold within a given amount of time.

arrears: late or overdue payments; in default.

arroyo: a dry ravine, found in arid areas, and formed by water runoff. Not suitable for building as they are prone to flooding when there is significant rainfall.

artesian well: a drilled well with water rising through the opening due to naturally occurring water pressure.

ASA: see *American Society of Appraisers.*

asbestos: a fire-resistant material, formerly used for insulation and some home products, which has been found to be a health hazard and is no longer used.

asbestos cement: fire-resistant cement made of a combination of asbestos fibers and Portland cement.

as-built drawing: a drawing made to show the actual dimensions and locations of installations.

ASHI: see American Society of Home Inspectors.

as-is condition: the transfer of *title* to a property in an existing condition with no *warranties* or representations.

asking price: the seller's initial price asked for a property.

aspect ratio: the ratio between the height of an object and the width.

assess:
   (1) to estimate value.
   (2) alternately, to levy a tax or fee on property.

assessed value: the value placed on a home by a government *tax assessor* in order to calculate a *tax base*.

assessment:
   (1) the estimated value of a piece of property.
   (2) alternately, a *levy* placed on a property in addition to taxes.

assessment cycle: the period of time a municipality allows between valuations of property for tax purposes.

assessment rolls: a list of taxable properties as compiled by the *tax assessor*.

assessor: an official who determines the assessed value of a property.

asset: an item of value, i.e., cash, securities, investments, real estate, etc. Any item of economic value owned by an individual or corporation, especially that which could be converted to cash. Examples are cash, securities, accounts receivable, inventory, office equipment, a house, a car, and other property. On a balance sheet, assets are equal to the sum of liabilities, common stock, preferred stock, and retained earnings.

asset coverage: the extent to which a company's net assets cover its debt obligations and/or preferred stock. Expressed in dollar terms or as a percentage.

asset depreciation range (ADR): a range of depreciable lives allowed by the IRS for a particular asset, which is used to determine class lives for property and equipment.

asset/equity ratio: total assets divided by shareholder equity.

assign: to transfer certain rights to another.

assignment: the transfer of a mortgage from one person to another.

assignment of mortgage: the transfer of a mortgage from the old owner to the new owner. This type of mortgage is an *assumable mortgage*.

assignment of rents: when a borrower gives his or her lender the right to receive rents collected from a tenant in the property owned by the borrower.

assignor: the person transferring rights and interests in a property.

assumable mortgage: a mortgage that can be taken over ("assumed") by the buyer when a home is sold. In most cases, the lender must approve the assumption. An assumption fee is usually paid to the lender—usually by the purchaser of the property—after the assumption of an existing mortgage. A borrower should evaluate the terms and conditions of an assumable mortgage to see if they are more competitive than the terms and conditions of a new mortgage offered by a lender.

assumption: the transfer of the seller's existing mortgage to the buyer. See *assumable mortgage*.

assumption clause: a provision in an assumable mortgage that allows a buyer to assume responsibility for the mortgage from the seller. The loan does not need to be paid in full by the original borrower upon sale or transfer of the property.

assumption fee: the fee paid to a lender (usually by the purchaser of real property) resulting from the assumption of an existing mortgage. The assumption fee is the amount paid to a lender resulting from a buyer taking over the payments on a seller's existing loan. The purchaser of the property usually pays this fee. Buyers pay an assumption fee when they take over the payments on a seller's existing loan.

ASTM: see *American Society for Testing Materials.*

at-risk rules: the tax laws that limit the amount of tax losses an investor—particularly a limited partner—can claim.

attached garage: a garage that is part of the same building as the dwelling.

attic: the space or room just below the roof of a building.

attorney-at-law: an individual who has been admitted to the bar and is allowed to practice law in his/her state and may perform all the services necessary to represent clients.

attorney of record: the attorney whose name appears in the permanent records of a case.

attorney's opinion of title: in some states, attorneys are required to examine the recorded documents relating to title and issue in what's called a "statement of opinion." This document outlines all the details of the attorney's search, the records examined, and what liens exist against the title, if any. This document does not insure against undisclosed defects—*title insurance* is still required.

attornment: an agreement by a tenant to accept a replacement landlord.

attractive nuisance: a feature that has the potential to be attractive and dangerous to children, such as an unfenced swimming pool.

auction market: where property is sold to the highest bidder.

audit: an examination and verification of a company's financial and accounting records and supporting documents by a professional, such as a *Certified Public Accountant*. An IRS examination of an individual or corporation's tax return, to verify its accuracy.

audited financial statements: a company's financial statements that have been prepared and certified by a *Certified Public Accountant*.

auditor: an individual qualified (at the state level) to conduct audits.

auditor's report: a section of an annual report containing an accountant's opinion about the accuracy of its financial statements.

audit trail: a step-by-step record by which financial data can be traced to its source.

automated underwriting: after a borrower completes a loan application with a lender, it is sent to "underwriting" for review. In short, underwriting is the process used to analyze how a borrower has handled credit obligations in the past and whether he has the ability to repay the mortgage he is applying for. That includes a full assessment of income and assets as well.

automatic renewal clause: a provision in an agreement, such as a lease, that allows renewal at the end of its initial term.

automatic sprinkler system: a fire protection system, required in some types of buildings, which is activated automatically by intense heat.

average accounting return: a measure of the return on an investment over a given period, equal to average book value over the duration of the investment.

average collection period: the average time period for which receivables are outstanding. Equal to accounts receivable divided by average daily sales.

average office occupancy: the average number of business days an office is in use.

average price: the price of a home, as figured by totaling the sales prices of the houses sold in an area, and dividing that number by the number of homes.

aviation easement: an easement over private property near an airport, limiting the height of structures or trees.

B

back-end fees: the *commission* received by a syndicator when real estate is sold, typically paid after the investors receive their initial investment plus return.

back-end ratio: lender calculations by which debt (*principal, interest, property taxes, insurance,* and other monthly bills) is compared with gross monthly income.

back taxes: unpaid property taxes.

back title letter: a letter given by the *title company* to an attorney to aid in his or her examination of a title.

back-to-back escrow: arrangements necessary when a person plans the sale of one property and the purchase of another, simultaneously.

backup contract: a second contract to complete a real estate deal if the first one falls through.

bad debt reserve: an amount set aside as reserve for bad debts.

bad debts: business accounts receivable that have been included in income in a prior year that are uncollectible; legally binding debts owed to the taxpayer that are totally worthless and uncollectible; and debts the taxpayer must pay that he or she guaranteed in connection with the business or for a profit may be deductible as bad debts.

bad faith: the intent to deceive from the beginning of a deal or contract.

bad title: a situation where clear ownership is marred by unsettled claims and liens, and that may prevent an owner from selling.

balance: the amount of money in an account, equal to the net of credits and debits at that point in time for that account.

balanced budget: a budget for which current expenditures are equal to or less than income. The concept is often discussed in reference to the federal government.

balance sheet: a statement of financial condition, which lists *assets, liabilities,* and stockholder's *equity.* The *net worth* of an individual is assets minus liabilities. Net worth is important because it determines the *credit-worthiness* of a borrower.

balloon mortgage: a loan that has level monthly payments based on a repayment schedule for a longer term (often 30 years), but that provides for a lump sum payment to be paid at the end of an earliar term (often 5 to 7 years). It is ideal for borrowers who want to sell or refinance a home within seven years and want a low monthly payment during that time. The interest rate paid on a balloon mortgage is usually lower than a comparable 30-year fixed-rate mortgage. Most balloon mortgages do have a refinance option, but it is wise to double-check.

balloon payment: the final lump sum payment of a *balloon mortgage.*

balustrade: a railing on a porch or stairway that is held up by a set of posts. (see *Appendix B*)

bank letter: a letter provided by a bank to another party to document the availability of funds to an individual or business.

bankrupt: being financially insolvent.

bankruptcy: a legal procedure by which an insolvent debtor can be relieved of repayment of certain obligations. Bankruptcies, depending on the type of filing, will remain on a credit report for seven to 10 years. This may become a problem in obtaining financing. For tax purposes, a formal petition filed in a bankruptcy court under Chapter 7, 11, 12, or 13 of Title 11 of the U.S. Code.

InfoBox: BANKRUPTCY FOR INDIVIDUALS

There are two types of personal bankruptcy filings.

Chapter 7: the most common for individuals. With this type of bankruptcy, most debts are wiped out. Yet state law becomes very important on the issue of whether individuals can keep real estate. Florida, for instance, allows filers to keep their homes. Others only allow a small amount of home equity to be exempt. Once the filer has been legally cleared of debts, Chapter 7 bankruptcies stay on a credit record for 10 years. Eventually, filers may qualify for new consumer loans, but they will never qualify for the best rates.

Chapter 13: also known as reorganization. The Chapter 13 debtor agrees to a repayment plan over a number of years. The real estate advantage is that Chapter 13 filers are allowed to retain some secured debt, such as a home or a car. Also, a Chapter 13 bankruptcy will be listed on the debtor's credit report for seven years instead of 10.

Bankruptcy will get tougher: at publication time, it was expected that lawmakers in Washington would make filing bankruptcy much tougher. Current legislation would have Chapter 7 filers meet a means test that would effectively force many Chapter 7 filers into Chapter 13 filings requiring more debts to be repaid.

---

baseboard: a strip or molding covering the joint of the wall and the floor. (see *Appendix B*)

baseboard heat: a heating unit, installed along the floor.

base loan amount: the total amount used to figure loan payments. If *closing costs* are financed, they are added to the base loan amount.

base rent: a monthly fixed rental payment, not including utilities.

basis: the amount assigned to an asset from which gain or loss is determined for income tax purposes when the asset is sold. For assets acquired by purchase, basis is cost. Special rules govern the basis of property received by virtue of another's death or by gift, the basis of stock received on a transfer of property to a controlled corporation, the basis of the property transferred to the corporation, and the basis of property received upon the liquidation of a corporation.

basis point: a unit of measure for the change in interest rates. One basis point equates to one percent of one percent, 0.01.

batt insulation: fiber or wool insulation in sheet form, usually with a paper lining, sold in large rolls.

Bauhaus style: the houses in this early twentieth century German style of architecture had no decoration and were smooth blocks constructed of steel, reinforced concrete, with integral walls of glass.

bay window: a window jutting out from the face of a wall.

beam: a long, straight piece of material, usually wood, used as a support in building.

bearer: the legal owner of a piece of property.

before-and-after rule: in the case of *eminent domain*, a property to be taken by the government is appraised before and after the taking.

before-tax cash flow: cash flow before making income tax payments or adding income tax benefits.

before-tax income: total income prior to deduction of taxes.

below the line: out-of-the-ordinary, non-recurring revenues or charges.

beneficial interest: a unit of ownership in a real estate investment trust.

beneficial use: the right of peaceful enjoyment of property by one party while the legal title is held by another. This is applicable when rental property is involved.

beneficiary: one who inherits the value of insurance policies and investment funds after the owner dies.

bequeath: pass property or personal effects to another through a *will*.

bequest: a gift by *will* of personal property. A bequest is not includable in the income of the recipient. *Basis* is usually set at the value of the property at the decedent's death. If a bequest of money is to be paid at intervals through property, it is taxable income to the recipient.

berm: a mound of earth, built to divert the flow of water during high water stages.

biannual: occuring twice a year. Also called *semiannual*.

bid: the stated price given to perform a job.

bidding war: multiple offers to purchase a piece of property or a house, or competition between realtors for the *listing* of a property or house.

bid out: prices that are obtained by contractors from subcontractors so that they can estimate the building cost of a house or project, prior to construction.

biennial: occurring every two years.

bifold door: a door composed of panels that are hinged vertically in the middle, which fold back upon themselves.

bilateral contract: a reciprocal contract in which the parties involved give mutual promises.

bi-level: a home built on two levels, often with the garage and storage or recreation room in the lower level and the balance of the home in the upper level. Homes of this style were built after 1950. (*see Appendix A*)

billing cycle: the period between billings for products and services, usually a month.

bill of assurance: a written guarantee of certain provisions, such as the size of individual homes, architectural standards, and quality of materials.

binder:
(1) an agreement, prior to *contract*, between buyer and seller.
(2) alternately, the report which is issued by a *title insurance* company detailing conditions of a home's title and giving guidelines for the title insurance policy.

binding arbitration: the judgment made by an independent third party to settle a dispute between two other parties; may be either voluntary or compulsory.

biweekly payment mortgage: a *mortgage* that requires payments to reduce the debt every two weeks (instead of the standard monthly payment schedule). The 26 (or possibly 27) biweekly payments are each equal to one-half of the monthly payment that would be required if the loan were a standard 30-year fixed-rate mortgage, and they are usually drafted from the borrower's bank account. The result for the borrower is a substantial savings in interest. Borrowers can qualify for a 30-year monthly payment amount but get a loan that pays off in approximately 22 years at current interest rates.

blanket insurance policy: an insurance policy covering multiple persons or pieces of property.

blanket mortgage: a *mortgage* that covers more than one parcel of real estate.

blended loan: mortgage refinancing in which the new interest rate takes into account the interest rate on the prior loan and the prevailing current market rate.

blended rate: the interest rate of a *blended loan*, which exceeds the rate on the old loan but is less than the rate on new loans.

blind entries: bookkeeping entries that show debits and credits but neglect to record other essential information.

blind pool: a *limited partnership* in which the specific properties are chosen by the *general partner*, after the funds become available.

blind pool syndicate: money raised by a promoter and placed into a fund prior to selection of investment properties.

blind trust: appointing a fiduciary to manage finances; used in cases where a conflict of interest is possible.

blockbusting: the illegal act of inducing homeowners to sell their homes or properties by representing that persons of another race are entering the neighborhood.

blown-in insulation: insulation that is inserted into walls or other areas by being "blown in." Commonly used in attic floors or other areas that are inaccessible for normal installation.

blueprint: a house plan that a builder follows.

blue sky laws: the state statutes that protect the public against securities frauds of real estate companies. These include regulations over the licensing of brokers, registrations, and new securities, and formal approvals by applicable government agencies.

board of appeals: a governmental body that reviews property tax assessments procedures.

board of directors: the people chosen by the shareholders to manage the enterprise.

board of equalization: a state board that ensures that local property taxes are assessed uniformly.

board of Realtors®: a local group of real estate brokers who are members of the State and National Association of Realtors®. They meet regularly to help determine licensing requirements as well as managing the multiple listing service of their area.

board of trustees: an appointed or elected body overseeing the management of an organization and rendering advice on issues. They are legally responsible for their decisions.

boilerplate: form language used in legal papers, such as deeds and mortgages, before they are individualized with personal details.

bona fide: (*Latin*) referring to persons or actions that are in good faith and honest.

bona fide purchaser: buyer who is acting in good faith.

bond: an agreement insuring one party against loss by actions or defaults of another.

bond for title (deed): a property sales contract that is mutually binding on both parties, where the title remains with the seller until the buyer pays the purchase price. It conveys the title once certain contract terms are satisfied.

bonus room: a room that can be used in many different ways, with no designated function, i.e. as kitchen or bedroom.

bookkeeping: the systematic recording of a company's financial transactions.

book profit: same as *paper profit*.

books: a company's accounting records, such as ledgers and journals.

book value: the value of an asset as it appears on a balance sheet, equal to cost minus accumulated depreciation. Book value often differs substantially from market price, especially in knowledge industries such as high-tech.

boot: cash or property of a type not included in the definition of a nontaxable exchange. The receipt of boot will cause an otherwise tax-free transfer to become taxable to the extent of the lesser of the fair market value of the boot or the realized gain on the transfer.

Examples of nontaxable exchanges that could be partially or completely taxable due to the receipt of boot include transfers to controlled corporations and like-kind exchanges.

borough: a section of a city having authority over local matters.

borrower risk: liabilities assumed by a borrower, such as loss of financial ability to repay a mortgage loan; rising interest rates on adjustable-rate loans; or home devaluation.

bottom line: same as *net profit*.

bottom plate: the bottom horizontal support for the studs.

bracket: a support, for a shelf or another structure, often against a wall.

breach: the violation of a law or obligation through commission or omission so that the responsibilities of an agreement or guarantee are not met.

breach of contract: the failure to fulfill the terms of a contract, without legal, excusable reasons.

breach of covenant: the failure to fulfill a legal agreement.

breach of warranty: the inability on the part of the seller to pass along *clear title* to a buyer.

break-even point: where total revenue equals total costs and there is no profit or loss, such as when an owner's rental income matches expenses and debt.

brick row house: a nineteenth century style of town house, made of brick, sharing common walls with other row houses.

bridge loan: a form of second trust that is collateralized by the borrower's present home (which is usually for sale) in a manner that allows the proceeds to be used for closing on a new house before the present home is sold. Also known as *swing loan*.

broker: a person who acts as a conduit between two parties. A *real estate broker* is licensed to handle property transactions. A *mortgage broker* matches, for a specific fee, borrowers to lenders and loan programs.

brokerage:
(1) the bringing together of two parties in exchange for a fee or commission.

(2) Also, a company or firm employing agents acting as brokers.

broker price opinion: a real estate broker's estimate of the price he or she can get for a property. When interviewing real estate brokers or agents, sellers may want several opinions before they agree to put their property on the market.

broker's agreement: a contract to act on behalf of a principal in selling real estate, wherein the principal agrees to pay a commission to the broker when a buyer is produced who is prepared to meet the terms of the sale.

brownstone: a nineteenth-century row house, usually having four to five stories with a front staircase from the street leading to the first floor. They share common walls with other brownstones. (*see Appendix A*)

BTU (British thermal unit): a measurement of heat or cooling. One Btu is the quantity of heat required to raise the temperature of one pound of water by one degree Fahrenheit.

budget: an itemized forecast of an individual's or a company's income and expenses expected for some period in the future.

budget deficit: the amount by which a government, company, or individual's spending exceeds its income over a particular period of time. Also called deficit or deficit spending. Opposite of budget surplus.

budgeting: the estimation of all income and expenses for an accounting period or for financial forecasting, planning, and controlling.

buffer strip or zone: a piece of land separating two or more properties from each other.

buildability: whether or not a home or other structure can be constructed on a piece of land.

builder breakdown method: a complete estimate of all costs in construction, including but not limited to land acquisition, material, labor, and preparation.

builder upgrades: better material or extras that are offered by the builder to the purchaser.

builder warranty: a limited-time warranty (one or two years) against defect, which is offered by builders to new homebuyers.

building capitalization rate: the rate of return of capital invested in building improvements.

building code: the laws that control the construction or remodeling of homes or other structures. A municipal or state ordinance which is enforceable under the police powers of the state and locality controlling *alterations*, construction methods and materials, size and *setback* requirements, use, and occupancy of all structures. Building codes have specific regulations covering all aspects of construction and are designed to maximize the health and welfare of the residents.

building density: the concentration (amount) of buildings in a given geographic area.

building inspector: an employee of a city or county who enforces building codes and ensures that construction is being performed correctly.

building life: the estimated useful life of a building.

building line:
(1) the guidelines limiting distance from the street or adjacent property a home or structure can be erected. Line established by a building or zoning code beyond which a building structure may not extend.
(2) alternately, the outer edge of the *rafter plate*.

building loan agreement: a loan agreement where a lender gives money to a builder at varying stages of construction; also referred to as a *construction loan*.

building moratorium: an enforced halt to construction, used to slow the rate of development in a town.

building permit: a permit, issued by local government, allowing construction or renovation of a house or other structure.

building residual technique: an appraisal method for determining a building's value on the basis of the residual building income after adjusting for land value.

building restrictions: the regulations limiting the type of use allowed on a piece of property.

building setback: a municipal ordinance stating the distance from a curb or property line where a building can be located.

build-to-suit: a situation where a landowner offers to build a specific structure on a site for a potential tenant and then lease the land and building to that tenant. This is done primarily for commercial property.

built-ins: appliances or other items that are permanently attached and framed into a home.

bullet loan: intermediate debt (five to 10 years) without periodic payments but with the entire amount (*balloon payment*) due at the maturity date.

bundle of rights: the various interests or rights an owner has in a property.

bungalow: a small one-story house or cottage, which often has either an open or enclosed front porch. The bungalow became the most common building style in the United States between the world wars. (*see Appendix A*)

Bureau of Land Management: the federal agency that oversees management of much of the government's undeveloped land. Web: www.blm.gov.

burned-out tax shelter: an aging tax shelter where depreciation deductions have grown smaller over time.

burn rate: for a company with negative cash flow, the rate of that negative cash flow, usually per month.

business-use property: a property used for the production of income. Examples include rental houses, machinery, factories, office buildings, and similar items.

buy-back: an agreement to sell real estate with a pre-arranged agreement to reverse the deal at an established price.

buydown mortgage: a home loan where the lender receives an up-front premium payment and, in return, reduces the interest rate during the early years of a mortgage.

buyer costs, other: see *other buyer costs.*

buyer's broker: the real estate broker who represents only the buyer's interests in a transaction and whose commission is paid by either the buyer or through the seller or listing broker, at closing.

buyer's market: a real estate market in which the buyers have the advantage over the builder due to slow sales.

buying power: the financial ability of a business or individual to afford a purchase; the worth of the dollar in real terms considering inflation.

buying power index (BPI): the average of income, retail revenue, and population of a locality as a percentage of the entire United States, which reflects the economic status of that region.

buy-out estimate: the estimated price at which one partner in a partnership can buy out another partner. Market comparisons, appraisals, or multiyear projections of market appreciation can be used to develop a buy-out amount.

buy-sell agreement: an agreement where the partners consent to purchase the interest of those leaving the partnership and those leaving consent to sell their interests to the other partners. Important in the event of death or disability of one or more partners, as well as other occurrences.

bylaws: *homeowners' association* rules and regulations governing activities in certain types of home communities, *condominiums*, and *townhouses*.

C

cadastral map: a map within a jurisdiction which shows the boundary lines and ownership of all real estate in the area.

CADD: also called *Computer Aided Design and Drafting*, a graphics program used on computers so that architectural drawing can be done in two or three dimensions.

CAGR: see *compound annual growth rate.*

calendar year: a year that ends on December 31.

California bungalow: a small, one-story early-20th-century house. See *bungalow.*

California ranch: see *ranch house*

call option/provisions: a loan agreement clause allowing the lender to ask for the balance due at any time.

cancellation clause: the details under which each party may terminate an agreement.

cap: a consumer safeguard that limits the amount the interest rate on an adjustable-rate mortgage can change in an adjustment interval and/or over the life of the loan. For example, if a per-period cap is 1 percent and a borrower's current rate is 5 percent, his newly adjusted rate must fall between 4 and 6 percent no matter what the change is in the *index* the lender uses to set rates.

capacity: the ability of lenders to know if a borrower is able to pay the debt he or she occurs. Lenders base their evaluation on employment and wage information as well as credit history. Much of this latter data is available electronically through each borrower's *credit report.*

Cape Cod: a style of wood-frame house with a central entrance and a steep roof. Cape Cods have one or two stories, often with bedrooms on the first floor; when they have a second story, they usually have dormer windows. *(see Appendix A)*

capital:
(1) the money used to create income, either as an investment in a business or an income property.

(2) the money or property comprising the wealth owned or used by a person or business enterprise.

(3) the accumulated wealth of a person or business.

(4) the net worth of a business represented by the amount by which its assets exceed liabilities.

When lenders review the "capital" portion of a borrower's loan application, they will be reviewing whether he has enough cash for a down payment and to pay closing costs. It's generally recommended that borrowers shouldn't spend every last dime, because there will be a significant need for cash after the borrower moves in.

capital appreciation: an increase in the market price of an asset.

capital assets: assets purchased for use over long periods of time, such as land and buildings, rather than for resale; can be fixed assets consisting of tangible assets, such as plants and equipment, and intangible assets, such as patents.

capital expenditure: the money spent on improvements on a property, which become part of the cost of an existing fixed asset. They generally may be depreciated or amortized.

capital gain: the investment profit made from the sale of investments or real estate.

capital gain distributions: the amounts paid by mutual funds, regulated investment companies, and *real estate investment trusts.* These amounts represent the shareholder's portion of gain from the sale of capital assets owned by these investment companies. Capital gain distributions are taxed in the year constructively received, and are always considered to be held long term.

capital gain or loss holding period: the length of time a capital asset is owned by the taxpayer. Assets owned 12 months or less are held short-term; those owned more than 12 months are held long-term.

capital gains tax: the taxes placed on profits from the sale of investments or real estate.

capital growth: same as *capital appreciation.*

capital improvement: an improvement made to boost the useful life of a property or add to its value. Major repairs, such as the replacement of a roof, are capital improvements. The costs of capital improvements to business property must be capitalized and may be depreciated.

capital investment: the money paid to purchase a capital asset or a fixed asset.

capitalization: a mathematical formula used by investors to compute the value of a property based on net income.

capitalization rate: the percentage rate of return estimated from the net income of a piece of property. Value = annual income ÷ capitalization rate.

capitalize: recording of an expenditure having a benefit of more than one year to the cost of a property, such as a new kitchen or new roof. Upon sale of the property, the gain or loss, for tax purposes, is the difference between the selling price and the adjusted cost basis. If used for business, depreciation on the capital improvements may be deductible for tax purposes.

capitalized cost: an equipment valuation used in depreciation calculations.

capitalized interest: the interest that is not immediately expensed, but instead is treated as an asset and amortized over time in the income statement.

capital liability: an obligation used to purchase fixed assets or to fund a specific project.

capital loss: the loss from the sale or exchange of a capital asset. Based on current law, up to $3,000 of net capital loss is deductible annually, with the excess carried forward to future years. Losses on personal-use assets are not deductible.

capital net worth: same as *net worth*.

capital recapture: the return of invested principal, excluding earned income or collection of a previously written-off bad debt.

capital recovery: the amount of an investment, made in real estate, which is recovered.

capital resource: any asset used in the production of products and/or services.

capital turnover: the number of times a given amount of capital assets turn over to generate sales over a given period of time.

cap rates (CAPS): the maximum interest rates a borrower might pay for an adjustable-rate mortgage.

carpenter: a craftsman skilled in woodwork, especially of the structural kind.

carpenter ant: an ant that gnaws and nests in wood. Nests are commonly found in porch pillars, window sills, and wood in contact with soil.

carryback/carryover: provisions in the tax code that allow certain losses or credits to be used in a tax year other than the tax year incurred. A carryover is to a future year. A carryback is to a prior year.

carryback financing: the financing of a property where a note, for a set amount, is held by the seller of the property.

carryover basis: the basis for the valuation of property, for tax purposes, acquired from a decedent.

casement window: a window that is hinged on the side, allowing it to swing open outward. A quadrant gear forces a lever to open and close the window when the crankshaft, attached to a gear that turns the quadrant gear, is turned. Windows will be held in any position by the gearing, which often can also be operated by remote control.

cash: currency and coins on hand, bank balances, and negotiable money orders and checks.

cash accounting: the keeping records of money received or expended.

cash asset ratio: same as *cash ratio*.

cash basis: a cash-based transaction. Generally cash basis bookkeeping is simpler than *accrual basis* bookkeeping, but makes securing financing more difficult.

cashbook: an accounting book that documents both cash receipts and disbursements.

cash budget: a forecast of estimated cash receipts and disbursements for a specified period of time.

cash control: the procedures used to verify the accuracy of cash receipts and disbursements.

cash conversion cycle: same as *cash cycle*.

cash cycle: the length of time between the purchase of raw materials and the collection of accounts receivable generated in the sale of the final product. Also called *cash conversion cycle*.

cash earnings: cash revenues minus cash expenses. This differs from earnings in that it does not include noncash expenses such as depreciation.

cash equity: the amount, in cash, invested in property.

cash equivalency: the price for which real estate would be sold if all cash was involved.

cash equivalent doctrine: generally, a cash-basis taxpayer does not report income until cash is constructively or actually received. Under the cash equivalent doctrine, cash-basis taxpayers are required to report income if the equivalent of cash (property, for example) is received in a taxable transaction.

cash flow: the income remaining on a rental property after the operating expenses and loan payment are deducted from the gross rental.

cash flow statement: the financial records of receipts and expenditures during a specific period. A summary of a company's cash flow over a given period of time.

cash journal: a journal where all transactions are initially recorded.

cash method of accounting: one of the two most common methods of accounting, the other being *accrual accounting*. Under the cash method of accounting, income is reported in the tax year it is actually or constructively received and expenses are deducted in the tax year they are paid.

cash out: any cash received at the time of a new loan beyond the balance of the mortgage, awarded based on the existing equity in the house. The cash out amount is calculated by subtracting the sum of the old loan, and fees from the new mortgage loan and is available for all types of property.

cash-out refinance: a refinance transaction in which the amount of money received from the new loan exceeds the total of the money needed to repay the existing first mortgage, closing costs, points, and the amount required to satisfy any outstanding subordinate mortgage liens. In other words, a refinance transaction in which the borrower receives additional cash that can be used for any purpose.

cash ratio: the total dollar value of cash and marketable securities divided by current liabilities. Also called liquidity ratio or cash asset ratio.

casualty: the complete or partial destruction of property resulting from an identifiable event of a sudden, unexpected, or unusual nature.

casualty loss: a casualty is the complete or partial destruction of property resulting from an identifiable event of a sudden, unexpected, or unusual nature. Examples are floods, storms, fires, earthquakes, and auto accidents. Individuals may deduct a casualty loss only if the loss is incurred in a trade or business, in a transaction entered into for profit, or is a personal loss arising from a disaster such as those mentioned above.

caveat emptor: (*Latin*), let the buyer beware, meaning that the prospective buyer must examine the property thoroughly and buy at his or her own risk.

CD-Indexed (Certificate of Deposit) ARMs: the Certificate of Deposit Index represents the weekly average of secondary market interest rates on six-month negotiable CDs. The initial interest rate and payments adjust every six months after an initial six-month period. ARMs with this index typically come with a per-adjustment cap of 1 percent and a lifetime rate cap of 6 percent.

cease and desist order: a judicial order prohibiting a person or business from doing something; usually issued by the court when unlawful activity is occurring.

cease and desist petition: a notice filed by a homeowner, which notifies the Secretary of State that a certain premises is not for sale, and puts *real estate brokers* on notice that the premises has no implied invitation to be solicited.

ceiling (ARM): the maximum allowable interest rate of an *adjustable-rate mortgage*.

ceiling rate: a controlled or administered price, which is set for property by a federal or local agency, usually in extraordinary circumstances.

census tract: a geographic area mapped out by the U.S. government for demographic data, which may be of interest to developers and other businesses.

CERCLA: see *Comprehensive Environmental Response, Compensation, and Liability Act*.

certificate: official, written documentation certifying that the fulfillment of certain requirements has occurred on a certain date.

certificate of beneficial interest: a document stating that someone has an ownership interest but not direct control, in an asset, business, or estate.

Certificate of Deposit (CD): a document representing that the bearer has a specified amount of money on deposit in a financial institution.

Certificate of Deposit Index: an index based on the *interest rates* on six-month *CD*s. Is often used to determine the interest rate on *adjustable-rate mortgages*.

Certificate of Eligibility: a document issued by the Veterans Administration to qualified veterans that verifies a veteran's eligibility for a VA-guaranteed loan. Obtainable through a local VA office by submitting form DD-214 (Separation Paper) and VA form 1880 (request for Certificate of Eligibility).

Certificate of Occupancy (CO): a document issued by the building department of the town, stating that the house has met all of the building codes and is habitable.

certificate of sale: a document issued by the court at a judicial sale, entitling the purchaser to receive a deed once the court approves the purchase.

certificate of title: a written opinion of the status of title to a property, given by an attorney or title company. This certificate does not offer the protection given by *title insurance.*

Certificate of Veteran Status: a *Federal Housing Administration* form filled out by the VA to establish a borrower's eligibility for an FHA Vet loan. Obtainable through a local VA office.

certification: a written statement of the correctness and reliability of something; written permission to do something.

Certified Assessment Evaluator (CAE): the credential awarded by the International Association of Assessing Officers to appraisers of real estate working for a government body.

certified historic structure: a structure listed on the National Register of Historic Places or located in a designated historic area. The IRS Code provides tax incentives for the rehabilitation of such structures.

Certified Public Accountant (CPA): an individual who has received state certification to practice accounting.

cession deed: a deed used to transfer property rights to a governmental authority.

CFA®: see *Chartered Financial Analyst.*

chain of title: the chronological order of conveyance of a property from the original owner to the present owner. Must be established before a lender will award a loan to a borrower.

chair rail: a wood molding separating the lower wall from the upper wall. It is so named because it prevents chair backs from scraping the wall.

change frequency: the adjustment schedule of an *adjustable-rate mortgage.*

change in accounting method: a change from one method to another, which usually requires prior approval from the IRS. A change generally requires adjustments to avoid omissions or duplications.

change in accounting period: a change from one period to another. Income for the short period created by the change must be annualized to calculate the tax for that period.

change order: any modification of a construction contract, which is signed by the owner, the architect, and the contractor. This would authorize a change in work, the amount of the contract, or a change in the contract time.

Chapter Seven (7): a type of *bankruptcy* filing, a provision of the 1978 Bankruptcy Reform Act, which provides for a person's property to be divided among creditors to satisfy unpaid debts.

Chapter Eleven (11): a type of *bankruptcy* filing allowing restructuring and reorganization of existing debts, which is used most often by businesses. Creditors must vote on a debt-paying plan and a judge must approve it.

Chapter Thirteen (13): a type of *bankruptcy* filing in which a person's obligations are paid back within a three-year period, allowing the obligated party to restructure and pay off debts without liquidating assets, particularly property.

charge off: same as *bad debt*.

Chartered Financial Analyst (CFA®): an individual who has passed an exam that measures fundamental knowledge of investment principles at a professional level. The CFA exam is administered annually in more than 70 nations worldwide. It is administered by the Association for Investment Management and Research (AIMR) is an international, nonprofit organization of more than 50,000 investment practitioners and educators in over 100 countries.

chart of accounts: a list of all account names and numbers used in a company's general ledger.

chattel: an item of personal property that is not affixed to the land or building; generally not included in the sale of property.

chimney: a vertical, noncombustible structure, extending above the roof, that carries smoke and other gases from combustion. (see *Appendix B*)

city plan: a large-scale map of an urban area detailing land use, which is essential for projecting the growth and development of the urban area.

civil action: a legal proceeding instituted by one party to exercise a right in a disagreement between individuals or businesses.

civil court: the state court where civil disagreements are decided by a judge or jury.

civil engineering: the specialization in the design of structures: buildings, bridges, etc.

civil law: the law involving noncriminal issues such as breach of contract, libel, accidents, etc.

cladding: material used for the outside covering of walls. (see *Appendix B*)

clapboard: a type of siding with long, narrow boards thicker on one side than the other. (see *Appendix B*)

Class A, B, and C properties: descriptions of various commercial properties based on their attractiveness—and pricing—in the marketplace.

- **Class A** buildings are well designed and situated, and sought after by top tenants. Class A buildings are one step down from *trophy buildings,* considered the most desirable of all commercial properties.
- **Class B** buildings are clean spaces without many amenities. They lack architectural flair and aren't in the most desirable locations.
- **Class C** buildings are usually unfinished spaces with only the basics in utilities and security; a draw for low-to-moderate income tenants who need affordable space and are willing to invest *sweat equity* in the project.

class action: a lawsuit brought by one or more persons of a large group for the benefit of all members of that group.

classified property tax: the tax rate that varies depending on the usage of the property in question.

cleaning deposit: a nonrefundable fee to pay for the painting and cleaning of an apartment or office after a tenant vacates the premises.

clear title: the title to property without liens, defects, or legal encumbrances of any kind.

closed-end lease: a lease with monthly payments over a given period of time with no charge when the lease expires. At the expiration of the lease, the lessor sells the leased property for a gain or a loss.

closed-end mortgage: a mortgage in which the collateralized property cannot be used as security for another loan.

closed mortgage: a mortgage in which the collateralized property cannot be used as security for another loan.

closing: the successful conclusion of a real estate transaction. It includes the signing of legal documents and the disbursement of the funds necessary to the sale of a home or loan transaction. See *settlement.*

closing agent: someone who coordinates the closing meeting and keeps track of the documents while the borrower and his representative sign the papers.

closing costs: the expenses (over and above the price of the property) incurred by buyers and sellers in transferring ownership of a property. Closing costs normally include an origination fee, an attorney's fee, taxes, an amount placed in escrow, and charges for obtaining title insurance and a survey. Before a property can be transferred from one owner to another, closing costs must be paid. Closing costs vary according to the area of the country. These costs may run anywhere from 3 percent to 6 percent of the total amount of the mortgage.

closing date: after a lender has approved a mortgage and the borrower accepts the commitment letter, the next step is to set a closing date. Many times, a real estate sales professional coordinates the setting of this date with the buyer, the closing agent, and the lender.

closing entry: the final bookkeeping entries made at the end of an accounting period to transfer income and expense items to the balance sheet accounts.

closing escrow: all of the conditions of the purchase and sale agreement have been fulfilled and the escrow agent has prepared a written summary of the funds received in escrow and those funds are now paid out.

closing of title: when a property's title has been fully investigated and it is confirmed that there are no problems that would prevent transfer to a new owner, closing of title is the legal procedure in which property ownership is transferred.

closing statement: see *HUD-1 Settlement Statement.*

cloud on title: any conditions revealed by a title search that adversely affect the title to real estate. Usually clouds on title cannot be removed except by a quitclaim deed, release, or court action.

CMO REIT: a *real estate investment trust* that invests in *collateralized mortgage obligations.*

co-brokerage: two or more authorized brokers who agree to cooperate together in representing a principal for the completion of a real estate sale.

code: an organized set of rules and regulation on a particular subject; often an accumulation of laws in a particular area of interest.

code of ethics: a statement of ethical behavior guidelines, which govern the day-to-day activities of a profession or organization.

codicil: an addition to a will, adding, subtracting, or clarifying provisions of the document.

COFI: see *cost of funds index.*

coinsurance: coverage involving the use of two or more insurers. Policy that states the minimum percentage of value to be insured in order to collect the full amount of loss. Policyholders must buy insurance in an amount equal to the value of the improvements to their property. Arrangement where the insured and insurer share on a proportional basis the payment for a loss.

coinsurance clause: a provision in an insurance policy that "caps" the insurer's liability by stipulating that the owner of the property that has experienced damage must have another policy that covers usually 80 percent of the cash value of the property at the time of damage, in order to collect the full amount insured.

collar beam: a horizontal beam near the top of a rafter system attached to the rafters. (see *Appendix B*)

collateral: assets (such as a home) pledged as security for a debt.

collateralized mortgage obligations (CMO): a security backed by a pool of mortgage loans of various classes and maturities and often packaged into *REITs*.

collateral loan: a loan secured by the pledge of specific collateral, such as borrowing $20,000 against a savings account of $50,000.

collateral security: additional security supplied by borrower to obtain a loan.

collection: a series of steps by a lender taken to bring a delinquent mortgage current.

Colonial: see *New England Colonial* and *Southern Colonial*.

color of title: unclear indications of ownership rights, which supplement a claim to title of property but do not actually establish it.

co-maker: a person who signs a promissory note along with the borrower. A co-maker's signature guarantees that the loan will be repaid, because the borrower and the co-maker are equally responsible for the repayment. See *endorser*.

combined financial statement: a financial statement covering multiple related or affiliated companies.

comfort letter: an accounting firm's statement provided to a company preparing for a public offering, confirming that unaudited financial data in the prospectus follows *GAAP*, and that no significant changes have occurred since the report was prepared.

commercial acre: an acre of property zoned for business income–producing purposes.

commercial bank: a financial institution, providing business loans, credit cards, checking and saving accounts, etc. Commercial banks are the largest financial intermediaries directly involved in the financing of real estate.

commercial broker: a real estate broker who specializes in the listing and selling of commercial property such as businesses, industrial, apartments, office buildings, etc.

commercial listing: lists of business properties.

commercial property: a business property, such as office buildings, medical centers, hotels, stores, etc., which are intended to operate with a profit.

commercial real estate: real estate usable in a trade or business.

commingling: the mixing together of money, held in trust for one reason, with other money.

commission: the money paid to real estate agents on the sale of a home, usually a negotiable percentage of the sale price.

commission split: the method for dividing a commission between a registered real estate person and the sponsoring real estate broker, and between the listing broker and the selling broker.

commitment: a formal offer by a lender stating the terms under which it agrees to lend money to a homebuyer. Also known as a loan commitment. The commitment letter states the dollar amount of the loan being offered, the number of years a borrower has to repay the loan, the loan origination fee, the points, the annual percentage rate, and the monthly charges. The letter also states the time the borrower has to accept the loan offer and to close the loan.

commitment fee: the fee charged by the lender to guarantee that the commitment, with its terms intact, is available for a certain period of time.

committee deed: a deed in which two or more people in an *indenture* agreement have reciprocity and obligations toward each other.

common area: the area in a housing or *condominium* development that is owned by all residents.

common area assessments: the fees paid by a housing or *condominium* development, which are used to maintain, operate, or repair common areas.

common elements: the parts of a *condominium* that are owned by all of the unit owners.

common law: a law based on custom, usage, and rulings of courts in various jurisdictions.

common-law state:
(1) a state in which the laws governing property rights are based on British common law.
(2) the property and income of each spouse belongs to him or her separately.

community association: a name given to any association of property owners sharing an interest in commonly owned property, which may be developed in condominiums, cooperatives, or housing subdivisions.

community income: the income of a married couple living in a community property state, which is considered to belong equally to each spouse, regardless of which spouse receives the income.

community property: a classification of property peculiar to certain states and referring to property accumulated through the efforts of both husband and wife.

community property laws: the statutes stipulating that the property accumulated during a marriage belongs equally to each spouse, irrespective of how much each contributed.

Community Reinvestment Act (Federal): the law that encourages the loaning of money in neighborhoods where minority depositors live.

co-mortgager: two or more parties sharing a joint financial obligation for a mortgage.

comparables: recently sold properties that are used to determine the value of a similar property.

comparable sales: a method widely used by real estate brokers where sales of similar properties in approximate neighborhoods are used to estimate value of the one being appraised.

comparative market analysis: the estimated value of property, based on the comparison of like properties.

comparative statements: financial statements that follow a consistent format but cover different periods of time. Useful for spotting trends.

competent parties: persons considered legally capable of entering into a binding contract.

competitive bid: bidding done to ascertain the best bid for work to be done.

completion bond: a form of surety bond that provides assurance to the financial backers of a real estate project that it will be completed on time and within all specifications.

compound annual growth rate (CAGR): the year-over-year growth rate applied to an investment or other part of a company's activities over a multiple-year period. The formula for calculating CAGR is (current value/base value)^(1/# of years). It's an imaginary number that describes the rate at which an investment grew as though it had grown at a steady rate.

compounding: the process of adding earned interest to the principal so that the interest is figured on a progressively larger amount. Paying interest on interest.

compound interest: the interest paid on the principal amount plus interest that has accrued and added to the total.

compound sum: the total amount, consisting of both principal and compound interest, due at maturity.

Comprehensive Environmental Response, Compensation, and Liability Act (CERCLA): the law, commonly known as *Superfund*, enacted by Congress on December 11, 1980. This law created a tax on the chemical and petroleum industries and provided broad federal authority to respond directly to releases or threatened releases of hazardous substances that may endanger public health or the environment. Over five years, $1.6 billion was collected, and the money went to a trust fund for cleaning up abandoned or uncontrolled hazardous waste sites.

compressed buy-down: a *buydown mortgage* where the level of rate reduction is changed every six months.

Computer Aided Design and Drafting (CADD): a graphics platform used on computers so that drawing can be done in two or three dimensions, with the three-dimensional designs able to be animated to be viewed from different angles, including from the inside of the drawing.

concession:

(1) the benefits granted by a seller/lessor to induce a sale/lease.

(2) alternately, right granted by a governmental body to use property for a particular type of business in a specific area.

condemnation: the process used by the government to take private property without the consent of the owner, for the use of the public.

conditional commitment: a written promise by a lender to make a loan, pending certain conditions to be met by the borrower.

conditional offer: an offer to purchase a piece of real estate provided certain conditions are met.

conditional sale: a contract stating that the title will remain with the seller until certain conditions are fulfilled by the buyer. Also referred to as conditional conveyance.

condition of the home: potential homeowners should know of major problems in a home before they make an offer. Potential buyers should carefully examine all elements of the home and ask questions of the seller and the real estate sales professional. A prospective buyer should consider writing a *contingency* in the sales contract that calls for a professional home inspection.

condominium: a form of property ownership in which the homeowner holds title to an individual dwelling unit and a proportionate interest in common areas and facilities of a multi-unit project.

condominium conversion: a change in title from single ownership of the entire building to multiple owners of multiple units, i.e. from a rental apartment house to individual condominium ownership. The tenant is usually given the right to purchase his/her unit at a favorable price, prior to open market sales.

condominium owners association: an association of the owners of condominium units that is concerned with the management of day-to-day matters in the complex.

conforming loan: loans under $322,700 are called conforming loans. Loans above that amount are called *non-conforming loans*, or *jumbo loans*, and typically carry a higher interest rate because of their size.

consideration:
(1) an inducement, consisting of a thing that is legal and has value, for a person to enter into a contract.
(2) alternately, the amount actually received from a sale after all expenses are deducted.

consolidated financial statement: a financial statement that covers a holding company and its subsidiaries.

Consolidated Metropolitan Statistical Area (CSMA): two or more metropolitan areas, which are adjoined and show some economic linkage. CMSA's are composed of individual metropolitan areas called *Primary Metropolitan Statistical Areas* (PMSA).

consolidation loan: a loan that combines smaller loans into one larger loan and is typical of a refinance of debt.

construction documents: drawings and specifications from an architect that provide the detailed requirements of a construction project.

construction drawings: includes architectural plans, building plans, working drawings, blueprints, etc. Construction drawings provide the information, drawings, and instruction needed to construct a building.

construction loan: a short-term loan used during the construction of a building or home. Funds are disbursed in stages, according to completed amount.

construction management contract: a contract between an owner and the general contractor who is responsible for hiring and supervising the trades and tasks necessary to build a structure.

construction specifications: commonly referred to as specs, these detailed descriptions consist of all items necessary to complete the construction of a building, including drawings and blueprints that outline the technical standards.

construction-to-permanent loan: a construction loan that can be converted to a long-term traditional mortgage upon completion of the construction.

Consumer Price Index (CPI): a U.S. government measure of the average change over time in the prices paid by urban consumers for a market basket of consumer goods and services. The CPI is the most widely used measure of inflation and is sometimes viewed as an indicator of the effectiveness of government economic policy.

contemporary home: homes built from the 1970s with very plain exteriors and wide-open space for the interior. While contemporary designs have evolved since then, most feature windows high on walls, large overhangs, split and drop floor levels, and unique wood and stone facings.

contingency: a condition that must be satisfied before a contract is legally binding.

contingency clause: a condition, which must be fulfilled, in a purchase contract.

contingency fund: money set aside for a possible loss.

contingency listing: a property listing with a special condition that must be met.

contingency reserve: most mortgages for purchase-renovation require an additional 10 percent of the total cost of the project to be put aside into a reserve account. This contingency reserve is only used when unforeseen repairs or deficiencies are found during renovation.

contingent fee: a fee that must be paid upon the occurrence of certain events.

contingent sale: a sale that is finalized only in the case of a particular occurrence.

continuation statement: a document submitted to a government agency to extend the time period for a previously approved document.

contract: an agreement between two or more parties to do something specific.

contract for deed: a contract where the seller agrees to defer all or part of the purchase price for a specified period of time.

contract for novation: in law, substituting a suitable person or entity for an original party of a contract, which terminates the old contract and begins a new one.

contract of sale: the written agreement between the buyer and the seller on the purchase price, terms, and conditions of a sale.

contractor: a person or firm supplying materials or work, for a stipulated sum, in the building trade. They are responsible for the entire job as a whole, while subcontractors are responsible for a certain trade and contract with the general contractor.

contract price: an amount payable to the seller and equal to the gross selling price when no mortgages are involved. If a mortgage is assumed, the contract price is the gross selling price minus the amount of the mortgage plus the excess (if any) of the mortgage over the seller's basis and expenses of sale.

contract specifications: the details of a contract of sale, including a legal description, type of deed, closing information, etc.

contract to purchase: a contract initiated by the buyer, which details the purchase price and conditions of the transaction, and is accepted by the seller. It is also known as an agreement of sale.

contractual lien: a voluntary obligation cumbrance, such as a mortgage.

conventional loan: a long-term loan made for the purchase of a home, which is not insured or guaranteed by a governmental agency and which generally conforms to the standards required for sale of the loan into the secondary mortgage market. Typically requires a substantial down payment, and is usually only available to those having good credit. It has fixed monthly payments for the life of the loan and usually has a 15-, 20-, or 30-year period of fixed interest rates.

conversion clause: a provision in some *ARM*s that allows a borrower to change an *ARM* to a fixed-rate loan, usually after the first adjustment period. The new fixed rate will be set at current rates, and there may be a charge for the conversion feature.

convertible adjustable-rate mortgages (ARM): a mortgage that begins as an *adjustable-rate loan* but can be converted to a fixed-rate mortgage during a specified period of time.

conveyance: the transfer of title of property from one person or entity to another.

conveyance tax: a tax imposed on the transfer of real estate.

co-op/cooperative: an apartment building in which each resident owns a percentage share of the corporation that owns the entire building. Also, a cooperative apartment.

cornice: the horizontal band around the ceiling, or on the eaves of a building. (see *Appendix B*)

corporate relocation: an arrangement for employers to pay for the transfer and move of employees.

corporation: a form of business organization consisting of an association of owners—called stockholders—who are regarded as a single entity in the eyes of the law.

correction deed: a deed issued to correct errors made in another deed.

cosign: to sign a note for the benefit of another, therefore assuming liability for the debt.

cost accounting: the process of identifying and evaluating production costs.

cost depletion: a method for recovering the taxpayer's investment in natural resources or timber.

cost of capital: the rate of return that is necessary to maintain the market value of a real estate project and is also used for project evaluation purposes.

cost of development: the expenditures incurred to develop real estate.

cost of funds index (COFI): an index of the weighted-average interest rate paid by savings institutions.

cost of maintaining a home: the expenses necessary to maintain a taxpayer's residence. These costs include rent or mortgage interest and real estate taxes, fire and casualty insurance on the dwelling, upkeep and repairs, utilities, paid domestic help, and food consumed in the home.

cost-plus percentage contract: a contract that determines the builder's profit based on a percentage of the labor and materials used in the construction of the building.

Counselors of Real Estate (CRE): real estate professionals who provide counseling on real estate purchases and investment decisions through a negotiated fee rather than a commission. Founded in 1953, with 1,100 members, it is located in Chicago, Illinois. Phone: 312-329-8427, Web: www.cre.org.

counterclaim: a counteraction by a defendant against a plaintiff in a legal action.

covenant: a binding agreement made by two or more parties to either do or keep from doing a specified thing.

covenant running with the land: a written agreement or guarantee annexed to the land, between two or more parties to do or not do something; it is transferred to successive titleholders.

Craftsman style: an architectural style that evolved near the turn of the century as part of the Arts and Crafts movement. Characterized by low-pitched, gabled roofs, large, overhanging eaves, usually with roof rafters exposed. *(see Appendix A)*

crawl space: unfinished space beneath the ground floor of a house. Often, there is access to plumbing and or wiring there.

creative financing: innovative financing arrangements to help sell a property.

credit: the money a lender extends to a borrower, who gives a commitment to repay the loan within a certain amount of time.

credit application: a form used to record information about an applicant seeking a loan.

credit bureau: the three main credit reporting agencies, or credit bureaus, are Equifax, Experian, and Trans Union. Consumers can order a copy of their credit report (usually for a fee) from Equifax: 800-685-1111, Web: www.econsumer.equifax.com; Trans Union: 800-888-4213, Web: www.transunion.com; Experian: 888-397-3742, Web: www.experian.com.

credit history: a record of an individual's open and repaid debts. A credit history helps a lender to determine whether a potential borrower has a history of repaying debts in a timely manner. When a lender reviews an applicant's credit history, the lender examines all the information in a credit report. These include credit cards, student loans, automobile loans, and other loans. The lender reviews whether payments have been made on time or late. A credit report also indicates if creditors discharged a debt because they believed it would never be repaid, or if the borrower declared bankruptcy or went through foreclosure.

credit life insurance: the insurance that pays off a mortgage in the event of the borrower's death.

credit limit: the maximum amount of money that can be loaned to a prospective borrower.

creditor: a person or institution to whom a debt is owed.

credit rating: the degree of creditworthiness assigned to a person, based on credit history and financial status.

credit report: a report detailing the credit history of a prospective borrower that's used to help determine borrower creditworthiness. See *credit scoring*.

credit repository: large companies that gather financial and credit information from various sources about individuals who have applied for credit.

credit score: a number based on all the information in a *credit report*.

This information is converted into a number that the lender uses to determine whether a borrower is likely to repay a loan in a timely manner. The scores used in mortgage lending are typically in the 300 to 900 range. The higher the score, the better. It is one of several measurements a lender will use to evaluate a loan application, but it has become more important over time.

InfoBox: WHAT LENDERS WANT TO KNOW

Lenders want more than a credit score when considering a borrower's loan application. They will look at the following in detail:

credit history: a track record of how past debts have been paid.

outstanding debt: a lender will want to know how many open charge accounts and other consumer loans a borrower has.

payment history: a lender will review whether bills were paid on time or after they were due.

types of credit: every type of credit a borrower uses will be under the microscope.

credit inquiries: every time a lender reviews a borrower's credit history, an "inquiry" is recorded in their credit report. Having many recent inquiries may suggest the use of credit is increasing, which is often viewed as more risky for the lender. However, auto and mortgage loan inquiries in the 30 days prior to the score being calculated are not used.

---

credit union: a nonprofit cooperative organization providing banking and financial services, such as home improvement loans, home equity loans, and mortgages to its members.

credit-worthiness: when lenders judge borrowers to be worthy of future credit.

crown: the summit or highest point, such as the highest point of an arch or the top of a structure. (see *Appendix B*)

crown molding: a decorative type of molding running atop the wall, where it meets the ceiling.(see *Appendix B*)

cul-de-sac: a street that is closed at one end; a dead-end street.

cumulative: an arrangement in which a payment not made when due is carried over to the following period.

curb appeal: when a property has an eye-catching quality from the street.

current assets: assets that can be converted to cash in less than one year.

current capital: same as *working capital*.

current debt: same as *current liabilities*.

current liabilities: expenses that are due to be paid.

current ratio: *current assets* divided by *current liabilities*. An indication of a company's ability to meet short-term debt obligations. The higher the ratio, the more liquid the company is.

current value: the value of a home at the time of appraisal.

custom builder: a builder who constructs a home or building with plans selected by the owner.

custom-built: a structure built specifically for an owner, to his or her specifications.

custom home: a structure designed by an architect selected by the owner.

D

damage deposit: a prepayment required to cover damage by a tenant, other than normal wear and tear.

days on the market: the period of time a property is listed for sale prior to being sold or removed from sale.

days payable: a measure of the average time a company takes to pay vendors, equal to accounts payable divided by annual credit purchases, times 365.

days receivable: a measure of the average time a company's customers take to pay for purchases, equal to accounts receivable divided by annual sales on credit, times 365.

DBA (doing business as): the certification by a state that a principal is doing business under an assumed name. The certification also contains the address where the business is being conducted.

dead bolt lock: a lock bolt having no spring action that is operated by a key or a turn piece.

dealer: a person or firm that regularly buys and sells property. A person is classified as a dealer if, at the time of the sale, that person held the property primarily for sale to customers in the ordinary course of business. Gains from the sale of such property are ordinary gains, not capital gains.

debit: an accounting entry that results in either an increase in assets or a decrease in liabilities or net worth.

debit note: a note indicating an amount owed by a person or company. Serves the same function as an *invoice*.

debt financing: the raising of money by loans and borrowing directly from financial institutions, providing increased financial leverage. Interest may be tax deductible.

debt limit: the maximum amount of debt an individual or business can borrow.

debtor: an individual or entity owing money.

debt ratio: debt capital divided by total capital.

debt service: the interest and principal paid on a loan.

debt-to-income ratio: the ratio of monthly debt payments to monthly gross income. Lenders use housing debt-to-income (DTI) ratio (housing payment divided by *monthly income*), and a total DTI ratio (*total debt payment*—including the house payment—divided by monthly income) to determine whether a borrower's income qualifies him/her as a buyer for a mortgage.

decedent: one who has died with a valid will in effect.

decimal feet: the measurement of length in feet and decimal portions. For example 5.5 in decimal feet is also 5 feet 6 inches or 5½ feet.

declaration of homestead: a statement filed with a government authority declaring the property a homestead for purpose of securing a homestead exemption; has no effect on the title and is not a conveyance.

declaratory judgment: a binding determination by the court as to whether there is an allowable action between the litigants. A subsequent trial determines relief.

declining balance depreciation: an accelerated method of depreciation. The type of property determines the percent. The depreciable basis for the next year is reduced by the depreciation deduction taken in the current year.

declining market: a market condition in which there are more sellers than buyers, causing prices to fall.

decree: a decision rendered by a court of law on sale, foreclosure, or other property issues.

dedication: a property given and accepted as a grant to the public.

deduction: an amount that may be subtracted from income that is otherwise taxable.

deed: a legal document transferring ownership of a piece of property from one owner to another. It contains a description of the property, and is signed, witnessed, and delivered to the buyer at closing.

deed covenant: any of a number of types of promises to do or not to do something, which are attached to the title and pass from one owner to the next, such as architectural style or type of material.

deed description: property description contained in a deed.

deed-in-lieu: a deed given by a mortgagor to the mortgagee to satisfy a debt and avoid foreclosure. Also called a *voluntary conveyance*.

deed in lieu of foreclosure: a legal document conveying property to the lender after the borrower defaults on his/her mortgage payment.

deed of confirmation: often referred to as a *correction deed*, it is used to rectify errors made in a previous deed.

deed of release: the deed that releases property, or a portion of it, upon satisfaction of a mortgage or other debt.

deed of trust: a document that gives the lender the right to foreclose on a piece of property if the borrower defaults on the loan. In some states, a deed of trust is used instead of a mortgage. When homeowners sign a deed of trust, they receive title to the property but convey title to a neutral third party—called a trustee—until the loan balance is paid in full. The deed of trust stipulates that, in the event of default, the trustee would liquidate the property for the benefit of the lender in a trustee's sale.

deed recording fee: a fee charged by the government to enter into the public record the deed and documents relative to the transfer of title to a piece of property.

deed restrictions: written statements in a deed that outline the limits of use of a property. Restrictions imposed against the race, sex, nationality, color, or creed of a person are illegal.

de facto contract: a contract, while not necessarily lawful, that exists in fact.

default: the failure of a debtor to pay principal/interest on a due date, or failure to fulfill a duty or discharge an obligation, such as mortgage payments.

default charge: a penalty charged if the amount owed on a purchase of real estate is not paid on time.

default judgment: a judgment issued by the court against a defendant who does not respond to the plaintiff's lawsuit and does not respond in his own defense.

defeasance clause: a provision guaranteeing the return of title to a mortgagor upon satisfaction of a mortgage's condition and terms. Causes the discharge of a mortgagee's estate interest in a property.

defeasible: a clause in a contract, title, or mortgage that is subject to be repealed or revoked upon the satisfaction of a claim or the completion of a future event.

defeasible title: a title that can be made null and void or defeated upon the satisfaction of a claim or the completion of some future contingency.

defective title: a title obtained through error or fraud, without proper signature or consideration, or other improper action. A defective title is null and void, having no effect on the original title.

defendant: in a *civil court*, the individual against whom a court action is brought by a *plaintiff* for restitution of property or satisfaction of a complaint. In a criminal court, it is an individual accused of a crime.

deferred charge: an expenditure that is considered an asset until it becomes relevant to the business at hand, such as prepaid rent, which is considered an asset until the rent is officially due.

deferred credit: revenue received by a firm but not yet reported as income.

deferred interest mortgage: a mortgage that has a lower interest rate and, thus, a lower monthly mortgage charge. When the house is sold, the lender receives the deferred interest plus a fee for postponing the interest that would have been paid monthly.

deferred maintenance: postponed repairs or maintenance on a piece of property, which result in a decline of property value.

deferred payments: money payments to be delayed until a future date or for an extended period of time.

deferred revenue: revenue that is considered a liability until it becomes relevant to the business at hand, such as a payment received for work that has not yet been performed.

deferred tax: a liability that results from income that has already been earned for accounting purposes but not for tax purposes.

deficiency: an additional tax liability that the IRS deems to be owed by a taxpayer.

deficiency judgment: a court finding that the debtor owes an amount exceeding the value of the collateral put up for the defaulted loan.

deficit: same as *budget deficit.*

deficit net worth: on a balance sheet, the excess of liabilities over assets and capital stock, usually resulting from operating losses. Also called negative net worth.

deficit spending: same as *budget deficit.*

delinquency: being behind in payment on a debt.

delinquent mortgage: a mortgage involving a borrower who is behind on payments. If the borrower does not bring the mortgage up to date within a specified amount of time, the lender may begin foreclosure proceedings.

delivery: the transfer of property from one to another.

delivery basis: a method of revenue recognition based on delivery instead of sale.

demand loan: a loan with no established maturity period, which is callable on the demand of the lender, for repayment. The interest is calculated on a daily basis, and paid periodically.

demise:
(1) the transfer of an estate by bequest or contract for a stated time period or life.
(2) alternately, the making of a charter or lease for a specified time period.

demised premises: leased or rented property.

demising clause: a provision in a lease whereby the landlord *(lessor)* leases and the tenant *(lessee)* takes the property.

demographics: statistics based on family size, ages, occupations, marital status and other population characteristics. This data is used by developers, lenders and other businesses to develop their products and services.

demolition insurance: an insurance policy that indemnifies the property owner, up to the limits of the policy, against fire or other hazard, requiring the total destruction and removal of the structure.

demurrer: a legal motion by a defendant that says there aren't enough facts to prosecute him/her or that the court has no jurisdiction to do so.

Department of Veterans Affairs (VA): an agency of the federal government that guarantees residential mortgages made to eligible veterans of the military services under certain conditions. The guarantee protects the lender against loss, and thus encourages lenders to make mortgages to veterans. To obtain more information, borrowers can contact the U.S. Department of Veterans Affairs. The VA guarantee allows qualified veterans to buy a house costing up to $203,000 with no down payment. Moreover, the qualification guidelines for VA loans are more flexible than those for either the *Federal Housing Administration* (FHA) or conventional loans. For qualified veterans, this can be an attractive mortgage program. Web: www.va.gov.

deponent: one who acts as a witness and gives written testimony under oath.

deposit: money given along with an offer to purchase property, or as security for the performance of some contract. Also called earnest money, it is intended to show willingness to follow through with the purchase agreement.

Depositary Institutions and Monetary Control Act (Regulation Q): a federal law that represented significant decontrol of federally regulated banks and *Savings and Loan Associations (S&Ls)*. It removed interest rate limitations, authorized interest-bearing checking accounts, reduced the applicability of states' usury laws, and widely expanded the services of S&Ls.

deposition: discovery, before trial, of information, in which a stenographer records the statements made, under oath, by a witness. These statements are made in answer to questions posed by the attorneys to both parties.

depreciable life: the economic or physical life of a fixed asset.

depreciable real estate: real estate subject to deductions for depreciation; under current tax law, is depreciated under either the *straight-line* method or the *MACRS* method.

depreciated cost: the original cost of an asset minus total its depreciation thus far. Also called net book value or written-down value.

depreciation: for tax purposes, the deduction of a reasonable allowance for the wear and tear of assets—including real estate—used in a trade or business or held for the production of income.

depreciation basis: an amount subject to depreciation, which equals the initial cost less the estimated salvage repair.

depreciation recapture: the part of a capital gain—the amount of a gain on depreciable assets—constituting tax benefits previously taken and taxed as ordinary income.

depressed market: a market condition in which the prices of real estate are declining because of a lack of demand.

derivative title: the transfer of title based on a preceding title transfer. A derivative conveyance increases, moderates, renews, or transfers the stake created by the original conveyance.

derived demand: a secondary demand that is created because of a primary agent or facility, such as an office building creating a need for a coffee shop.

descriptive memorandum: a type of description of a real estate property offering by a developer, rather than a prospectus.

design/build: a project where the owner contracts with a company to perform design and construction services.

design drawings: plans that are used in the building business that give, in detail, all needed information for the construction or fabrication of a building or structure.

designer: a home design professional. Designers are limited to drawing blueprints, unlike architects, who are able to certify plans.

design load: the maximum amount of weight that can be supported by a structure.

desist and refrain order: a court order to stop a specific activity.

detached housing: freestanding residential housing constructed on its own building lot.

developer: the person or company that builds new homes, shopping centers or commercial buildings for profit on a specific area of land. A developer will organize and plan the development, supervise its construction, and manage all the business elements of the project.

developer's equity: the financial interest a developer has in a project.

developer's profit: the sum of money a developer earns, after all costs are deducted, in a development project.

development: planning and building homes, shopping centers, business facilities, schools, or churches. The process includes the construction of streets, sewers, utilities, parks, etc. In some cases, it may simply describe the process of obtaining the required governmental approvals for construction to proceed. The phrase "developed land" usually describes property for which approvals have been secured but no physical improvements have been constructed.

development loan: a loan used by a developer for the purposes of paying development costs and repaid by sale proceeds. Also referred to as a *construction loan*.

devise: a gift of real estate as stipulated in a will.

devisee: one who receives real estate under a will.

devisor: someone who donates real estate.

dictum: a judge's remark that illustrates or amplifies the ruling. Also describes a ruling made by an *arbitrator*.

dimension plans: initial plans that show the layout of a house but are less detailed than full blueprints.

direct capitalization: divides a property's first-year net operating income by an estimated general capitalization rate to develop a total property estimate. If an income property produces a first-year net operating income of $30,000 and the market indicates a general capitalization rate of 10 percent for comparable properties, the direct capitalization estimate of the value of the total property would be $300,000 ($30,000 x 10).

direct costs: site preparation or building construction costs, including fixtures. This doesn't include such costs as building permits, land survey, and overhead costs such as insurance and payroll.

direct overhead: the cost of doing business on one specific job.

direct reduction mortgage (DRM): a fully amortized mortgage necessitating equal periodic payments of both interest and principal. In the early years of the loan, the share of payment to the principal is smaller and the interest larger. This gradually reverses toward the end of the loan period.

disability insurance: an insurance policy that covers an individual's ability to produce income.

disaster loss: if a casualty is sustained in an area designated as a disaster area by the President of the United States, the casualty is designated a disaster loss. For tax purposes, a disaster loss may be applied to the previous year before the disaster occurred, so the victims can get immediate benefits.

disbursement: paying out in the discharge of a debt or expense.

discharge: removing a debt by making payment.

discharge of bankruptcy: a court order whereby the bankrupt debtor is forgiven of his or her debts. Depending on the form of bankruptcy, a bankruptcy remains on a credit report for seven to 10 years.

discharge of lien: an order to withdraw a property lien after a claim is paid by other means.

disclaimer: a renunciation of a claim to real estate ownership.

disclosed principal: a person who uses an agent for his/her negotiations with a third party, often when the agent pretends to be acting for himself/herself. As a result, the third party does not know he/she can look to the real principal in any dispute.

disclosure statement:

(1) a written statement of a borrower's rights under the *Truth-in-Lending Act*.

(2) alternately, a statement of all financing charges, which must be disclosed by a lender.

(3) also, a statement that lists information relevant to a piece of property, such as the presence of radon or lead paint.

discount: deducting a certain amount from a payment, based on negotiation or the introduction of new information that could lower the cost of the item.

discounted cash flow: a method to estimate the value of a real estate investment, which emphasizes after-tax cash flows and the return on the invested dollars discounted over time to reflect a discounted yield. The value of the real estate investment is the present worth of the future after-tax cash flows from the investment, discounted at the investor's desired rate of return.

discount loan: a loan in which the entire financing charge is subtracted from the initial loan proceeds. The total amount of funds received is the face value of the loan less this deduction. For example, a $50,000 one-year loan borrowed at a discount rate of 12 percent would mean $44,000 being disbursed at the loan closing. The effective interest rate would be 13.6 percent, not the 12 percent discount rate, since only $44,000 is received.

discount points: a type of fee that lenders charge. Discount points are additional funds borrowers pay the lender at closing to get a lower interest rate on their mortgage. A point equals 1 percent of the loan amount. For a mortgage of $100,000, one point would equal $1,000. Typically, each point paid for a 30-year loan lowers the interest rate by .125 of a percentage point. If the current interest rate on a 30-year mortgage were 7.75 percent, paying one point would lower the interest rate to 7.625. It often makes more sense to pay discount points upfront if the borrower plans to stay in the home for a long time.

discount rate: the interest rate charged by the Federal Reserve Bank to its member banks for loans. Changes in this rate will have a significant impact on the real estate market.

discrimination: the unequal treatment and denial of opportunity to individuals based on race, color, creed, nationality, age, or sex.

disinflation: a lessening in the rate of inflation that may occur during a recession.

disposable income: personal income minus personal income tax payments and other governmental deductions, it is the money available for people to spend or save.

dispossess proceedings: a legal action by the owner of property to oust or exclude an individual or business from using the property.

distressed property: a property in poor financial or physical condition; foreclosed real estate or property in a bankruptcy; *income property* that is making an inadequate return.

distribution approach: the apportioning, disbursing, dividing, or parceling out of property among individuals. Probate: court approval to divide and distribute the contents of an estate after all claims against it are satisfied. The estate is then divided between all distributees. Statutes of distribution: state laws controlling the distribution of the estate of an individual who dies intestate.

divestiture:
(1) the surrender, voluntarily or involuntarily, of ownership of property or of an interest therein.
(2) alternately, a court order to give up possession or the right to property, such as in the case of an antitrust action.

doctrine: a legal rule, principle, or tenet.

document: recorded materials, including letters, photos, reproducible computer files, legal forms, etc. A document is any tangible information, including letters, contracts, electronic or paper files, x-rays, receipts, or other material evidence.

documentary evidence: any written evidence or tangible material that is coherent and related to the subject at hand. This includes documents, contracts, electronic and paper files, photographs, and other non-oral evidence.

document needs list: a list of documents that a lender requires from a potential borrower, such as paycheck stubs and credit card statements.

document stamp: a tax imposed by some state and local governments to record property deeds and mortgages into the public records.

dollar amount paid: cash plus the principal amount of a loan on the property that the taxpayer is legally obligated to pay.

dollar and percentage adjustments: a modification in the amount of money involved, for some justifiable reason.

dominant tenement: property that has an easement right through another adjoining property. The property through which the easement passes is considered to have the servient tenement.

donee: one to whom a gift or bequest is made.

donor: one who donates or gives a gift or bequest.

dormer: a window that projects from a sloped roof, expanding the livable space in an attic. (see *Appendix B*)

double budget: an accounting system that keeps capital expenses and operating expenses separate.

double-declining balance depreciation: an accelerated depreciation method in which a fixed percentage factor of two times the straight-line rate is multiplied each year by the declining balance of the fixed asset's book value. To compute the annual depreciation expense, the asset's book value at the beginning of the period is multiplied by the double declining rate. Although salvage value is not included in the initial calculation for depreciation, a fixed asset cannot be depreciated in the last year below its salvage value.

double-digit inflation: an annual rate of inflation of 10 percent or higher.

double-entry bookkeeping: an accounting technique that records each transaction as both a credit and a debit.

double-hung window: a window with two overlapping sashes that slide vertically in tracks. The most common style of operable window.

down payment: the amount of a home's purchase price a borrower needs to supply up front in cash to get a loan. Most conventional loans require 20 percent of the new home's value as a down payment.

down zoning: the rezoning of land from a higher density use to a lower density use.

dragnet clause: a mortgage clause that compels the mortgagor to pledge additional properties, mortgaged or not, as additional collateral to a different mortgage loan. Failure to pay any of the mortgages can result in a foreclosure on the dragnetted property, even if it is otherwise unmortgaged or its own payments are current.

dry mortgage: creates a lien against the mortgagor's property, but does not permit a lien against his/her personal assets.

drywall: a wall constructed of plasterboard.

dual agency: the representation of both parties by the same real estate agent or broker.

dual contract: the illegal practice of having two contracts for the same transaction. For example, having one contract for a higher amount so that more money can be borrowed.

dual divided agency: the representation of two or more parties in a transaction by the same real estate broker.

dual listing: a listing where a real estate broker represents both the buyer and seller, creating two principals.

due diligence: investigating fully the terms of a contract or a business deal before signing.

due-on-sale provision: a provision in a mortgage that allows the lender to demand repayment in full if the borrower sells the property that serves as security for the mortgage.

due-on-transfer provision: terminology usually used for second mortgages. See *due-on-sale provision*.

due process: the course of legal proceedings established by the legal system of a nation or state to protect individual rights and liberties.

duress: the act of forcing an individual or business to do something against their will; can be used as a legitimate defense in court to reverse the effect of the compelled act.

Dutch auction: the descending-price auction, commonly known in academic literature as the Dutch auction, uses an open format rather than a sealed-bid method. Bidding starts at an extremely high price and is progressively lowered until a buyer claims an item by calling "mine" in some form. When multiple units are auctioned, normally more takers press the button as the price declines. In other words, the first winner takes his prize and pays his price and later winners pay less. When the goods are exhausted, the bidding is over.

Dutch Colonial style: a design that features a barnlike gambrel roof, overhanging eaves, a ground-level front porch. And, if it has more than one story, it will have dormers. (*see Appendix A*)

E

Early Georgian: see *Georgian*.

early occupancy: the occupation of the property by the buyer before the sale is completed.

earned income: income from personal services, as distinguished from income generated by property or other sources. Earned income includes all amounts received as wages, tips, bonuses, other employee compensation, and self-employment income, whether in the form of money, services, or property.

earnest money: a deposit in advance of a down payment, given as an indication of good faith.

earnest money deposit: a deposit made by the potential home-buyer to show that he or she is serious about buying the house. The earnest money deposit is a good-faith payment submitted with an offer on a home to show the seller that the borrower is serious. The earnest money is deposited in an escrow account and will be applied to closing costs. Sometimes, a lender will want the borrower to bring a receipt for the earnest money deposit, along with the sales contract, to the initial loan application meeting.

earning asset: an asset that provides income.

earnings: revenues minus cost of sales, operating expenses, and taxes, over a given period of time. The reason corporations exist, and often the single most important determinant of a stock's price. Also called *income*.

earnings before interest and taxes (EBIT): same as *operating income*.

earnings report: an official quarterly or annual financial document published by a public company, showing earnings, expenses, and net profit. Also called income statement or profit and loss statement.

earthquake load: a measurement of how much stress a building can stand during an earthquake. Also referred to as a seismic load.

easement: a right of way giving persons other than the owner access to or over a property.

easement by necessity: a legal right to travel to a landlocked parcel of land.

easement by prescription: a legal right acquired by adverse land use for a statutory period of time.

easement in gross: a personal right to use the land of another, but not attached to any one parcel of land.

Eastlake house: a nineteenth-century house with plenty of distinctive three-dimensional ornamentation, an open front porch, and a turret. (*see Appendix A*)

easy credit: when lenders reject very few prospective buyers of real estate—this is usually due to an ample money supply and lower interest rates that relax credit standards.

eave: the lower section of the roof, forming an overhang and comprised of a fascia, soffit, and soffit molding. The word *eave* comes from the Old English word *off*, meaning over. (see *Appendix B*)

eave vent: a roof opening or opening in an eave that allows for passage of air so that condensation does not form in a tightly insulated house.

EBIT: see *earnings before interest and taxes.*

EBITDA: *earnings before interest, taxes, depreciation, and amortization.* A calculation used to analyze *REITs.*

ECOA: see *Equal Credit Opportunity Act.*

economic base analysis: an appraisal method of deriving property values where the current and future economic conditions are measured in a particular area.

economic capacity of land: the ability of the size of the property to accommodate the desired economic purpose.

economic force: the ability of economic factors to influence the real estate market.

economic indicators: reports made by the government and leading industry groups that measure the past, current, and future direction of the economy and may have an impact on the real estate market. They include the following:

- **measures of general economic performance:** these include Gross Domestic Product (GDP), Personal Income, Capital Expenditures, Corporate Earnings, and Business Inventories.
- **price indices that illuminate the inflation rate:** the *Consumer Price Index (CPI),* a well-known inflation measure for everyday retail pricing; the Producer Price Index (PPI) monitors raw materials and semi-finished goods at the early stage of the distribution cycle. It reflects changes in the general price level, or the CPI, before they actually occur.
- **measures of labor market conditions:** national and state Unemployment Rates, Average Manufacturing Workweeks, Applications for Initial Jobless Claims, and Hourly Salary Rates.
- **money and market indicators:** the Dow Jones Industrial Average (DJIA), the 30-year Treasury Bill rate, and various measurements of the nation's money supply.
- **combined indicators:** the Index of Leading Economic Indicators consists of 11 data series comprising the money supply, business formation, stock prices, vendor performance, average work week, new orders, contracts, building permits, inventory change, layoff rate, and change in prices. Business activities are examined as an indication of a change in the economy.
- **measures for major industries:** Housing Starts, Resale Housing, Construction Permits, Auto and Retail Sales.

economic life: the expected period that property will provide benefits; typically less than the physical life of the property. *Depreciation* is usually based on the economic life.

economic surplus: the extent to which assets exceed liabilities. Profits remaining after subtracting for operating expenses, taxes, interest, and insurance.

economic value: the value of an asset deriving from its ability to generate income.

economies of scale: a situation by which the average per square foot cost of construction declines as a building's size and volume expand.

edge venting: providing of ventilation to the attic space by regularly placing vents around the eave line of the roof.

effective age: an appraiser's estimate of the physical condition of a building. The actual age of a building may be shorter or longer than its effective age.

effective debt: the total debt that a company owes, including the capitalized value of any lease payments it has to make.

effective gross income: normal annual income, including overtime that is regular or guaranteed. The income may be from more than one source. Salary is generally the principal source, but other income may qualify if it is significant and stable.

effective interest rate: a consumer-oriented rate that takes into account the projected amount of time the borrower will hold the loan (if he or she holds it to term) as well as the specific costs, fees, and potential rate changes associated with it. The effective rate is <u>not</u> the *APR*. It is similar in that it factors in interest, mortgage insurance, and other fees (including points); however, the APR assumes that a borrower keeps the loan for the entire term, while the effective rate takes into account how long the borrower tells a lender he or she plans to be in the property he or she is financing.

effective net worth: net worth plus subordinated debt.

effective tax rate: tax divided by taxable income equals the tax effective rate. If the tax is $30,000, and the taxable income is $120,000, then the effective tax rate is 25 percent.

efficiency ratio: operating expenses divided by fee income plus tax equivalent net interest income.

efficiency unit: a small unit—usually without full bath or kitchen facilities—in a multifamily unit.

egress: access from a land parcel to a public road or other means of exit. Right to exit and enter through land owned by another.

ejectment: steps taken to remove from the real property someone who does not have a contractual basis to be there.

electrical drawings: plans that show the location of the wiring layout, the types and position of all electrical equipment and the location of the fixtures.

electrical power: the flow of current at a voltage, which is measured in watts (watts = amps x volts).

electric service: electric power supplied by a utility, which may be any of three capacities, and is either overhead on poles or buried in the ground.

electronic transfer: the transfer of mortgage or other payment automatically by deduction from a checking or savings account.

electrostatic painting: in this type of painting, electrically charged powder is sprayed on a surface that is charged with the opposite electrical charge and then bakes on the coating.

eleemosynary: a charitable gesture, such as real estate donated to a charity, whose value would then be tax deductible.

elevation: the height of a structure above an established reference point.

elevation map: the representation on a flat surface of any region that depicts the elevation of that region.

elevations: the exterior view of a home design, showing the position of the house relative to the grade of the land from the front, sides, or back.

Elizabethan style: English architecture that generally has two levels, with the second level typically overlaying the first story. With a high roof and a sculptured chimney, it usually has half-timber stucco walls. See *Tudor.*

embankment: mounded soil used as a support along a roadway, or to retain water.

emblements: annual crops raised by a land tenant. Even if the lease expires before the crop has matured, the tenant has the right to the crop.

embrasure: an opening for a door or window with the sides slanted, so that it is wider on the inside than on the outside.

eminent domain: the right of a government to take private property for public use upon payment of its fair market value. Eminent domain is the basis for condemnation proceedings.

employer-assisted housing: a program to help employees purchase homes through special plans developed with lenders.

empty-nesters: couples who have raised their families and will possibly downsize their dwelling.

encroachment: an improvement that intrudes illegally on another's property.

encumbrance: a claim or lien or interest in a property that complicates the title process, interfering with its use or transfer. Anything that affects or limits the fee simple title to a property, such as mortgages, leases, easements, or restrictions.

end loan: the conversion of a construction loan to a permanent mortgage, on a multi-unit project, after all units have been completed.

endorsement:
(1) a signature on a draft or check by a payee prior to the transfer to a third party.
(2) also, a statement attached to an insurance policy that changes the terms of the policy.

endorser: a person who signs over ownership of property to someone else.

endowment: funds or property bestowed upon a person or institution, whereupon the income is used to serve a specific purpose for which the endowment was intended.

energy-efficient window: a window that has at least two parallel panes of glass so that the loss of heat through the window is slowed.

energy tax credit: a tax credit given to encourage the conservation of natural resources, as well as the development of alternative resources.

energy tax credit/business property: an energy tax credit allowed for the purchase of certain business-use property utilizing solar, geothermal, or biomass energy.

energy tax credit/residential property: prior to 1986, taxpayers were eligible for a credit against the cost of energy-saving devices or renewable energy source property installed in their principal residences. Residential energy credits claimed in prior years must be subtracted from the basis of the residence.

enforceable: an agreement, debt, judgment, or law that can be put into effect, such as a lien put upon a property upon default of a loan.

engineered masonry: a masonry design based on structural analysis.

engineered 24" framing: building framing using 24" spacing rather than the standard 16" spacing between studs.

engineering: the science concerned with putting scientific knowledge to practical uses; divided into different branches, such as civil, electrical, mechanical, or chemical engineering. Planning, designing construction or management of machinery, roads, bridges; building waterways, etc.

engineering controls: valves, switches, regulators, or levers used to manipulate, regulate, or run a system.

entity:
(1) a separate economic unit subject to financial measurement for accounting purposes.
(2) alternately, an individual, partnership, corporation, etc., permitted by law to own property and engage in business.

entrance cap: a waterproof cap, also called weatherhead, mast head, or rain cap, which is placed at the upper part of an electrical mast at the point where the wires are run to the inside electrical meter. Wires hang from the pole to the entrance cap so that the entrance cap is not the low point in the downhill run from the pole, because water will run to the low point before dripping to the ground. Wires enter the entrance cap at an upward angle through a tight insulator. Water is further stopped from getting through the entrance cap because of this entrance angle.

entrepreneur: an individual who starts an enterprise, with the associated risks and responsibilities.

environmental codes: laws that govern any part of building that would have an effect on the environment.

environmental impact statement: a government mandated evaluation of the effects a development will have on the environment of a proposed site.

Environmental Protection Agency (EPA): an agency of the U.S. government established to enforce federal pollution abatement laws and to implement various pollution prevention programs. The agency supervises environmental quality and seeks to control the pollution caused by solid wastes, pesticides, toxic substances, noise, and radiation, and has established special programs in air and water pollution, hazardous wastes, and toxic chemicals. It also sponsors research in the technologies of pollution control. Ten regional offices facilitate coordination of pollution control efforts with state and local governments. Web: www.epa.gov.

Equal Credit Opportunity Act (ECOA): a federal law requiring creditors to make credit equally available without discrimination based on race, color, religion, national origin, age, sex, marital status, or receipt of income from public assistance programs.

equalization: a mass appraisal of all property within a jurisdiction for the purpose of equalizing values to assure that each taxpayer is bearing a fair share of the tax load.

Equifax: Equifax Credit Information Services, Inc., one of the Big Three credit reporting bureaus that operate nationwide. Equifax: 800-685-1111, Web: www.econsumer.equifax.com.

equitable conversion: in some states, under a contract of sale, buyers and sellers are treated as though the closing had taken place, even though the legal title has not passed. When there has been an equitable conversion, whereby equity adjusts the title to a property according to the parties' intentions, the property is vested in the buyer.

equitable lien: a written contract or court judgment placing a lien on a parcel of property as collateral for a loan.

equitable owner: the person identified to receive the benefit of property held in trust.

equitable title: the right to demand that title be conveyed upon payment of the purchase price.

equity: the difference between the fair market value of the property and what the borrower still owes on the mortgage. A lender determines how much equity is in the home by taking the appraised value of the home and subtracting any mortgage debt. For example, if a house is valued at $150,000 and the mortgage balance is $90,000, the borrower has $60,000 in equity. That equity is considered the basis for any *second mortgages* or *home equity line of credit* the borrower may ask for later.

equity buildup: the increase in a person's equity in real estate due to the reduction in the mortgage loan balance and price appreciation.

equity cushion: the ownership interest in property that is above the minimum need to meet uncertainties or a downward trend in a real estate market.

equity in property: the amount by which the appraised value of property exceeds the debt balance. If property has a fair market value of $500,000 and the mortgage balance is $200,000, the owner's equity in the property is $300,000.

equity kicker: the privilege of a real estate investor or lender to participate in the profitability generated from property, in addition to any principal, interest, or dividends.

equity lending: bank financing to a homeowner based on his dollar equity in the home. If a home is worth $500,000 and the owner owes $200,000, his equity is $300,000.

equity of redemption: a borrower's right to redeem his property by immediately paying off the loan balance and any related costs.

equity participation: when a lender has an equity interest in the property that is the subject of the loan. This is in addition to principal and interest payments on the mortgage. The lender shares in the increase in market price of the property as well as any net income generated.

equity purchaser: an individual or business that buys someone else's equity in property but may not assume any responsibility for a loan balance.

equity rate of return: the return before taxes on the capital invested in real estate property.

equity REIT: a type of *real estate investment trust (REIT)* whose investment money is used for the purchase of a portfolio of specific properties to be managed in order to generate investment return through current income and capital gain.

equity sharing: an arrangement whereby a party providing financing gets a portion of the ownership.

equity-to-value ratio: the percent of the purchase price of property to its total appraised value. If property is appraised at $500,000 and the price paid is $400,000, the ratio is 80 percent.

equity trust: also called *equity REIT.*

equity yield rate: the rate of return on the equity portion of an investment, taking into account periodic cash flow and the proceeds from resale. Considers the timing and amounts of cash flow after annual debt service, but not income taxes.

errors and omissions insurance: a policy that pays for mistakes by a builder or architect.

errors in credit report: a credit report may contain inaccuracies. The best way to prevent or remove errors is to request copies every year, or before a major purchase, and review the information. Since each of the main credit bureaus keep their own records, it may be wise to request copies from all three: Equifax: 800-685-1111, Web: www.econsumer.equifax.com; Trans Union: 800-888-4213, Web: www.transunion.com; Experian: 888-397-3742, Web: www.experian.com. Expect to pay a fee. See pages 86 and 87 for information on how to fix a credit report.

InfoBox: CORRECTING YOUR CREDIT REPORT

Under the *Fair Credit Reporting Act* (FCRA), a borrower has the right to correct any errors found on a credit report. Here are steps to follow:

• Tell the credit agency in writing that the information they have is inaccurate. The letter you send the agency should clearly identify each disputed item in the report, state the facts, and enclose copies of any evidence supporting the claim. The borrower should explain why he disputes the information, and request deletion or correction. Circle the relevant information in the credit report and attach.

• Mail this information by certified mail to ensure you have proof the agency received it.

• At the same time, a borrower should write to the specific creditor he believes acted in error and include the same evidence sent to the agency. This could speed action on the matter. Many creditors have specific addresses and phone numbers for disputes, so check that information so the borrower's case ends up in the right hands.

• The credit agency must reinvestigate the items in question—usually within 30 days—unless they consider the dispute frivolous. They also must forward all relevant data you provide about the dispute to the information provider. After the information provider—the credit card company, utility, bank, etc.—receives notice of a dispute from the agency, it must investigate, review all relevant information provided by the agency, and report the results back to the agency.

• If the information provider finds it did make an error, it must notify all credit agencies so they can correct the information. Disputed information that cannot be verified must be deleted from the borrower's file.

- Important: If a borrower was late with a payment but is now current with a particular account, the credit report must reflect it.

- When the agency's reinvestigation is complete, it must provide the borrower with written results and a free copy of the revised credit report reflecting the change. If an item is changed or removed, the agency cannot put the disputed information back in a borrower's file unless the information provider verifies its accuracy and completeness and supplies contact numbers.

- If a borrower requests, the agency is also required to send correction notices to anyone who received this report in the past six months. Job applicants can have a corrected copy of their report sent to anyone who received a copy during the past two years for employment purposes.

- Lastly, most accurate negative elements of a credit report must be removed after seven years. The exceptions:

  - Information about criminal convictions: no time limit.

  - Depending on the type of bankruptcy filed, bankruptcy can remain on a credit report for seven to 10 years.

  - Credit information reported in response to an application for a job with an annual salary of more than $75,000: no time limit.

  - Credit information reported because of an application for more than $150,000 worth of credit or life insurance: no time limit.

  - Information about a lawsuit or an unpaid judgment can be reported for seven years or until the state's statute of limitations runs out, whichever is longer.

escalation clause:

(1) a provision in a lease that requires the tenant to pay more rent based on an increase in costs.

(2) alternately, a provision in a loan agreement or mortgage in which the entire debt becomes immediately due upon the occurrence of an item, such as missing three consecutive monthly payments or when the current ratio falls below 1.0.

escape clause: an optional provision in any contract that allows one or both parties to abandon their agreement if certain listed events or situations happen.

escheat: when the ownership of a property reverts to the state because the owner dies without leaving a will.

escrow: the holding of documents and money by a neutral party for a real estate transaction. This ensures that all conditions of the sale are met.

escrow account: an account that the lender or mortgage servicer establishes to hold funds for the payments for property taxes and insurance. In some states, this is also known as an *impound account.*

escrow agent: a neutral third party who ensures that all condition of a real estate transaction are completed satisfactorily. A person with fiduciary responsibility to the buyer and seller, or the borrower and lender, to ensure that the terms of the purchase/sale or loan are carried out.

escrow analysis: the periodic examination, by the lender, of an escrow account for purposes of determining if the amount withheld from a borrower's monthly mortgage payment is sufficient to pay for expenses, such as property taxes and insurance.

escrow closing: when all the conditions of a real estate transaction are completed and title of the property is transferred to the buyer, *escrow* is considered closed.

escrow company: a company that acts as a neutral third party, ensuring that all conditions of a real estate transaction, established by the buyer, seller, and lender, are fulfilled.

escrow fees: the amount earned by the escrow agent for accumulating and monitoring data from various sources and for distributing it to the parties.

escrow payment: the funds withdrawn from a borrower's escrow account by the mortgage servicer, to pay property taxes and insurance.

escrow statement: a declaration by an escrow agent that instruments or property are being held in accordance with the agreement of the parties in a real estate deal.

estate: a taxable entity that is established upon the death of a taxpayer. It consists of all the decedent's property and personal effects. The estate exists until the final distribution of its assets to the heirs and other beneficiaries. The executor must complete his administration of the estate with the disbursement of assets and the filing of a tax return.

estate at sufferance: the wrongful occupancy of property by a tenant after the lease has expired.

estate at will: the occupation of real estate by a tenant for an indefinite period, which can be terminated by either party at will.

estate for life: the interest in property which ends with the death of a specified person.

estate for years: an interest in land allowing possession for a specified period of time.

estate of inheritance: an estate that descends to heirs in perpetuity.

estate on condition: a land property estate contingent upon the occurrence or lack of occurrence of a particular event, whereupon it can be created, augmented, or dismantled.

estimate: an appraisal value of property; an approximation of market values. Alternately, to calculate the approximate computation of the cost of completion of construction.

estimated closing costs: an estimate of the expenses incidental to the sale of real estate, including loan, title, and appraisal fees. These costs exist in addition to the price of the property and are paid at closing. Some are one-time expenses and some are recurring.

estimated hazard insurance: an estimate of hazard insurance, known as homeowner's insurance or fire insurance, to cover physical damage such as from fire or wind. Coverage is usually required to equal the replacement value of the home.

estimated property taxes: an estimate of property taxes to be paid. Amount is based on local tax rates and assessed property value (based on most recent sale price plus assessment updates).

estimated taxes and insurance: the calculation of estimated taxes and insurance, which is used by lender to evaluate a borrower's effective monthly housing expense.

estimated useful life: the period of time over which an asset will be used by a particular taxpayer. Although that period cannot be longer than the estimated physical life of an asset, it can be shorter, if the taxpayer does not intend to keep the asset until it wears out. The estimated useful life of an asset is essential to determining the annual tax deduction for depreciation and amortization.

estoppel: the prevention of a person from making a statement of affirmation or denial because it is contrary to a previous statement. The barring of an act.

estoppel by deed: restraining a person or business from denying an appropriate conveyance of property

estoppel certificate: a mortgagor's signed statement that the stated remaining balance of a mortgage is correct. It is a property lien, which later prevents him/her from stating that the facts were misrepresented, therefore making the mortgage invalid.

estover: the right of a tenant to make use of a property's wood- or food-producing capacity to provide for his/her own necessities.

et al: (*Latin*) an abbreviation meaning and others.

et con: (*Latin*) a legal abbreviation meaning with husband.

et ux: (*Latin*) a legal abbreviation meaning with wife.

evict: the removal of a tenant through legal process.

eviction: a legal procedure for removal of a tenant for reasons that would include, but not be limited to, failure to pay rent.

eviction, actual: the act of removing or dispossessing or expulsion of an individual from premises by force or by law.

eviction, constructive: the altering of rented or leased premises by a landlord, rendering it unsuitable for habitation, in order to effectuate the tenant's vacating.

eviction, partial: the removal of a tenant from a portion of a rented or leased premise.

evidence of title: a document, such as a deed, that demonstrates property ownership.

examination of title: a title company review of public records and other documents to determine the chain of ownership of a property. The report on the title of a property from the public records or an abstract of the title.

exception:
(1) the waiver of a requirement in an agreement.
(2) alternately, a right or portion of property reserved to the grantor in a conveyance by deed.

exceptional depreciation: the damages to a building that exceed that of normal wear and tear.

excess condemnation: taking more property in a condemnation proceeding than was originally required or planned.

excess depreciation: costs taken over and above what one is entitled to; can occur either by claiming depreciation costs exceeding the actual depreciable value or by depreciating items that cannot be depreciated.

excess income: rental income, received from property that exceeds the costs of owning and maintaining the property.

exchange: a transfer of property for other property or services. Exchanges of like-kind property are a popular method for deferring taxes.

excluded gain: generally applies to gains realized on the sale of a principal residence.

exclusionary zoning: property zoning that has the net effect, intended or not, of excluding the poor and minority groups from living in a particular area. Large property size requirements are often responsible exclusionary zoning.

exclusive agency: the employment of a particular broker. If a sale by another broker is accepted, both are entitled to commissions.

exclusive buyer's agent (EBA): an agent or company that works exclusively for buyers. They do not represent sellers, or list properties.

exclusive listing: a written contract that gives a licensed real estate agent the exclusive right to sell a property for a specified time, but reserves the owner's right to sell the property himself or herself without the payment of a commission.

exclusive right to sell: a contract with a real estate agent that pays a commission to the agent even if the property is sold to a buyer found by the owner.

exculpatory clause: a provision in a mortgage that allows the borrower to surrender the property to the lender without personal liability for the loan.

execute: to sign, complete, perform, and carry out all the terms of a contract, including signing the contract and delivering it to the proper party.

executed contract: a contract whose terms and provisions have been completely fulfilled and satisfied by all involved parties.

executor: someone appointed to carry out instructions left in a will. If no executor is named in the will, one is named by the probate court.

executor's deed: a deed to convey property, which is done by the executor of a will once it is authorized by the probate court.

executory cost: the cost excluded from the minimum lease payments to be made by the lessee in a capital lease. The *lessee* reimburses the *lessor* for the lessor's expense payments.

exemplary damages: see *punitive damages*.

exempt: real estate that is not subject to property tax, such as that owned by nonprofit entities, including charitable, governmental, and religious institutions.

exemption:

(1) an amount provided by law that reduces taxable income or taxable value.

(2) Alternately, removal of property from the tax base, partially or completely.

expansible house: a house designed to be easily expanded, such as having a basement that may be finished after, or an attic that can be expanded into more bedrooms.

expenditure: a payment, or the promise of a future payment.

expense: any operating cost, such as rent, utilities, and payroll, as distinguished from capital expenditure for long-term property and equipment. The cost of maintaining property.

expense ratio: the percentage of assets used to build or operate a piece of property.

expenses: for federal income tax purposes, expenses are divided into four categories:

• trade or business expenses;
• expenses in connection with production of income or in connection with management, conservation, or maintenance of property held for production of income;
• expenses in connection with the determination, collection, or refund of any tax; and
• personal, family, or living expenses.

Expenses in the first three categories are generally deductible in determining taxable income. Expenses in the fourth category are not deductible, except in a few cases (medical expenses, charitable contributions, etc.) in which they are specifically allowed by law. Expenses are to be distinguished from *capital expenditures*.

expenses of sale: when paid by the seller, these expenses reduce the sale price of property. Examples are commissions to a broker or real estate agent, title search, title insurance, legal fees, and transfer taxes.

Experian: formerly known as TRW Information Systems and Services; one of the Big Three credit reporting firms. Experian: 888-397-3742, Web: www.experian.com.

ex post facto: (*Latin*) an act occurring after the fact.

exposure: a person or business susceptible to loss on an investment, such as a high-risk speculation. The advertising, whether free or paid, of property that is for sale. Open to the elements, unhidden from view.

express agreement or contract: a contract where all parties express their intentions in words, orally or written.

extended coverage: protection over and above that of a standard policy or warranty; covers things that might otherwise be excluded.

extension (tax): a filing made with the Internal Revenue Service to pay taxes after the deadline. In the extension form, a taxpayer must make a reasonable estimate of his tax liability for the year. Failing to do so will result in a penalty.

extraordinary item: a nonrecurring event that materially affected a company's finances in a reporting period. Must be explained in the annual report or quarterly report.

F

façade: the external front of a building that faces the street or courtyard; usually used to describe bigger, elegant buildings.

face brick: an exterior decorative surface, made of brick that is not rendered, painted, or plastered, and of various brick materials, including clay, to give a desired effect.

faced masonry: a masonry structure that has different types of material as backing and facing, such as brick on concrete, bonded together.

face velocity: the measurement of the air velocity as measured at the face of the inlet or outlet in an *HVAC* system.

facilitator: a real estate professional who aids in a transaction but does not have an agency relationship with that party and can be known as an intermediary or transaction broker.

factoring: the purchase of the accounts receivable of a business, or, alternately, taking the accounts receivable of a business as collateral for a loan.

factor of safety: the ratio of the maximum strength of a piece of material or a part to the probably maximum load to be applied to it. If a maximum of 2,000 pounds can be tolerated, a load of 500 pounds will have a four-to-one factor of safety.

Fair Credit Billing Act: a federal law governing credit and charge card billing errors. If the credit card company violates this law, consumers can sue for damages.

Fair Credit Reporting Act: a consumer protection law that regulates the disclosure of consumer credit reports by consumer-credit reporting agencies and establishes procedures for correcting mistakes on one's credit record.

Fair Debt Collection Practices Act: a federal law outlawing debtor harassment and regulating collections agencies, original creditor's collection offices (if separate), and creditor's lawyers. Original creditors may be covered under state law.

Fair Housing Act: a federal law making it illegal to refuse to rent or sell to anyone based on race, color, religion, sex, or national origin. 1988 amendments expanded protections to include family status and disability.

Fair, Issac, and Co.: a leading company that creates the *credit score* technology used by lenders. The company's predictive modeling, decision analysis, intelligence management, decision management systems, and consulting services are behind more than 25 billion lending decisions a year. The company was founded in 1956.

fair market rent: the rent a property commands in a free and open market setting.

fair market value: the amount at which property would change hands between a willing buyer and a willing seller, neither being under compulsion to buy or sell and both having reasonable knowledge of the relevant facts.

fair rental value: the amount the owner of property could reasonably expect to receive from a stranger for the same type of lodging; generally, the amount at which a home with its furnishings could be rented to a similar size family in a similar location.

falling out of escrow: a situation where one of the parties is unable to satisfy the conditions of the purchase and sale contract.

false personation: a criminal act of falsely representing another individual to gain profit or an advantage.

family limited partnership: a limited partnership whose interests are owned by members of the same family so that gift and estate taxes may be reduced, although the freedom or transferability of ownership is not available.

fanlight: a half-circle window, often with sash bars resembling the ribs of a fan; usually used above doorways and large windows.

Fannie Mae: see *Federal National Mortgage Association.*

Farmer's Home Administration (FmHA): see *U.S. Department of Agriculture Rural Development.*

Farm Service Agency (FSA): an agency of the U.S. Department of Agriculture that offers direct and guaranteed loan programs to help farmers unable to obtain credit. Qualified farmers obtain their credit through the use of loan guarantees, where a local agricultural lender makes and services the loan, and FSA guarantees the loan up to a maximum of 90 percent. Web: www.fsa.usda.gov.

FASB: see *Financial Accounting Standards Board*.

fascia:

(1) horizontal, flat trim pieces that are used around the outer end of roof rafters at eave/wall junctures.

(2) horizontal bands, with each band projecting out from a wall a bit more than the one below; this creates a tiered molding around a window or door.

(3) board connecting the ends of the roof rafters and providing a surface to support gutters.

FDIC: see *Federal Deposit Insurance Corporation*.

feasibility study: research on the prospects that a proposed development will fulfill the objectives of a particular investor. This study should estimate the demand for the product, the absorption rate, legal considerations, cash flow, and approximate investment returns likely to be produced. Analysis is also made of alternative means of accomplishing the task.

Federal Agency Securities: debt instruments of U.S agencies such as the Federal Home Loan Bank, the Federal National Mortgage Association, the Federal FARM Credit Bureau, and the Tennessee Valley Authority. Although these issues are not direct obligations of the U.S. Treasury, they still have a high credit rating.

Federal Deposit Insurance Corporation (FDIC): an independent governmental agency that insures up to $100,000 per depositor in participating banks and savings and loan associations. Web: www.fdic.gov.

Federal Fair Housing Law: originally passed as Title VIII of the Civil Rights Act of 1968, it prohibits discrimination in the sale or rental of residential dwelling units or vacant land on the basis of color, national origin, race, religion, or sex.

Federal Home Loan Bank Board (FHLBB): a federal agency that monitors the federal savings and loan associations and federally insured state-chartered S&Ls and acts as a central bank. In addition, it operated the Federal Savings and Loan Insurance Corporation (FSLIC).

Federal Home Loan Bank System (FHLBS): a federally created banking system intended to assure liquidity to qualified thrift lenders; twelve regional Federal Home Loan Banks are directed since 1932 by the *Federal Home Loan Bank Board (FHLBB).* The regulatory functions went to the Office of Thrift Supervision, which was established to replace the Federal Home Loan Bank Board as part of the *Financial Institutions Reform, Recovery and Enforcement Act (FIRREA).*

Federal Home Loan Mortgage Corporation (FHLMC, or Freddie Mac): this agency buys loans that are underwritten to its specific guidelines, pools them, and sells shares to investors. These guidelines are an industry standard for residential conventional lending. Web: www.freddiemac.com.

Federal Housing Administration (FHA): a federal agency within the *Department of Housing and Urban Development (HUD),* which insures residential mortgage loans made by private lenders and sets standards for underwriting mortgage loans. Web: www.hud.gov.

Federal Housing Administration Insured Mortgages: mortgages insured by the *Federal Housing Administration (FHA).* FHA insurance is intended to make more housing available and to safeguard the lender against risk of nonpayment.

Federal Housing Finance Board: the U.S. government agency that regulates the 12 banks created in 1932 to improve the supply of funds to local lenders that, in turn, finance loans for home mortgages. This agency also tracks average mortgage rates around the country. Web: www.fhfb.gov.

federally related mortgage: a mortgage loan that must follow federal guidelines because it is guaranteed, insured, or otherwise regulated by a government agency.

federally related transaction: a real estate transaction that is overseen by a federal agency.

Federal National Mortgage Association (FNMA): dubbed Fannie Mae, this congressionally chartered, shareholder-owned company buys mortgages from lenders and resells them as securities on the secondary mortgage market. This agency buys loans that are underwritten to its specific guidelines. These guidelines are an industry standard for residential conventional lending. The current limit for a Fannie Mae one-family loan is $322,700. Phone: 800-732-6643, Web: www.fanniemae.com.

Federal Reserve Board: a group of economists who set the nation's monetary policy through its ability to control interest rates, thereby controlling inflation. Web: www.federalreserve.com.

Federal Savings and Loan Association: a charter issued by the Office of Thrift Supervision, under the U.S. Department of Treasury, to an institution to act as a savings and loan association. A federally chartered savings and loan association, in contrast to one with a state charter, may have the ability to branch across state lines as well as to make certain investments a state-chartered thrift institution cannot.

Federal style: an American architectural style, which evolved after the Revolutionary War and includes bigger windows and a glass-surrounded front doorway, topped with an arched window.

federal tax lien: a lien placed on an individual's real property by the federal government, for federal income or estate tax violations. If these taxes are not paid, the government may seek a tax warrant, causing a federal tax lien to be placed against the taxpayer's property. In the event of death, the estate is liable for the lien.

Federal Trade Commission (FTC): a government agency that regulates companies and industries, including collections agencies, timeshare operators, etc. National headquarters: 600 Pennsylvania Avenue NW, Washington, D.C. 20580. Phone: 202-326-2222, web: www.ftc.gov.

fee ownership: a form of ownership giving the owner complete control, including the development of an inheritable estate; also known as a fee estate.

fee simple: this type of ownership, which is the maximum interest a person can have in a piece of real estate, entitles the owner to use the property in any manner as long as it is in accordance with state and local laws.

fee simple absolute: an estate limited absolutely to an owner and his or her heirs in perpetuity and without limitation. This status entitles the owner to full ownership of the property and the unrestricted ability to divide it among the heirs.

fee simple conditional: a fee estate conditioned by the provisions of the grantor or the grantor's heirs that some action occur in order to complete its conveyance. If this condition does not occur, the estate returns to the original grantor.

fee simple defeasible: a fee simple ownership that can be defeated and returned to the grantor should a particular event occur.

fee simple determinable: a fee estate limited by the happening of a certain event.

feng shui: an ancient Chinese philosophy that believes that the positioning and physical characteristics of a home affect the fortunes and well-being of the owner.

FHA: see *Federal Housing Administration.*

FHA loans: mortgage loans that are insured by the *Federal Housing Administration (FHA).* The FHA operates loan plans for purchasers of rural property, as well as providing low-rate mortgages to buyers who make down payments as low as 3 percent. With FHA insurance, a borrower can purchase a home with a low down payment of from 3 to 5 percent of the FHA-appraised value or of the purchase price, whichever is lower. FHA mortgages have a maximum loan limit that varies depending on the average cost of housing in a given region. In general, the loan limit is less than what is available with a conventional mortgage through a lender. Web: www.hud.gov.

fidelity: the accuracy of a description, translation, reproduction.

fidelity bond: insurance coverage purchased by an employer to cover employees who are entrusted with valuable property or funds, and to protect against specified losses arising from any dishonest act by these employees.

fiduciary: a person or institution acting in a legal capacity in the best interests of someone, including to hold or administer property owned by another.

fiduciary duty: the holding in trust of something by one person for another. Also applies to legal, real estate, and business relationships.

fifteen-year mortgage: a fixed rate, level-payment mortgage loan where, for a slight increase in monthly payments, the loan can be paid off in only 15 years. The overall savings in interest paid to the lender, between the 15-year and 30-year mortgage, can be quite substantial without making the monthly payment significantly higher.

final value estimate: a final property appraisal estimate arrived at by the use of appropriate appraisal methods.

final walk-through inspection: a sales contract should include a clause that allows a buyer to examine the property he wants to purchase within the 24 hours before closing. Real estate professionals typically accompany their clients on this walk-through, which is the last chance to ensure that the seller has vacated the house and left behind whatever property was agreed upon before papers are signed. During the walk-through, a buyer should:
- make sure to check that all lights, appliances, and plumbing fixtures are in working order;
- double-check that all conditions of the sales contract have been met;
- plan to delay the closing if problems are discovered and not cleared up before a specific time.

finance charge: interest and any other charges, including points that make up the fees incurred when borrowing money.

financed closing costs: the costs for closing of title that are added to the loan amount rather than being paid up front. This practice adds to the amount borrowed, increasing the monthly payment.

Financial Accounting Standards Board (FASB): an independent agency that establishes *GAAP.*

financial asset: a nonphysical asset, such as a security, certificate, or bank balance; the opposite of nonfinancial asset.

financial calculator: a calculator that has numerous built-in financial functions, including cash flow analysis, mortgage amortization, present and future yield, yield to maturity, and many other business statistics and financial ratios.

financial capital: funds that are available to acquire real capital.

financial condition: the status of a firm's assets, liabilities, and equity positions at a specific point in time, often described in a financial statement.

financial feasibility: a study of the economic ability of a proposed land use to justify itself.

financial index: an index is a number to which the interest rate on an *adjustable-rate mortgage (ARM)* is tied. It is generally a published number expressed as a percentage, such as the average interest rate or yield on U.S. Treasury bills. A margin is added to the index to determine the interest rate that will be charged on ARMs. This interest rate is subject to any caps associated with the mortgage. The interest rate changes on an ARM are tied to some type of financial index. Some of the most common type of indexed ARMs are:

• Treasury-Indexed ARMs;
• CD-Indexed ARMs (Certificate of Deposit);
• Cost of Funds-Indexed ARMs (COFI);
• LIBOR-Based ARMs.

When comparing ARMs, look at how the index to which it is tied has performed recently. A lender can provide information on how to track the index and a history of the index they use.

Financial Institutions Reform, Recovery and Enforcement Act (FIRREA): a law restructuring the regulatory apparatus dealing with savings and loan associations.

financial intermediary: a financial entity, usually a bank, that facilitates the transfer of funds between borrowers and lenders, depositors and investors.

financial leverage: the ability of borrowed money to magnify the effects of profits.

financial markets: a market for creating and exchanging capital and credit in the economy.

financial statement: a report that shows income and expenses for an accounting period; normally consists of a balance sheet, income statement, and statement of cash flows. A bank may request a financial statement from a prospective borrower for commercial property or any other business use.

financial structure: the right side of a firm's balance sheet, detailing how its assets are financed, including debt and equity issues.

financing: the loaning and borrowing of money to buy property.

finder's fee: a fee or commission paid to a mortgage broker for finding a mortgage loan for a prospective borrower.

fire division wall: a wall designed and rated to delay passage of fire, which extends continuously from the bottom to the top of a structure.

fire door: a door designed to resist the passage of fire. Fire doors are rated by the amount of time they can resist the penetration of fire, with the time ranging from one-half to three hours. Fire doors are used to close openings in firewalls, so that the door area is no more vulnerable to fire than the wall.

fire extinguisher: a device containing fire-suppressing material under pressure, which is directed at the fire to extinguish it by means of oxygen deprivation and/or cooling. Extinguishers are rated as follows:
- Grade A—ordinary material fires;
- Grade B—flammable liquids fires;
- Grade C—electrical fires;
- Grade D—materials that need an extinguishing compound to absorb heat and not react with the fuel.

fire lines: the use of a wet standpipe, which is a vertical pipe, always full of water, that reaches to the upper floors of a building and can be immediately accessed to distribute water in the event of a fire.

fire rating: a rating system that shows the fire resistance of a material or system as tested by a recognized laboratory against applicable *ASTM* standards.

firewall: a fireproof wall placed to prevent the spread of fire.

firm commitment: a written promise made by the lender to loan money. It usually contains all of the terms relevant to the transaction.

FIRREA: see *Financial Institutions Reform, Recovery, and Enforcement Act.*

first mortgage: the primary mortgage on a property, which takes priority over any other liens and is satisfied before any secondary liens. In the case of a foreclosure, the first mortgage will be repaid before any other mortgages.

first refusal right: being offered the right to buy something before it is offered to others. The opportunity of a party to match the terms of a proposed contract before the contract is executed.

first user: the initial user of real estate, such as the first occupant of a newly built home.

fiscal: pertaining to money, especially government taxation and spending policies.

fiscal year: an accounting period of twelve months, but not necessarily starting on January 1.

five c's of credit: a historic guideline lenders have used to award credit that still holds today: character (willingness to pay); capacity (financial cash flow); capital (wealth); collateral (security); and conditions (economic status).

fixed asset: a long-term, tangible asset held for business use and not expected to be converted to cash in the current or upcoming fiscal year, such as real estate, business equipment, and furniture.

fixed-charge coverage ratio: the profits before income taxes and interest payments, divided by long-term interest, for a given period of time.

fixed cost: a cost that does not vary depending on production or sales levels, such as rent, property tax, insurance, or interest expense.

fixed expenses: those expenses that remain the same regardless of circumstances.

fixed installment: monthly home loan payments.

fixed payment mortgage: a mortgage with fixed periodic payments of interest and principle.

fixed-period adjustable-rate mortgages: this type of *adjustable-rate mortgage (ARM)* maintains the same initial interest rate for the first three, five, seven, or 10 years of the loan, depending on the term offered. Afterward, the rate adjusts annually, and can move up or down as market conditions change. Borrowers should make sure there is a cap that prevents such a mortgage from becoming unaffordable.

fixed-rate mortgage: a loan with an interest rate that remains at a specific rate for the entire loan. Approximately 75 percent of home mortgages are this type. Also see *balloon mortgage* and *biweekly payment mortgage*.

fixer-upper: a house that needs repair and remodeling and sells at below market price.

fixing-up expenses: the expenses incurred to enhance the appearance and condition of real estate to prepare it for sale.

fixture: shelving or display pieces in a commercial enterprise.

flame spread rating: tests, done in accordance with *ASTM* Standard E84, for establishment of fire-resistant values of building materials by measuring how fast and far flames will spread over certain surfaces.

flashing: metal strips used to prevent water seepage, and installed around chimneys, vents, windows, doors, and skylights, along seams in the roof, and beneath shingles. The purpose of flashing is to prevent the penetration of water as well as to provide a drainage passageway between joints, most commonly the joint between a roof and a wall.

flat: an apartment within a multi-family house, usually on one floor.

flat fee: a set amount charged by a broker, as opposed to a percentage.

flat lease: a lease agreement having level payments during the contractual period; does not have an escalation clause, which would allow for increased costs due to increases in inflation, taxes, or other related costs.

flexible loan insurance program (FLIP): a *graduated-payment mortgage (GMP)* developed to overcome the negative amortization aspects of the GMP. The buyer's own down payment is deposited in a pledged, interest-bearing account, where it is used as both cash collateral and a source of supplemental payments during the initial years of the loan. During this time, predetermined amounts are withdrawn by the lender from the savings account and added to the borrower's reduced payment, making a full mortgage payment. Decreasing every month, it disappears at the end of a predetermined period. Using this type of program is likely to make a borrower able to qualify for a larger loan than with a conventional fully amortized mortgage.

flexible payment mortgage: a loan allowing the borrower to pay only the interest for the first few years of the loan.

flexible rate mortgage (FRM): a mortgage with an interest rate that changes based on certain events, such as changes in the prime rate.

floating interest rate: an interest rate that is not fixed over the term of a loan, bond, or other fixed-income security but is allowed to vary according to the change in a specified index, such as the prime interest rate or the Treasury bill rate.

flood certification: the determination as to whether or not a property is located in a flood zone. If it is, the lender will require federally provided *flood insurance*.

flood insurance: special coverage that is required for property in a designated flood plain or zone since that risk is typically not covered under standard hazard insurance.

flood plain or zone: a level land area subject to periodic flooding because of its proximity to body of water. During the flood stage, the property may be underwater.

floor area ratio (FAR): the ratio between a structure's total floor area and the total land area of the land upon which it is constructed. The FAR is calculated by dividing the total building floor area by the total building lot square area: floor area ratio = building floor area/building lot area. A maximum allowable floor area ratio is typically specified by the local building code or zoning.

floor joists: the beams that provide structural floor support. The flooring is directly attached to the floor joists. (see *Appendix B*)

floor load capacity: the amount of weight that the floors can support.

floor loan: the minimum amount of money a lender is willing to provide on a commercial loan for a building that is to be tenant occupied. This loan is progressively funded as the building is constructed and occupied.

floor plan: the arrangement of rooms in a structure. A two-dimensional scale drawing of the arrangements, size, and orientation of doors, rooms, walls, and windows of a single floor of a building structure.

Florida room: a glass-enclosed porch at the rear or side of a home, usually in warm-weather areas.

flue lining: heat-resistant lining, usually of fire clay or terra cotta pipe, used for the inner lining of chimneys.

flue pipe: an airtight conduit constructed within a chimney using fireproof materials to carry away combustion gases and smoke occurring in a furnace or firebox.

flush door: a door with plywood facing over the internal core of wood or wood products. A hollow core door is one with plywood facing over framework without a solid core.

foam insulation: foam produced by catalyzed chemical reactions that hardens in the walls. The term includes both spray-applied and injected applications, such as spray-in-place foam and pour-in-place foam.

forbearance: a lender's decision to refrain from taking legal action on a delinquent loan in hopes the default will be remedied in a timely manner.

forced air heating system (forced hot air): a heating system that circulates warm air from a heat source, through the ducting by means of a blower fan.

forced sale: the sale of property where the seller is under duress and is unable to allow current market prices and conditions to determine the selling price.

force majeure: a delay or failure to perform an obligation in time, due to an unpreventable, overwhelming, and irresistible force. This is sometimes called an Act of God delay.

foreclosure: a legal process in which a lender ends the borrower's interest in a property after a loan is defaulted. The lender takes the property and then sells it to cover the mortgage amount and legal costs from the proceeds of the sale. Any other proceeds may be returned to the borrower. Foreclosure is usually a last step that lenders will take after efforts to work out a delinquent loan have been exhausted.

foreclosure sale: the public sale of a property after the legal process of foreclosure is completed.

forfeit: to relinquish a right.

forfeiture: the loss of money, property, rights, or privileges due to a breach of legal obligation.

for sale by owner (FSBO): a homeowner acting as salesperson for his/her own property. No listing commission is paid, but a sales commission may be paid to a buyer's agent.

foundation: the support structure of a house. The base or portion of a structure that is in contact with the ground, usually extending below grade. A support on which something stands.

foundation bolt: a bolt that is set into wet concrete, to be used for the attachment of the pressure-treated boards (called the mud sill or sill plate) once the concrete has hardened. Once in place, these boards will be the base of the framing structure.

foundation plan: a drawing, used for construction, which shows all the dimensions and placement of the foundation.

four-way switch: a switching device that uses three switches to permit an outlet to be operated from all three switches. Also called a double-pole reversing switch, this electrical switch is used in conjunction with two three-way switches in cases where three points for controlling an electrical circuit are needed.

frame:

(1) the basic, skeletal structural around which a building is built and which gives it its shape or form.

(2) the border or case into which a window or door is set, which serves as a structural support.

(3) to enclose or to provide a border for.

framing: the structural skeleton of a building, including interior and exterior walls, floor, roof, and ceilings.

franchise: a license granted by a company to a smaller firm to operate a business within a specific area; many real estate agents operate as franchisees for larger national real estate franchisers.

Freddie Mac: see *Federal Home Loan Mortgage Corporation (FHLMC).*

free and clear title: a property title that has no encumbrances, including mortgages, judgments, or financial liens.

free cash flow: operating cash flow (net income plus amortization and depreciation) minus capital expenditures and dividends.

freehold estate: an estate in which ownership is for an indefinite length of time. Unlimited interest in a property. Examples of freehold estates include: a fee simple absolute—which is inheritable and lasts as long as the individual and heir want it; and a life estate—in which the land remains in possession of the individual for his or her lifetime.

French Provincial: a formal, two-story house with a high, steep roof and curve-headed upper windows that come through the cornice.

frieze: decorative molding around the tops of walls, columns, etc.

frontage: the linear measurement of a parcel of land along a lake, river, street, or highway.

front-end ratio: a lender calculation comparing a borrower's monthly housing expense (principal, interest, taxes, and insurance) to gross monthly income.

front footage: the number of feet of street frontage of a parcel of land.

front money: the amount of money necessary to start a project. Money invested in the initial stage of a business transaction to demonstrate good faith as well as to help offset some expenses.

FSBO: see *for sale by owner.*

full covenant and warranty deed: a type of property deed containing five warranties:
- covenant of seisin—assurance that the purchaser has possession of the property in quantity and quality as promised;
- covenant of quiet enjoyment—assurance of hostile claims to the property title;
- no liens and encumbrances;
- covenant of further assurance—assurance by the seller to the purchaser that all necessary actions to perfect the title will be undertaken, should any claims arise against the title; and
- warranty of title.

full disclosure: the requirement to reveal any and all pertinent information

full-service broker: a real estate broker who performs all services, including listing and selling.

full warranty: a warranty that entitles a homeowner to full remedies for defective work by a contractor.

fully amortized adjustable-rate mortgage: a mortgage that pays down (amortizes) the balance of a loan.

fully amortized mortgage: a mortgage that has been paid in full and has no balance due.

fully depreciated: of an asset, having already allocated the maximum allowable amount for the purposes of depreciation.

fully indexed rate: the interest rate that is used to calculate monthly payments in the absence of constraints imposed by the *initial rate* or caps. Fully indexed rate, in conjunction with adjustable-rate mortgages, is the interest rate indicated by the sum of the current value of the index and margin applied to the loan.

functional deficiency: the negative characteristics about a property that do not meet the needs of the usual occupant.

functional depreciation: the loss of value, except for those due to physical deterioration.

Functional Modern house: a post–World War II house incorporating modern technology, material, and architecture, including energy conservation methods, to achieve a highly functional structure.

funded debt ratio: the percentage of working capital from funds that have been borrowed to the working capital available from equity.

furring: narrow strips fastened to the walls and ceilings to form a straight surface upon which to lay the lath or other finish.

future advance clause: a clause in an open-ended mortgage that permits the mortgagor to borrow additional sums of money in the future by pledging the same real estate as collateral. Construction loans have a future advance clause providing additional loan guarantees as the building project progresses.

future interest: a property or estate right that may not be enjoyed until sometime in the future when a certain event occurs, such as a life estate that will pass to another individual having a future interest as a fee simple estate.

G

GAAP: see *Generally Accepted Accounting Principles.*

gable: a triangular wall enclosed by the sloping ends of a ridged roof and the top wall plate. The entire section, including wall, roof, and space enclosed, is referred to in that manner. (see *Appendix B*)

gain: the excess of the amount realized from a sale or exchange over the adjusted basis of the property sold or exchanged.

gambrel roof: a roof with two differently angled slopes on each side, similar to a barn roof.

gap: a defect in the chain of title, such as a missing document, raising doubt as to true ownership.

gap loan: temporary financing bridging the difference between the construction loan and the permanent loan. Also called a *bridge loan* or *standby loan.*

garden apartment:
(1) a below ground-level apartment with a view of the lawn or backyard.
(2) also refers to a particular type of housing project where all residents have access to a lawn area.

gated community: an exclusive, fenced-in housing development featuring a security guard at the entrance.

gazebo: a small roofed structure, usually round and open-sided, providing a place for resting.

GDP: see *Gross Domestic Product.*

GEM: see *Growing Equity Mortgage.*

general contractor: a contractor who assumes responsibility for completing a construction project, under contract to the owner, and hires, supervises, and pays all subcontractors. A borrower using mortgage funds to renovate a home may be required by a lender to review whether the contractor meets all federal, state, and local registration, and licensing and certification standards. Also known as *prime contractor.*

general depreciation system: the most commonly used *MACRS* system. Personal property is depreciated using the *declining-balance* method (double or 150 percent, depending on the recovery class), switching to *straight line* when that method results in the larger deduction. Residential rental property is depreciated using the straight-line method over 27.5 years, and nonresidential real property is depreciated using the straight-line method over 39 years (31.5 years for property placed in service before May 13, 1993).

general ledger: a book of final entry summarizing all of a company's financial transactions, through offsetting debit and credit accounts.

general lien: a lien that includes all of the property owned by the debtor, rather than a specific property; it may be obtained either through a judgment lien, where the court issues a judgment, a lien by creditors on an estate, or through federal and state tax liens.

Generally Accepted Accounting Principles (GAAP): a widely accepted set of rules, conventions, standards, and procedures for reporting financial information, as established by the *Financial Accounting Standards Board*.

general partner: a partner in a limited partnership who has the right to manage its operations and has unlimited personal liability.

general straight-line depreciation system: a *MACRS* system of depreciation using the *straight-line* method over the normal MACRS recovery period for the asset.

general warranty deed: a deed in which the grantor agrees to protect the grantee against any other claim to title of the property. The covenants assure good title, freedom from encumbrances, and quiet enjoyment.

Georgian style: a large, English-style home, originally built in the eighteenth century. Georgian homes are usually two to three stories, and are characterized by paneled front doors, double hung windows, and a simple exterior. (*see Appendix A*)

gift tax: a federal tax placed on a gift, monetary or property. The tax is based on the appraised value (if other than monetary) at the time of transfer. Under current tax law, each person may gift up to

$11,000 tax-free annually to another person.

G.I. Loan: a loan made through the *Department of Veteran Affairs*.

G.I. Loan Guarantee: see *VA Guarantee*.

Ginnie Mae: see *Government National Mortgage Association (GNMA)*.

girder: a very large beam that supports other beams; a timber beam used to support wall beams or joists.

good and marketable title: same as *clear title:* free of problems.

good faith: the concept that each party in a real estate transaction is presumed to be honest and fair with no deceit, and their intentions are presumed honorable and realistic.

good-faith estimate: a report from a lender that outlines the costs a borrower will incur to get a mortgage. It is based on the lender's typical loan origination costs for the area where the home is located. The estimate usually changes between application and closing, so borrowers should review the settlement form before the closing meeting. The settlement form will list the actual amount of money the borrower will need to bring to closing. *Closing costs* will need to be paid with a certified or cashier's check, because personal checks usually are not accepted.

good repair clause: a contract clause indicating that the property must be properly maintained to keep the contract valid, which creates liability for the *seller* or *lessee* if the subject property is found to be in need of repairs.

goodwill: the ability of a business to generate income in excess of a normal rate on assets due to superior managerial skills, favorable relationships, market position, new product technology, etc. In the purchase of a business, goodwill represents the difference between the purchase price and the value of the net assets. Goodwill acquired after August 10, 1993, must be amortized over a 15-year period and is subject to recapture when the business is sold.

government mortgage: a mortgage that is insured by the *Federal Housing Administration (FHA)* or guaranteed by the *Department of Veterans Affairs (VA)* or the *Rural Housing Service (RHS)*.

Government National Mortgage Association (GNMA): a government-owned corporation within the U.S. Department of Housing and Urban Development (HUD). Created by Congress on September 1, 1968, GNMA assumed responsibility for the special assistance loan program formerly administered by *Fannie Mae.* Popularly known as Ginnie Mae, the corporation funds high-risk mortgages typically in areas approved for government construction projects that have no other funding sources. The government body also buys home loans issued by others, such as commercial banks, mortgage banks, and insurers, and, after pooling them together, sells shares to investors. Unlike Fannie Mae and *Freddie Mac,* Ginnie Maes are backed by the United States and thus have a higher credit standing. Web: www.ginniemae.gov.

Government Rectangular Survey: see *rectangular survey.*

GPM: see *graduated-payment mortgage.*

grace period: a period of time during which a loan payment may be made after its due date without incurring a late penalty. The grace period is specified as part of the terms of the loan in the lending agreement.

graded tax: increasing tax rates as levels of taxable income rise.

graduated lease: a lease that provides for increases at stated intervals.

graduated-payment adjustable-rate mortgage (GPARM): an *adjustable-rate mortgage* that requires lower payments in the early years of the loan than later. It benefits borrowers who are strapped for cash at the outset of the loan.

graduated-payment mortgage (GPM): a mortgage where the monthly payments are low for the first few years, gradually rise for a few years, and then remain fixed.

Graduate Realtor® Institute (GRI): a designation issued by the *National Association of Realtors® (NAR)* to members meeting specific performance and education requirements for residential real estate sales.

grandfather clause: a clause in a statute exempting already-existing violations.

grant: the technical term used in a deed of conveyance of property to indicate a transfer to another party.

grantee: one to whom an interest in a piece of property is conveyed.

grantor: a person conveying interest in a piece of property to another.

grantor/grantee index: a search engine or library of public records that cross-references *grantors* and *grantees* of properties with each other and their common properties. Many communities allow these searches to be done online.

Greek Revival style: a nineteenth century style whose most prominent feature is a pillar-anchored pediment forming a portico in front of the house. (*see Appendix A*)

grid:
(1) a pattern of lines laid out at right angles to each other.
(2) alternately, a series of intersecting lines dividing a map or chart into equal sections.
(3) also, the intersecting bars, wires, or supports, as in a grating or supports in a dropped ceiling.

gross area: the total floor area of a structure, expressed in square feet, usually measured by taking outside measurement.

Gross Domestic Product (GDP): the measurement of the value of all goods and services produced by the economy within its boundaries; the nation's broadest gauge of economic health. GDP is normally stated in annual terms, though data are compiled and released quarterly. The government gives a preliminary figure every quarter and revises it twice. GDP is one measure of the state of the economy.

gross income: the total revenue of a household before expenses and taxes are subtracted.

gross income multiplier: the method used to compute the price of an income-producing property by dividing the asking or market price of the property by the current gross rental income. If the current gross rental income is $30,000 and the asking price is $300,000, the gross income multiplier is 10. Also known as *gross rent multiplier.*

gross leasable area (GLA): a building's total floor area, in square feet, available for tenant leasing.

gross lease: a rental in which the landlord pays all operating costs, such as taxes, utilities, insurance, and maintenance.

gross margin: gross income divided by net sales, expressed as a percentage.

gross profit: the profit remaining after the deduction of direct costs but before the deduction of expenses.

gross rent multiplier: see *gross income multiplier.*

gross rents: the total income from rents before expenses or the depreciation or cost recovery deduction.

ground lease: a lease of land only.

ground plan: a view of a plot showing the structures located upon it.

ground rent: the amount of money that is paid for the use of land when title to a property is held as a leasehold estate rather than as a fee simple estate.

group home: a residence used to house unrelated people needing special care or supervision. The structure provides long-term housing and support services.

growing-equity mortgage: a mortgage that provides scheduled payment increases over an established period of time, with the increased amount of the monthly payment applied directly toward reducing the remaining balance of the mortgage. The loan will be retired in less time than a loan with a fixed payment.

guarantee: a financially binding guaranty assuring that the guarantor will fulfill an obligation or contractual agreement.

guaranteed payment loan: an assurance that a loan's financial obligation will be secured by a third party.

guaranteed sales program: a real estate brokerage program that purchases the seller's equity if a property does not sell during a certain period of time.

guarantee mortgage: a loan that is guaranteed by a third party, for example a government institution.

guaranty: a promise to uphold a guarantor's contractual and financial obligation in the event of default.

guardian: one who is appointed to administer the personal affairs and property of an individual who is incompetent.

guardian's deed: a deed used to convey property of a minor or legally incompetent person.

gutter: a shallow channel to collect rainwater and melted snow at the eaves of a roof; the gutter diverts water away from the house.

gypsum: a naturally occurring mineral that is the main component of drywall.

H

habendum clause: the "to have and to hold" clause that defines or limits the quantity of the estate granted in the deed. Declares whether the type of ownership conveyed is fee simple, a life estate, or something different.

half-bath: a room with only a toilet and a washbasin but no shower or tub.

handyman's special: this generally refers to a property that requires significant renovation, though it often sells at an attractive price.

hard money:
(1) currency that has wide acceptance, such as the U.S. dollar.
(2) alternately, gold or silver coins, as compared to paper currency.
(3) also, actual cash exchanged in a loan; term sometimes used to describe extremely high-interest-rate mortgage loans made to desperate borrowers.

hazard: a condition that affects the probability of losses or perils occurring, such as flood damage to a house.

hazard insurance: essentially, homeowner's insurance or fire insurance. Hazard insurance covers physical risks such as those from fire or wind. Usually required by lenders for the full replacement value.

header:
(1) a structural support over an opening. (see *Appendix B*)
(2) a joist that supports other joists.

heavy timber construction: the use of heavy timbers, connected with bolting and metal plates at their intersections, for main structural pieces in construction. The heavy timbers carry the structural load, so studs are added to form partitions and not for weight bearing.

hectare: a metric measurement, equaling 2.471 acres, or about 107,637 square feet, or 10,000 square meters.

heir: an individual legally entitled to inherit money and property on the death of another person.

heirs and assigns: language commonly used in a *fee simple* title conveyance. The significance is whether the title is clear and can be passed on to the purchaser's estate, including all heirs and those who may have any interest in the estate, the assigns.

hereditaments: property, real estate or personal, tangible or intangible, which may be inherited.

heterogeneous:
(1) a mixed assortment of housing styles in a residential development.
(2) alternately, mixed zoning uses in an urban development plan.

hiatus: a gap between two parcels of land, which is not included in the legal description of either parcel.

hidden asset: an asset not immediately apparent from a balance sheet.

hidden clauses: ambiguous contractual language that may result in an unsuspecting buyer of real estate incurring obligations or risks not clearly evident.

high density: the concentration of housing units on a specific property or in a specific area.

highest and best use: an appraisal term meaning the legally and physically possible use that will produce the greatest current value.

high loan-to-value loan: a loan covering more than 100 percent of the market value of the home. Such loans are used as a refinancing tool, essentially making them a *home equity loan*.

high-rise: a building, usually taller than six stories, serviced by elevators. The designation as to high-rise is determined by local codes.

highway easement: the construction of a highway right of way over a privately held parcel of land. Property owners are compensated for the value of the property usurped by a highway easement.

historical cost: an accounting principle requiring all financial statement items to be based on original cost.

historic district: an area designated by government to have historical importance. Various incentives are provided, including tax breaks to rehabilitate and preserve the area,

historic preservation: a movement begun in the 1960s in the United States to protect landmarks and to unify neighborhoods. To physically rehabilitate a historic building.

historic structure: a home or building that is listed in the *National Register of Historic Places* and certified as historic by the U.S. Secretary of the Interior. A building that is officially recognized for its historic significance has special status under the 1997 Tax Reform Act, which encourages rehabilitation and discourages demolition or substantial alteration of the structure.

holdback: a portion of a construction loan withheld by a lender from a contractor until all construction work is satisfactorily completed or sufficient space is leased in a floor loan.

holder in due course:

(1) a legal ruling providing protection to homebuyers of defective homes bought from a seller who then sold the contract to a third party.

(2) alternately, one who acquires a bearer instrument in good faith and is eligible to keep it even though it may have been stolen.

hold harmless clause: a contractual clause where one party assumes a liability risk for another and thus effectively indemnifies the named party from any liability.

holding company: a company formed for the purpose of owning or controlling other companies.

holding funds: the funds retained in an account until a certain event occurs.

holding period: the period of time property has been owned for income tax purposes. The holding period determines if gain or loss from the sale or exchange of a capital asset is long or short term.

hollow-core door: a door that has the thin plywood of the veneer of the door supported by a wood frame.

home affordability index: a measure of the typical U.S. family's ability to buy a home, published by the *National Association of Realtors*. When the Index measures 100, a family earning the median income has exactly the amount needed to purchase a median-priced, previously owned home, using conventional financing and a 20 percent down payment. Some experts say that every one-point increase in the home mortgage interest rates results in 300,000 fewer home sales.

home equity conversion mortgage: also known as a *reverse mortgage*, this loan is made to older owners—62 and over—to convert their equity into money. Borrowers are qualified on the basis of the value of their homes. This is not the same as a *home equity loan*. In addition, the loan does not have to be repaid until the borrower no longer occupies the property. The equity can be paid to the homeowner in a lump sum, in a stream of payments, drawn from a line of credit, or a combination of monthly payments and line of credit.

- **advantages:** there are no restrictions on how the funds should be spent, and the funds don't affect Social Security or Medicare benefits. Any remaining equity at the time of the borrowers' death may be passed on to heirs.
- **requirements:** borrowers must be 62 or older and must have their home mostly paid off. Eligible properties include a single-family home, a two- to four-unit dwelling, a condominium, or a manufactured home. All housing types must meet *Federal Housing Administration (FHA)* guidelines. This home must be the borrower's principal residence. In general, a borrower can get between one-third and one-half of total equity as a line of credit or as a lump sum payment.

home equity line of credit (HELOC): an open-ended line of credit based on a homeowner's equity. Most loan amounts are limited to 75 or 80 percent of the appraised value. Withdrawals can be made at any time with the guidelines.

home equity loan: a loan allowing owners to borrow against their equity in the home; usually a second mortgage.

home improvement loan: a loan used to pay for major remodeling, reconstruction, or additions to the home, usually a second mortgage.

home inspection: an examination of a home's condition, internal systems, or construction prior to purchase. This should be done by a professional contractor or an appraiser knowledgeable about the following:
- roof and siding;
- windows and doors;
- foundation;
- insulation;
- ventilation;
- heating and cooling systems;
- plumbing and electrical systems;
- walls, floors and ceilings;
- common areas in a condominium or cooperative.

Prospective buyers should view the home inspection report as a way to identify problems before purchase, to help negotiate adjustments in the purchase price if problems exist, and to help get the buyer to make any needed improvements before the deal is finalized.

home inspector: a professional who evaluates the structural soundness and operating systems of a home.

home inventory: the listing of items of an individual's possessions at his or her residence, and their costs.

home loan: also known as a *mortgage*, it is a lien that makes property security for the repayment of a debt, such as the one incurred upon purchase of that home.

home office expenses: expenses of operating a portion of a residence used for business or employment-related purposes. For more information on home office expenses and the home office deduction, go to www.irs.gov.

homeowners' association (HOA): a group that governs a planned community or condominium and collects monthly fees from all owners to pay for common area maintenance, to handle legal and safety issues, and to enforce the conditions and restrictions set by the developer.

homeowners' fee: a fee charged to homeowner to belong to a Homeowners' Association, which includes the cost of maintenance and other services.

home ownership: the state of living in a structure that one owns.

homeowners' insurance policy: a type of insurance policy covering the risks of homeowners, including damage, theft, fire, personal liability, etc. Homeowner's insurance—also called *hazard insurance*—should be equal to at least the replacement cost of the property. Replacement cost coverage ensures that a home will be fully rebuilt in case of a total loss. Most homebuyers purchase a homeowner's insurance policy that includes personal liability insurance, in case someone is injured on their property; personal property coverage, for loss and damage to personal property due to theft or other events; and dwelling coverage, to protect the house against fire, theft, weather damage, and other hazards. If the home is located near water, a lender might require flood coverage. This insurance is generally expensive. Lenders often want the first year's insurance premium to be paid at or before closing. Sometimes a lender may require this payment to be made monthly in a required escrow account.

Homeowners Protection Act of 1997: an act that requires private mortgage companies to tell borrowers of their right to cancel mortgage insurance when the loan amount is no more than 80 percent of the value of the home. Covers loans originated after July 31, 1999.

homeowners' warranty (HOW): a type of insurance that covers repairs to specified parts of a house for a specific period of time. It is provided by the builder or property seller as a condition of the sale.

homeowners' warranty program: a private insurance program that protects purchasers of newly, constructed homes against structural and mechanical defects and provides reimbursement for the cost of remedying the situation, if the builder does not do so.

home price: the price agreed upon by seller and purchaser, and for which title is exchanged.

home rule: the power of the local government to implement its own land-use regulations.

home sale exemption: when President Clinton inked the Taxpayer Relief Act of 1997 on August 5, 1997, he dramatically changed the way home sales are taxed. Prior to the change, homesellers could delay paying tax on a home sale if they rolled-over the gain and purchased a more expensive home within 2 years of the sale. A separate rule applied to those over age 55 that gave them a once-in-a-lifetime $125,000 exclusion. However, under the new tax code, both the rollover provision and $125,000 exclusion are replaced with a new exclusion that should allow most homeowners to sell their primary residence without tax.

homestead: the legal status provided by certain states on a home-owner's principal; in some states provides protection against credi-tor claims or forced land sale as long as the homeowner continues to maintain his/her residence there.

Homestead Law: the law that exempts a homestead from forced sale to meet general debts.

homestead rebate: usually offered to elderly and low-income homeowners, a homestead rebate is money paid back from the state from surplus payments of property taxes.

home warranty: warranties issued by contractors, sellers, and real estate agencies that protect homebuyers from specified defects in a house, as per the contract.

homogenous: the term for an area where property types and uses are similar and compatible. A thing constructed with parts of the same material.

horizontal property laws: the body of law relating directly to con-dominiums and cooperative developments. Most property law provides vertical ownership of property in the sense that property owners own mineral rights as well as air rights to the property. Horizontal property laws state that property owners own only the confines of the apartment unit within a condominium or cooperative building complex. Thus, horizontal property laws do not allow property owners to own the land on which their apartment unit is located.

household: a domestic unit living in one home.

household employee: an individual who performs nonbusiness services for the taxpayer in or around the taxpayer's home. Such services include child and dependent care, house cleaning, cooking, and yard work.

household expenses: a portion of total support; the value of lodging, plus food consumed in the home, utilities paid, and repairs made. The total is divided equally among all family members. Each member's share of household expenses is part of his or her total support.

house poor: purchasing a more expensive house than a buyer can afford based on his/her income.

housing code: a federal, state, or local government ordinance that sets minimum standards of safety and sanitation for existing residential buildings, as opposed to building codes, which govern new construction.

housing discrimination: the illegal practice of denying the right to buy or rent a home to an individual based on race, religion, color, national origin, sex, disability, or family status.

housing expense ratio: the percentage of gross monthly income that goes toward paying housing expenses.

housing starts: an estimate of the number of dwelling units on which construction has begun during a stated period.

HUD: see *U.S. Department of Housing and Urban Development.*

HUD median income: the median family income for a particular county or *metropolitan statistical area (MSA)*, as estimated by the *Department of Housing and Urban Development (HUD).*

HUD-1 Settlement Statement: a document that provides an itemized listing of the funds that are payable at closing. Items that appear on the statement include real estate commissions, loan fees, points, and initial escrow amounts. Each item on the statement is represented by a separate number within a standardized numbering system. The totals at the bottom of the HUD-1 statement define the seller's net proceeds and the buyer's net payment at closing. The blank form for the statement is published by the *Department of Housing and Urban Development (HUD).* The HUD-1 statement is also known as the closing statement or settlement sheet.

HUD-1 Uniform Settlement Statement: see *Uniform Settlement Statement.*

HVAC: an acronym that refers to the climate control system, which governs heating, ventilation, and air conditioning.

hybrid method of accounting: a combination of accounting methods, usually of the *cash* and *accrual* methods.

I

illiquid: an investment that cannot be quickly sold or converted to cash without incurring a significant loss. Real estate is generally an illiquid investment.

illiquidity: inadequate cash to meet obligations. Real estate is an illiquid asset because of an inability to sell or convert to cash in a short period.

immunization: protection against interest rate risk by holding assets and liabilities of equal durations.

impact fees: fees that must be paid by developers of new homes and subdivisions to pay for town facilities such as schools and parks.

impaired credit: a decline in the credit status of a prospective borrower.

implied condition: a provision not explicitly stated in an agreement but considered an important item.

implied contract: an agreement created by actions of the parties involved but not written or spoken.

implied easement: property that is used consistently for many years without challenge by the actual owner.

implied warranty: under law, there is an express warranty that real estate sold is appropriate for sale and is in proper condition, even if not stated.

implied warranty of habitability: a legal doctrine: all new homes are assumed to meet all building codes and are fit for habitation.

impound account: an account held by the lender to which the borrower pays monthly installments, collected as part of the monthly mortgage payment, for annual expenses such as taxes and insurance. The lender disburses impound account funds on behalf of the borrower when they become due. Also known as *escrow account*.

improved land: land that has been developed for use and has had installation of such utilities as water, sewer, roads, and building structures. These improvements increase the raw land's usability, thereby increasing its market value.

improvement: a change to a house that adds value, prolongs its use, or adapts it to different use.

improvement ratio: the relative value of improvements to the original value of the unimproved property.

imputed (or unstated) interest: in the case of certain long-term sales of property, the IRS has the authority to convert some of the gain from the sale into interest income if the contract does not provide for a minimum rate of interest to be paid by the purchaser. Such converted interest is called imputed interest.

imputed value: the value of an asset that is not recorded in any accounts but is implicit in the product. For example, when making historical comparisons, an imputed value can be estimated for any period for which data is not available.

inactive: said of an asset that is not continuously in use. Said of a thinly traded security.

inactive asset: an asset that is not generally being utilized, such as a backup power generator or a secondary system used only when the primary system malfunctions.

income: funds received from the use of property, skill, or business. The excess of revenue over expenses and losses for an accounting period.

income approach: an appraisal method of determining the market value of real estate based on the property's anticipated future income; market value equals expected annual income divided by the capitalization rate.

income producing property: an investment property. Real estate held for investment potential or in order to earn income by leasing or letting it, rather than for its own use.

income property: a property that is used to generate income, i.e., rented to others as either commercial or residential.

income statement: a profit-and-loss statement. Financial statement depicting a business entity's operating performance; reports the components of net income, including sales of real estate, rental income, operating rental expenses, income from rental operations, and income before tax. The income statement shows the cash flow for an entire accounting period, usually a quarter. The income statement is included in the annual report of the real estate corporation.

income stream: a regular flow of money generated by a business or investment.

income yield: also known as *capitalization rate*, it is the percentage rate of return estimated from the net income of a piece of property.

incompetent: one who is not legally capable of completing a contract. This includes the mentally ill, and minors.

incorporate: to form a *corporation* under state regulations.

incorporeal property: the legal interests and rights in real estate that do not include the right of possession, such as air and mineral rights, riparian rights, easements, and access rights.

incurable defect: a defect in a property that cannot be fixed or is too expensive to repair.

incurable depreciation: when the cost of repairing a component of a structure exceeds the value of the structure, making it economically impractical to repair.

indemnify: to protect another person against loss or damage, or to compensate a party for loss sustained.

indenture: an agreement between two or more parties conveying real estate where both parties assume obligations. Similar to a contract.

independent appraisal: a value estimate provided by an appraiser who has no interest in ownership of the property in question.

independent auditor: a *Certified Public Accountant* who provides a company with an accountant's opinion but who is not otherwise affiliated with the company.

independent contractor: one who is self-employed and contracts to do work according to his own methods and is not subject to control except as to the results of such work. An employee, by contrast, is subject to the control of the employer as to the methods to be used to obtain the desired results.

index: a number used to compute the interest rate for an *adjustable-rate mortgage (ARM)*. The index is generally a published number or percentage, such as the average interest rate or yield on Treasury bills. A margin is added to the index to determine the interest rate that will be charged on the ARM. This interest rate is subject to any caps that are associated with the mortgage.

indexed loan: a loan in which the term, payment, interest rate, or principal amount may be adjusted periodically according to a specific index, which is stated in the loan agreement.

index lease: a rental contract in which the tenant's rental is tied to a change in the price level, such as the Gross National Price Deflator, a component of the Gross National Product.

Index of Leading Economic Indicators: this index indicates the direction of the economy in the next six to nine months and helps to forecast business trends. This series of 11 indicators is calculated and published monthly by the U.S. Department of Commerce.

index of residential construction cost: an index of the costs to construct residential properties.

indirect costs: construction costs not directly associated with the home or building, such as waste disposal, permits, and other expenses rendered during the planning and building stage.

indirect overhead: costs that are not related specifically to one particular job but are a general cost of doing business.

industrial park: an area zoned for the purpose of industrial development. Usually located outside the main residential area of a city, and normally provided with adequate transportation access, including roads and railroad.

industrial property: a property that is zoned and used for industrial use, such as factories, manufacturing, research and development, warehouse space, and industrial parks.

industrial tract: land zoned for industrial use, such as manufacturing, factory office and warehouse space, and research and development.

industrial zoning: a category of property zoning that designates property to be used for industrial purposes.

in escrow: a phrase used for the period in which the escrow agent communicates to both the buyer and the seller as to what documents or moneys have to be deposited with the escrow agent to satisfy the terms of the purchase and sale. The items collected include moneys to cover mortgage insurance premiums, taxes, hazard insurance, and title insurance.

in-file credit report: a computer-generated report from credit repositories, which is regarded as an objective history.

infill development or housing: new construction in an already established area.

inflation: an increase in the amount of money or credit available in relation to the amount of goods or services available, which causes an increase in the general price level of goods and services. Over time, inflation reduces the purchasing power of a dollar, making it worth less.

inflation accounting: showing the effects of inflation on financial statements, a FASB requirement for large companies.

inflation equity: the increase in the value of property brought on by inflation.

information reporting: income reporting to the Internal Revenue Service using Form 1099, stating income earned.

information returns: returns, such as Form W-2 and the various 1099 forms, that report income and property transactions to the IRS. The payer, broker, or other designated person is required to file these returns, and is subject to penalties for noncompliance.

infrastructure: the basic public works in a community, including roads, parks, bridges, schools, utilities, and communication systems.

ingress and egress: access from a land parcel to a public road or other means of exit. The right to exit and enter through land owned by another.

inheritance: as distinguished from a *bequest* or *devise*, an inheritance is property acquired through laws of descent and distribution from a person who dies without leaving a will. Property so acquired usually takes as its basis, for gain or loss on later disposition or for depreciation, the fair market value at the date of the decedent's death. An inheritance of property is not a taxable event, but the income from an inheritance is taxable.

inheritance tax: a tax imposed by the government, based on the value of the property received from the deceased.

initial interest rate: the original interest rate of the mortgage at the time of closing. This rate changes for an *adjustable-rate mortgage (ARM)*. Sometimes known as a *teaser rate.*

initial payment: the down payment on the price of a piece of real estate.

initial rate: the rate charged during the first interval of an *ARM* loan.

initial rate cap: a specific limit of some *adjustable-rate loans* (ARMs) defining the maximum amount the interest rate may increase at the expiration of the original interest rate.

initial rate duration: a time period, lasting either months or years, before the initial interest rate for a loan expires and an increase takes place.

injunction: a court order issued to a defendant in an action either prohibiting or commanding the performance of a defined act. Violation of an injunction could lead to a contempt of court citation.

in re: *(Latin)* in regard to; in the matter of.

in rem: *(Latin)* against the thing. Legal term describing proceedings against property rather than proceedings against people.

insolvent: a financial condition in which a taxpayer's total liabilities exceed the total fair market value of all his or her assets. A taxpayer is insolvent to the extent that his or her liabilities exceed his or her assets.

inspection: see *home inspection*.

inspection fee: a fee paid to a professional to determine the physical condition of a home, and to supplement the information in the appraisal report; is often required by the lender.

inspection report: after an inspection, a written report is submitted, detailing the condition of the home's foundation, framing, plumbing, electrical system, heating, air conditioning, fireplaces, kitchen, bathrooms, roof, exterior, and interior.

inspector: a person who inspects. An official examiner.

installment:
(1) any of several parts appearing at intervals.
(2) periodic payments of debt in equal parts.

installment contract: a purchase agreement where the buyer does not receive title to the property until all installments are paid.

installment loan: borrowed money that is repaid in equal payments, known as installments. A furniture loan is often paid for as an installment loan.

installment method: a method of accounting enabling a taxpayer to spread the recognition of gain on the sale of property over the payment period. Under this procedure, the seller computes the gross profit percent from the sale (that is, the gain divided by the contract price) and applies it to each payment received, to arrive at the amount of the gain to be recognized.

institutional lender: a financial institution that invests, either directly or indirectly, in mortgages and other mortgage-backed securities on behalf of their depositors.

instrument: a formal, written legal document.

insurable interest: any interest a person or owner-entity has in a property that is the subject of insurance, so that damage to the property would cause the insured a financial loss or other tangible deprivation. Generally, an insurable interest must be demonstrated when a policy is issued and must exist at the time of a loss.

insurable title: a property title that a title insurance company agrees to insure against defects and disputes.

insurance: policies that guarantee compensation for losses from a specific cause. Various forms of insurance cover against fire, flood, earthquake, liability, etc.

insurance binder: a temporary insurance arrangement used until a permanent policy can be issued.

insurance dividends: amounts paid to policyholders are not dividends on capital stock, but are a rebate of a portion of the premiums paid for the insurance. Such dividends reduce the cost of the insurance, and are not taxable unless in excess of the total premiums paid. Interest paid when the dividends are left with the insurance company is reported to the taxpayer as interest, and is taxable.

insured mortgage: a mortgage that is protected by the *Federal Housing Administration (FHA)* or by *private mortgage insurance (PMI)*. If the borrower defaults on the loan, the insurer must pay the lender the lesser of the loss incurred or the insured amount.

intangible asset/property: nonphysical assets, such as contracts or mortgages, employee loyalty or customer goodwill, as distinguished from physical property such as buildings and land.

intangible personal property: property, other than real property. Examples include cash, insurance, stock, investments, goodwill, and patents.

interest: the charge paid for borrowing money, calculated as a percentage of the remaining balance of the amount borrowed.

interest accrual rate: the percentage rate at which interest accrues on the mortgage. In most cases, it is also the rate used to calculate the monthly payments, although it is not used for an *adjustable-rate mortgage (ARM)* with payment change limitations.

interest cover: the annual rate of interest on the loan, expressed as a percentage of 100.

interest-only loan: a loan where only the interest is paid each month. Therefore, the outstanding amount of principal is not reduced.

interest rate: a percentage expressing the relationship between the interest for one year and the principal.

interest rate buydown plan: an arrangement wherein the property seller (or any other party) deposits money to an account so that it can be released each month to reduce the mortgagor's monthly payments during the early years of a mortgage. During the specified period, the mortgagor's effective interest rate is "bought down" below the actual interest rate.

interest rate cap: consumer safeguard that limits the amount that the interest rate on an *ARM* loan can change in an adjustment interval and/or over the life of the loan. For example, if a per-period cap is 1 percent and the current rate is 7 percent, then the newly adjusted rate must fall between 6 percent and 8 percent regardless of actual changes in the index.

interest rate ceiling: the highest interest rate allowed to be charged on an *adjustable-rate mortgage (ARM)*.

interest rate floor: for an *adjustable-rate mortgage (ARM)*, the minimum interest rate, as specified in the mortgage note.

interest rate for HECMs: the interest rate on a *home equity conversion mortgage (HECM)* adjusts monthly or yearly. It is tied to the weekly average yield of U.S. Treasury securities adjusted to a constant maturity of one year. The interest charged on the HECM loan will be payable to the lender when the loan terminates.

interest received: an amount received for the use of money that is to be repaid in full at a specified time or on demand.

interim financing: financing used for a short term to bridge the gap between the purchase of a home and the sale of a home; also called a *bridge loan*. Construction loans are interim financing.

interim loan: a loan that is to be replaced by a permanent loan.

interim statement: a financial report covering less than one year, such as a quarterly report.

interim use: the temporary use of property in a nonconforming use, which can be overturned by a formal zoning ruling.

intermediation: a court order on an issue directly related to the immediate action.

internal rate of return (IRR): the real annual return on a real estate investment. It equates the initial investment with the present value of future net cash inflows from the investment.

Internal Revenue Code: United States federal tax law, consisting of rules and regulations to be followed by taxpayers; continually revised and amended.

Internal Revenue Service (IRS): the branch of the federal government responsible for collecting taxes, including corporate and personal. It also administers tax rules and regulation, and investigates tax irregularities. Web: www.irs.gov.

International style: a type of architecture originating in Europe in the 1920s. Its design was very functional and emphasized buildings constructed of steel, reinforced concrete, and glass. Smooth white surfaces with very large wall windows and no decoration advertised that functionality was important and "less is more." It was a reaction to the highly decorated houses of the Victorian period. (see *Appendix A*)

intestate: a person who dies without a will and having unknown intentions regarding the disbursement of his estate. In this case, a court-appointed administrator typically acts as an executor.

in toto: *(Latin)* in the whole, or as a whole

inventory: goods held for sale or materials to be used in the manufacture of goods held for sale.

investment:

(1) expenditure to buy property or other capital assets that generate income.

(2) alternately, securities of real estate companies or capital assets.

investment analysis: an analysis of the risks and rewards to an individual in making a particular property investment. It considers the cost of the original investment, the investment return over a period of time, the suitability of the investment, and the probability of success.

investment flows: cash flows associated with the buying and selling of fixed assets and business interests.

investment interest: interest paid on loans acquired to purchase or hold investment property. Investment interest is deductible as an itemized deduction to the extent of net investment income.

investment life cycle: the time interval between buying a real estate investment and selling it.

investment property: real estate, such as rental properties, that generates income.

invoice: a bill issued by one who has provided products and/or services to a customer. In asset-based lending, invoice means account receivable.

involuntary alienation: the loss of property due to attachment, condemnation, foreclosure, sale for taxes, or other involuntary transfer of title.

involuntary conversion: the receipt of money or other property as reimbursement for the loss or destruction of property through theft, casualty, or condemnation. Any gain realized on an involuntary conversion can, at the taxpayer's election, be considered nonrecognizable for federal income tax purposes if the owner reinvests the proceeds within a prescribed period of time in similar property.

involuntary lien: a lien on property, such as for the nonpayment of real estate taxes or mechanic's lien.

i persona: *(Latin)* I am the person, meaning that is actually the person himself/herself.

ipso facto: *(Latin)* the result of an act or a fact.

irrevocable: something that cannot be taken, returned, or revoked.

Italian architecture: a style of architecture, originally introduced into the U.S. prior to the Civil War; it is modeled after Renaissance country homes in northern Italy. They were usually relatively large brick houses, characterized by having an off-center square tower and a flat roof, with heavy overhanging eaves supported by braces.

itemized deductions: certain personal expenditures allowed by the *tax code* as deductions from adjusted gross income. Examples are certain medical expenses, qualified interest on home mortgages, and charitable contributions. Itemized deductions are reported on Schedule A, Form 1040. A taxpayer who itemizes deductions may not claim the standard deduction.

J

jamb: the vertical side post of a door or window. (see *Appendix B*)

jeopardy: danger, risk factor.

J factor: the factor used by appraisers and investors to determine the changes needed in operating income to obtain a desired rate of return. This factor is determined after consideration of the location, rental, similar properties, and cost of maintenance.

joint:

(1) a combined action of two or more people who are either for or against something.

(2) alternately, used to indicate a common property ownership interest in real estate. Indicates a shared liability in terms of a contractual relationship.

joint and several liability: a situation wherein each borrower on the same note is held fully liable for the entire amount of the debt, not just a portion. The creditor may demand full repayment from any individual.

joint liability: liability shared among two or more people, each of whom is liable for the full debt.

jointly owned property: a property held in the name of more than one person.

joint note: more than one maker on a note where, if one or more of the makers default on the note, all of the makers are sued jointly, rather than just one or all, to make restitution.

joint ownership: ownership of real estate with two or more individuals having equal ownership. Upon the death of one owner, the property is transferred to the survivor.

joint tenancy: a form of joint ownership. Each tenant has an undivided interest in the entire property. On death of one of the owners, the survivor becomes the owner of the whole. A joint tenancy may involve more than two persons.

joint venture: an agreement between two or more parties to invest in a specific single business or property. Although it may not be a continuing relationship, it is treated as a partnership for income tax purposes.

joists: parallel supporting beams that hold up the planks of a floor.

journal: an accounting book of original entry in a double-entry system where all transactions are initially recorded.

journeyman: a worker who has already served his apprenticeship to work in a trade such as plumbing or carpentry, but who is not yet a supervisor.

judgment: a decision made by a court of law. In judgments that require the repayment of a debt, the court may place a lien against the debtor's real property as collateral for the judgment's creditor.

judgment creditor: the party to whom the court awarded a financial judgment against a debtor.

judgment debtor: the party against whom the court has issued a financial judgment.

judgment lien: a court order in which the *judgment creditor* is granted a lien against the property of the *judgment debtor* for the nonpayment of the amount due.

judicial foreclosure: a type of foreclosure proceeding used in some states, is handled as a civil lawsuit and conducted entirely under the auspices of a court.

jumbo loan: a loan exceeding the limits set by *Fannie Mae* and *Freddie Mac*. The current limit for a single-family home is $322,700, except in Hawaii, Alaska, and the Virgin Islands, where it is $484,050.

junior lien: a lien that is subordinate to a senior lien and cannot be satisfied until the senior lien is paid.

junior mortgage: a loan that is subordinate to the primary loan and cannot be satisfied until the primary loan is paid.

jurisdiction: the geographic area of authority and responsibility for a specific government entity.

just compensation: the fair market value of a property, paid to the owner when it is acquired in an eminent domain action.

K

keystone: the central supporting block at the top of an arch. (see *Appendix B*)

kicker: a payment required by a mortgage in addition to normal principal and interest. Also called an *equity kicker* or *participation loan*, it allows the mortgagee to participate in income from the mortgagor.

kick-out clause: a sales contract clause that allows a seller to accept a contingent offer and then back out to accept a second and better offer, without penalty.

kiosk: a small, freestanding stand with open sides, used for selling merchandise or services.

kitchenette: a tiny kitchen area that is often built into the end of another room, such as in an efficiency apartment.

kitchen triangle: an imaginary triangle extending from the sink to the stove to the refrigerator. The kitchen triangle helps maximize the efficiency of a kitchen by reducing the traveling distance between these appliances.

kit home: a structure built from prefabricated parts, which is assembled by a contractor.

L

labor burden: an employer's charges for employee benefits, wages, taxes, insurance, etc.

laches: the delay or negligence in asserting one's legal rights, potentially leading to *estoppel* of the negligent party's suit.

land:

(1) the surface of the earth.

(2) real estate that is often held for investment purposes.

land contract: a type of creative financing in which a down payment is made and periodic payments are made at intervals to pay off the balance. The purchaser may use, occupy, and enjoy the land, but no deed is given by the seller until the total price is paid off.

land cost: the total cost of purchasing a land parcel, including purchase price, closing costs, commission, and finance charges.

land development: the process of developing raw land by planning and building homes, shopping centers, schools, or churches. Initially, the development process includes construction of streets, sewers, utilities, and other resources.

land economics: the study of how land is used and allocated. Some areas of study include the role of homeownership on children's development, the impact of land use regulation on housing affordability, and research into how certain types of land use spur commercial development.

land lease: a lease that includes only the land and no structures.

land loan: a loan used to purchase land. There is more risk connected with the purchase of unimproved land than improved property, therefore, a mortgage for unimproved land will usually have a higher interest rate.

landlocked: a parcel of land that has no access to a public thoroughfare except through adjacent property.

landlord: a person or business owning property that is rented out to tenants.

landlord's lien: a landlord's right to receive the value of the tenant's property to pay for unpaid rents or for damages to the lease premises.

landmark: a fixed object serving as a boundary mark for a tract of land.

landmark district: an area so designated because it is a location for historic and/or architecturally significant buildings.

land reclamation: the process of upgrading unusable land through making physical improvements, such as draining and filling a swamp.

land residual technique: an appraisal method of estimating the value of land when given the net operating income and the value of improvements.

land sale-leaseback: the sale of land and immediate leasing back by the original owner, whereupon the original owner can realize the capital value of the property and still retain its use.

landscape: the area surrounding a home, consisting of grass, plantings, etc.

landscape architect: a professional, with a degree, who is trained in the design and planning of using the land. In addition to lawns and plantings, a landscape architect may be responsible for drainage, parking, and the building sites.

landscape contractor: one who implements the plans of the landscape architect or designer by doing the planting and upkeep.

landscape designer: a professional, without a degree, who is trained in the design and planning of using the land.

landscape fencing: the use of shrubs or trees as a boundary around property.

landscaping: the design and planting of trees, gardens, lawns, or other plants on a property.

land use intensity: a description of whether a parcel of land has been correctly developed within zoning ordinances.

land use map: an official map indicating intensity of land use in a zoned urban area.

land use planning: activity, generally by a local government, that provides public and private land use recommendations, used to guide decisions on zoning.

land use regulation: local law that outlines ordinances, codes, and permit requirements that govern use of public lands and natural resources.

land use succession: changes in the predominant use of a neighborhood or area over a period of time. Contributing factors to this change include the physical aging of residents, leading to the turnover of ownership; business districts expanded into the area; and the physical aging of the building structures.

land value: the value of the land in a sale where the total sale price includes land as well as any improvements to the land.

land value map: a map delineating property values over a designated area.

late charge: the penalty a borrower must pay when a payment is made a stated number of days (usually 10 or 15 days) after the due date.

latent: something that is hidden or overlooked and may only be realized at a later time.

latent defect: a problem that is not obvious but may manifest itself at a later point in time, such as lead paint or bad wiring.

late payment: a payment received after the due date.

latitude:
(1) surveying measure of the angular distance, as measured in degrees north or south from a fixed point.
(2) it can also mean the loosening of rules and restrictions in certain loan covenants.

lawful object: an object or action, which is authorized, approved, and not prohibited by law.

lawn sprinkler system: pipes, valves, sprinkler heads, etc., that are installed in a lawn, above or below ground, to water the grass and shrubs.

laying out: using a plan to determine, prior to actual work, the manner in which pieces of a structure or system relate to each other.

lay of the land: an idiomatic expression indicating the desire of an individual to understand new surroundings and all of its nuances including its quality and character.

leach field: a porous soiled area, through which septic tank leach lines run, emptying out the treated liquid waste, forced from the tank, which then percolates through the soil.

leach lines: lines that carry effluent from the septic system out to the leach fields where it empties into the area of porous soil.

lead: a potential contaminent, which can be found in the water and paint, especially in older homes. Lead is no longer used in paints and piping.

lease: a written agreement between the property owner and a tenant that stipulates the conditions under which the tenant may possess the real estate for a specified period of time and rent.

lease agreement: a binding agreement containing the terms of a renter's occupancy.

leased fee: an owner's interest in a property he or she is leasing; refers to those rights retained by the landowner of the leased land which include the right to receive rent and the right to get the land back at the end of the lease.

leasehold: when a tenant signs a lease on a property, the tenant's interest in that property for that period is called a leasehold. Some leaseholds may be used as collateral in business loans.

leasehold estate: a way of holding title to a property wherein the mortgagor does not actually own the property but rather has a recorded long-term lease on it.

leasehold improvements: property improvements made by the tenant that can be removed by the tenant as long as he or she doesn't damage the property in the course of removing those items.

leasehold mortgage: a mortgage collateralized by a tenant's interest, usually structural improvements, in a lease parcel of property.

A leasehold mortgage is subordinate to the landlord's land lease since it is a second lien by order of priority on the property.

leasehold value: how much the tenant's interest in a lease is worth, particularly when the lease is long-term and the amount of rent moves below the current market rate.

lease option: an agreement, specified in the lease, that provides the tenant the option to renew the lease for a given time period upon the expiration of the initial lease.

lease-purchase mortgage loan: an alternative financing option that allows low- and moderate-income home buyers to lease a home from a nonprofit organization, with an option to buy. Each month's rent payment consists of *principal, interest, taxes and insurance (PITI)* payments on the first mortgage, plus an extra amount that is earmarked for deposit to a savings account in which money for a down payment will accumulate.

lease-purchase option: nonprofit organizations may use the lease-purchase option to purchase a home that they then rent to a consumer, or "leaseholder." The leaseholder has the option to buy the home after a designated period of time (usually three or five years). Part of each rent payment is put aside toward savings for the purpose of accumulating the down payment and closing costs.

ledger: an accounting book of final entry where transactions are listed in separate accounts.

legacy: a gift by will. Something handed down by an ancestor.

legal age: the official age of maturity upon which one is held legally responsible for one's acts, including contracts for the sale or lease of real estate. In most states, the age is 18.

legal blemish: a problem with a piece of property, such as a title claim or zoning violation.

legal description: a legally acceptable description of real estate including metes and bounds, government rectangular survey, or lot numbers of a recorded plat. All property deeds have a legal description.

legal instrument: a formal legal document, such as a contract.

legal name: the name one has for official purposes, usually the first and last name given at birth, which must be used to sign documents, deeds, or contracts.

legal notice: notification of others using the method required by law, which can include a registered letter, advertisement in a designated newspaper, telegram, or other methods.

legal residence: normally, the home that is considered one's permanent home.

legal title: the rights of ownership as defined by law or that could be successfully defended in a court of law.

legatee: a person who inherits property from a will.

lender: the bank, mortgage company, or mortgage broker offering the loan.

lender participation: a mortgage that allows the lender to share in part of the income or resale proceeds. Also referred to as *participation mortgage*.

lending agreement: a contract in which a borrower agrees to the terms of a loan, which include payment dates, interest rate, total cost of the loan, and late payment fees.

lessee: an individual who rents property from another. In the case of real estate, the lessee is also known as the *tenant*.

lessor: one who rents property to another. In the case of real estate, the lessor is also known as the *landlord*.

let:
(1) to rent a property to a *tenant*.
(2) alternately, awarding of a contract to the bidder for the property with the best offer.

letter of attornment: a letter outlining a tenant's formal agreement to be a tenant of a new landlord.

letter of commitment: an official notice to a borrower of the lender's intent to grant a loan; it also specifies the terms of the loan and usually sets a date for the closing.

letter of credit: an arrangement where a bank agrees to substitute its credit for a customer's.

letter of intent: a written statement expressing a desire to enter into a contract, without actually doing so.

level payment income stream: an *annuity*. A series of equal or nearly equal periodic payments or receipts.

level payment mortgage: a mortgage where each payment made by the borrower is equal for each period.

levy: an additional tax, penalty, or fine applied by a public or private entity.

liabilities: debts and financial obligations incurred but unpaid.

liability: a financial obligation, debt, claim, or potential loss.

liability insurance: insurance coverage that offers protection against claims alleging that a property owner's negligence or inappropriate action resulted in bodily injury or property damage to another party.

liable: legally responsible or obligated for something.

libel: written statements about a person or company that are unfounded, untrue, malicious, or damaging.

LIBOR-based ARMs: the London Interbank Offered Rate (LIBOR) is based on the interest rate at which major international banks are willing to lend and borrow funds for a specified period of time in the London Interbank market. The LIBOR is similar to the prime-lending rate posted by major U.S. banks. A borrower can select an *adjustable-rate mortgage (ARM)* that adjusts to the LIBOR at specified periods, usually every six months. This type of ARM typically has a per-adjustment period cap of 1 percent and is offered with either a 5 percent or a 6 percent lifetime rate cap.

license: legal authorization to do something.

licensed appraiser: an appraiser who meets certain state requirements but is not at the level of a certified appraiser.

licensee: one who holds a license.

license laws: laws that govern activities, such as in real estate.

lien: a legal monetary claim against a property that must be paid off when the property is sold.

lien, junior: a lien that will be paid after other, more senior liens have been paid.

lienholder: one who holds a lien.

lien period: the time period in which one may carry out a lien on property.

lien release: a written document terminating the terms of a lien, which is normally issued after payment has been made in full.

lien theory state: a state whose laws give a lien on property to secure debt.

life cap: a limit on the amount that a loan rate can change during the term of the mortgage. A mortgage whose interest initially begins at 6 percent and has a life cap of 7 percent cannot go over the amount of 13 percent.

life estate: a freehold equity in an estate, restricted to the duration of the life of the grantee or other stipulated individual.

life tenant: one who is allowed the use of real estate during his lifetime or the lifetime of another designated party.

lifetime rate cap: the maximum interest rate that may not be exceeded on an *adjustable-rate mortgage (ARM)* over the life of the loan.

like-kind exchange: an exchange of property held for productive use in a trade or business or for investment—except inventory and stocks and bonds—for property of the same type. Unless different property is received—called *boot*—the exchange is nontaxable in the current year. Any gain or loss is not recognized until the property received in the exchange is sold or disposed of.

like-kind property: similar property that can be exchanged in a nontaxable transaction. See *1031 exchanges*.

limited liability: the restriction of a person's potential losses to the amount invested.

limited partner: a member of a partnership whose liability for partnership debts is limited to the amount invested in the partnership.

limited partnership: a partnership in which there is at least one partner who is passive and limits liability to the amount invested (limited partner), and at least one partner whose liability extends beyond the monetary investment (general partner). Investment groups of various kinds, including real estate syndicates, use this manner of ownership where a general partner makes the decisions for the group and is primarily liable for losses.

line of credit: the maximum pre-approved amount that an individual or business can borrow without filing another application.

lintel: a horizontal structure which supports the load over an opening.

liquidate:
(1) to convert assets into money.
(2) to dispose of or get rid of.

liquidated damages: an amount agreed upon that one party would pay the other in the event of a breach of a contract.

liquidation: the conversion of assets into money. The breaking-up and selling assets of a company for cash distribution to its creditors and then owners. *Chapter 7 bankruptcy* is a liquidation.

liquidation price: cash value or other consideration that can be received in a forced sale of assets. Liquidation value is typically less than that which could be received from selling the assets in the normal course of business.

liquidation value: see *liquidation price*.

liquidity: the ability to obtain close to the true value of an asset by converting it into cash quickly.

liquidity ratio: same as *cash ratio*.

liquid market: a situation where there is plenty of housing stock on the market, meaning that there is less price volatility in the market.

lis pendens: *(Latin)* suit pending. Recorded notice of the filing of a suit.

listed property: includes passenger autos and other property used

for transportation, property generally used for purposes of enter-
tainment, recreation, or amusement, computers not used exclusively at a regular business establishment, cellular telephones, and
other property to be specified by the IRS. Restrictions apply to
the depreciation of listed property.

listing: a property for sale.

listing agent: the sales agent who had obtained the right from a seller to handle the marketing of a piece of property.

listing broker: the real estate broker who is responsible for the listing
of a property and who is to represent the interests of the seller.
Brokers are licensed, and able to run their own companies. Not all
agents are brokers.

listing form: the prepared form used to specify terms of the listing
agreement.

listing inventories: the amount of houses for sale within a given
market.

litigation:
(1) the act or process of carrying on a lawsuit.
(2) alternately, the lawsuit itself.

littoral: land abutting a large body of water, such as an ocean or a
lake.

littoral rights: the rights concerning property adjoining a large
body of water, such as an ocean or a lake, that concern the ability
of the littoral property owner to use the shore and the adjoining
water.

live-in partnership: two unrelated people purchasing a home.

live-work space: a dwelling designated to conduct a home-based
business.

living unit: one single dwelling, condo, apartment, house, etc.

load-bearing wall: a wall that supports the weight of other parts of
a home, in addition to its own weight; also called a bearing wall.

loan: a sum of money lent for a specified period of time, and
repayable with interest.

loan application: an itemization of basic financial information presented to a lender by a potential borrower. It is lengthy and requires such information as: bank account balances and account numbers, employment data and outstanding debts—including loans and credit cards—with names and addresses of creditors.

loan application fee: a fee charged by a lender to cover the initial costs of processing a loan application. The fee may include the cost of obtaining a property appraisal, a credit report, and a lock-in fee. Additional fees will be charged at *closing*.

loan commitment: the commitment letter stating the dollar amount of the loan being offered, the number of years a borrower has to repay the loan, the loan origination fee, the points, the annual percentage rate, and the monthly charges. The letter also states the time the loan offer must be accepted and the time until closing. Once signed, the borrower has accepted its terms and conditions.

loan officer: an official representative of a lending institution who is empowered to loan money within certain guidelines.

loan origination: the process by which a mortgage lender brings into existence a mortgage secured by real property.

loan origination fee: commonly referred to as *points,* the loan origination fee covers the administrative costs of processing the loan. One point is 1 percent of the mortgage amount. For example, a $100,000 mortgage with a loan origination fee of 1 point would mean the borrower pays $1,000.

loan rate: the interest rate charged for a loan.

loan term: the amount of time that is set for the repayment of the mortgage or loan. *Conforming loans* are usually 15 or 30 years.

loan-to-value (LTV) percentage: the relationship between the principal balance of the mortgage and the appraised value (or sales price, if it is lower) of the property. For example, a $100,000 home with an $80,000 mortgage has a LTV percentage of 80 percent.

lock-in: a lender's guarantee of an interest rate for a set period of time. The time period is usually that between loan application approval and loan closing. The lock-in protects the borrower against rate increases during that time.

lock-in clause: a clause inserted in a loan agreement guaranteeing a quoted interest rate for a specific period of time.

lock-in period: a period of time during which a lender guarantees to the buyer a specified interest rate, regardless of a rise in market rates. The longer the time period of the guarantee, the more points charged.

lodging: includes the fair rental value of a room, apartment, or house in which the dependent lives, a reasonable allowance for the use of furniture and appliances, and all utilities.

loft: residences created from old manufacturing or warehouse facilities prized for their high ceilings and open floor plans.

log cabin: a house built with unfinished logs.

longitude: a measurement of the distance east or west of the prime meridian.

long-term assets: also called fixed assets, they are assets, such as office equipment, that can be depreciated. On a balance sheet, the value of a company's property, equipment, and other capital assets expected to be usable for more than one year, minus depreciation.

long-term capital gain: an income tax term, which applies to the gain on an investment, held long enough to qualify for a special tax rate.

long-term capital gains and losses: gains and losses on the sale or exchange of capital assets that have been held for more than 12 months. A net long-term capital gain is the excess of long-term gains over long-term losses.

long-term financing: normally a mortgage that lasts at least ten years.

long-term lease: a lease contract that lasts for at least five years.

long-term liabilities: debts that are payable beyond a one-year period.

low-documentation loan: a mortgage requiring only minimum verification of income and assets.

low down payment loan: a home loan requiring only a small down payment to obtain financing for purchase of a home.

low-income housing: housing specifically intended for those people living below a specified income level.

LTV: see *loan to value ratio*.

lump sum contract: a contract that provides for a set fee for the service to be performed.

M

MACRS: see *Modified Accelerated Cost Recovery System.*

main home: a regular, permanent place of residence

maintenance: the periodic expenditure needed to preserve a property's original status rather than to improve that property. Activity required to compensate for wear and tear.

maintenance bond: a warranty bond given to guarantee that the necessary work will be done by the contractor doing repairs. This type of bond normally has a specific period of time.

maintenance fee: a monthly assessment by a homeowners' or a condominium owners' association on owners, used for maintenance and repair of common areas.

maker: any person, company, or legal entity that signs a check or note to borrow money.

mall:
(1) a public area connecting individual stores in a shopping center. Modern malls are often enclosed, enabling all-weather access.
(2) also refers to an entire regional shopping center.

mall stores: retail stores in a shopping center other than the anchor tenant, which is normally a larger store.

management agreement: a contract between the owner of a property and the party who agrees to manage it. Fees are usually 4 percent to 10 percent of the rental income.

management fee: the cost of professional property management. The fee is typically set at a fixed percentage of rental income.

management survey: a survey of the maintenance requirements for a commercial or industrial rental property for the purpose of preparing a management agreement.

mantel:
(1) a projecting shelf above the fireplace opening.
(2) the entire finish around a fireplace.

manufactured housing: homes and dwellings that are not built at the home site but are moved to the location are considered manufactured housing. Manufactured housing units must be built on a permanent chassis at a factory and then transported to a permanent site and attached to a foundation. All manufactured homes must be built to meet standards set forth by the U.S. Department of Housing and Urban Development (HUD). The standards focus on such aspects as design, strength, energy efficiency, and fire resistance. Manufactured housing represents one of the fastest-growing housing markets in the United States. Nearly all of the mortgage products are available for owners of manufactured housing.

Map Act: local government requirements regarding the subdivision of construction.

margin:
(1) the difference between the cost and selling price.
(2) for an *adjustable rate mortgage (ARM),* the amount that is added to the index to establish the interest rate on each adjustment date, subject to any limitations on the interest rate change.

marginal land or property: a property that is barely profitable; poor income potential.

marginal tax rate: the income tax—expressed as a percentage—that comes off the top of your next dollar of incremental taxable income. Put another way, the percentage of that next dollar of income that you'll actually be allowed to keep is 100 percent minus your marginal tax rate.

marginal utility: the additional worth or utility received when purchasing an additional unit of a commodity or service identical to the one being purchased. There is often no need for the second item; therefore its value is marginal.

margin of security: a buffer amount between the value of the collateral and the principal balance of the obligation.

marital deduction: the tax-free amount transferable by will to a spouse, which, under current law, is unlimited.

marketable title: a title so free from defects that there is no question as to the owner. Any court would enforce this title.

market absorption rate: the rate at which a market can absorb additional units of supply without causing market saturation and sever price distortions.

market analysis: research of the supply and demand condition of the real estate market and specific properties in a specific area to discover future trends.

market approach: the method of valuing a property through examination and comparison of recent sales of comparable properties.

market area: a regional area from which one can expect the greatest demand for a specific product or service.

market comparison approach: the method of appraising real estate based on a market comparison of neighboring properties having similar characteristics, to ascertain the cost for the current one.

market conditions: factors that, at a particular point in time, affect the sale or purchase of a home.

market data approach: the analysis of real estate sales data to appraise real estate values. see *market comparison approach.*

market delineation: the process of defining the geographic extent of the demand for a specific property.

market price: the actual open market price paid in a transaction where real estate is traded.

market rent: the rent that a comparable unit would command if offered in a competitive real estate rental market.

market research: surveys of the area in which a product or service is to be offered, which are done to determine the cost of doing business, any competition, potential sales, etc.

market risk: an uncertainty in the value of real estate due to market, economic, political or other conditions.

market segmentation: defining the socio-economic characteristics of the demand for a specific property.

market study: a study of real estate activities, including demand, price, locational influence, and current trends.

market value:
> (1) the independently appraised value of real estate in a free competitive market.
>
> (2) the highest price a buyer would pay and the lowest price a seller would accept, assuming that both were willing but not compelled to do so.

markup: the additional amount added to a bid or price, which contains overhead, profit, excess costs, etc.

masonry wall: a wall comprised of brick, stone, cement, etc.

Master Association: a homeowners' association in a large *condominium* or *planned unit development (PUD)* project that is made up of representatives from associations covering specific areas within the project. In effect, it is a second-level association that handles matters affecting the entire development, while the first-level associations handle matters affecting their particular portions of the project.

master deed: a deed filed by the developer or converter of a *condominium* for the purposes of recording all of the individual condominium units owned within a condominium complex.

master lease: a controlling lease in an apartment or commercial building, which controls subleases.

master limited partnership: an unincorporated combination of limited partnerships in real estate together as a group. It is generally formed by a roll-up of existing limited partnerships that own property, and typically has the advantage of ownership interests that are more marketable than individual limited partnership.

master mortgage loan: the remaining debt on a loan used for the original purchase of a building that's been taken *co-op*. Each resident is obligated for a portion of this loan, which is separate from the individual debt he or she may have taken on to buy his co-op unit.

master plan: a document, such as the one prepared by a local government, that describes the overall development concept, including both present property uses as well as future land development plans. It is a guide for private and public development.

master planned community: a development built according to a plan that includes commercial buildings, educational facilities, homes, and community facilities.

material defect: a problem in a specific property that could affect the property's value or salability.

material fact: information about a piece of property that could affect its salability and might change an individual's decision to purchase.

material participation: a tax term defined as year-round active involvement in the operations of a business activity on a regular, continuous, and substantial basis.

material participation income: active income, as distinguished from passive income, from employment, as well as business and other for-profit activities, in which the taxpayer takes a significant and active role.

maturity: the date on which the principal balance of a loan, bond, or other financial instrument becomes due and payable. The due date.

maximum financing: a mortgage amount that is within 5 percent of the highest *loan-to-value (LTV)* percentage allowed for a specific product. Thus, maximum financing on a fixed-rate mortgage would be 90 percent or higher, because 95 percent is the maximum allowable LTV percentage for that product.

median:
   (1) a strip of land that separates the lanes of opposing traffic.
   (2) alternately, the midpoint in a range of numbers.

median price: a house price that falls in the middle of the pricing of the total number of homes for sale in a specific area.

mediate: to settle a matter by conciliation with the use of a neutral third party.

mediation: a method of resolving disputes, in which a neutral party tries to resolve contract differences.

Megan's Law: a federal law requiring states to maintain on a public register when convicted sex offenders are released and move into their neighborhoods. It is the Child Protection Act of 1996.

merged credit report: a credit report that obtains information from the Big Three credit-reporting companies, Equifax, Experian, and Trans Union Corp.

merger of title: forming two or more parcels of property under one title.

meridian: an imaginary line drawn from the North Pole to the South Pole; the measurement of longitude.

metes and bounds: the boundary lines of land.

metropolitan statistical area (MSA): one or more counties having a population of at least 50,000. A consolidated metropolitan statistical area (CMSA) is an area with two or more primary metropolitan statistical areas (PMSA). A CMSA must also include at least 1 million people.

MGIC: see *Mortgage Guaranty Insurance Corporation.*

millwork: doors, moldings, jambs, etc., which are formed into their finished shapes by removal of excess material, and manufactured in a lumber mill or planing plant.

mineral rights: the ownership rights to the oil, gas, and minerals or other resources in property.

minimum lot area: the smallest lot area required or allowed for building under the zoning code.

minimum rated risk: in insurance, charging the lowest rate accorded an insurance policy covering a minimum risk classification situation.

mini-warehouse: a warehouse building separated into small lockable individual units that provides storage. Units are usually rented on a monthly basis.

minority discount: when the value of an asset is discounted because the holder doesn't hold the majority of voting shares or a leadership role in directing the asset.

minority interest: ownership of less than 50 percent.

mint condition: a house (or anything) that is as close to new as possible.

misrepresentation: an untrue statement, whether unintentional or deliberate. Misrepresentation is a form of fraud that could lead to cancellation of a contract or could bring other liability.

Mission house: a late nineteenth and early twentieth century style of housing that resembles the old mission churches of Southern California. It has a tile roof, widely overhanging eaves, arch-shaped windows and doors, stucco walls, and a pyramid roof. (*see Appendix A*)

mixed-income housing: an area of houses at widely varying prices.

mixed use commercial project: a commercial building having several different uses blending together, such as retail shops on the first floor, professional offices on the upper floors, and a restaurant on the top floor.

mixed-use development: a combination development of several different functions within one area, such as residential space combined with a commercial establishment.

MLS: see *multiple listing service*.

mobile home: a premanufactured structure, often constructed of metal, that is designed to be transported to a site and semipermanently attached.

mobile home park: a site where *mobile homes* are located in an area as mandated by municipal zoning laws. They provide necessary utilities and often include recreational facilities.

model furnishings: the interior furnishings included in a model unit, which are chosen to highlight the features of the model unit and show it to its best advantage.

model unit (home): a representative home, apartment, or office space built for a sales campaign to show the design, structure, and appearance of units to potential purchasers.

modernize: to upgrade a facility by installing up-to-date equipment, making contemporary cosmetic improvements, and deleting obsolete facilities.

modification: a change in the terms of an agreement.

Modified Accelerated Cost Recovery System (MACRS): the method of depreciation introduced by the Tax Reform Act of 1986. MACRS is not an entirely new system of depreciation but rather a series of significant modifications to the *ACRS* system. MACRS is mandatory for most depreciable assets placed in service after December 31, 1986, and was available on an optional basis for assets placed in service after July 31, 1986, and before January 1, 1987. Under MACRS, costs of qualified property are written off over predetermined periods.

Examples of Property Classes:

- 20-year property—this class includes property such as farm buildings.
- Residential rental property—this class is comprised of rental buildings or structures (including mobile homes) for which 80 percent or more of the gross rental income is derived from dwelling units. It excludes hotels and motels. Residential rental property is depreciated over 27.5 years.
- Nonresidential real property—this class includes real property that is not residential rental property. This property is depreciated over 31.5 years.

modified annual percentage rate: an index of loan cost based on the standard *APR* but adjusted for the time the borrower expects to hold the loan.

modify: to change or alter, slightly or partially.

modular: units of standardized size or design, which can be arranged or fitted together in a variety of ways.

modular housing: dwelling units constructed from components prefabricated in a factory and erected on the site.

molding or moulding: the decorative trim around windows and door openings, ceilings and floors, etc., used to give a better appearance as well as provide protection from jagged edges, and helping in preventing drafts. Molding may be made from any material, but the most often used material is wood.

money market account: an account that provides individual investors with many of the advantages of a money market fund.

money market fund: a mutual fund that allows individuals to participate in managed investments in short-term debt securities, such as certificates of deposit and Treasury bills.

Monterey style: a two-story house with a balcony design adopted from the early California Spanish period; the railed balcony runs across the front of the house at the second-floor level. Roofs are low pitched or gabled, and exterior walls are constructed in stucco, brick, or wood. (*see Appendix A*)

monthly association dues: a monthly payment paid to homeowners' association and used for maintenance and repair in housing that has communal areas.

monthly fixed installment: that portion of the total monthly payment that is applied toward principal and interest. When a mortgage negatively amortizes, the monthly fixed installment does not include any amount for principal reduction.

monthly payment mortgage: a mortgage that requires payments to reduce the debt once a month. A monthly mortgage payment is composed of four components:
- *Principal* refers to the part of the monthly payment that reduces the remaining balance of the mortgage.
- *Interest* is the fee charged for borrowing money.
- Taxes and *insurance* refer to the amounts that are paid into an escrow account each month for property taxes and mortgage and hazard insurance.

All four of these elements are often referred to as PITI. The lender may mail a book of coupons each year to make it easier for the borrower to organize his payments.

month-to-month tenancy: a *tenancy* in which no written lease is involved, and rent is paid monthly. It can be renewed for each succeeding month or terminated at the option of either party with sufficient notice.

monument: a fixed object and point marking a boundary or position.

mortgage: a legal document by which real property is pledged as security for the repayment of a loan. The items stated in the mortgage include the homeowner's responsibility to: pay principal; pay interest; pay taxes; pay insurance on time; pay to maintain hazard insurance on the property; and adequately maintain the property. The mortgage also includes the basic information found in the *note*. Should a borrower consistently fail to meet these requirements, a lender can seek full repayment of the balance of the loan, foreclose on the property, or sell the property and use the proceeds to pay off the loan balance and foreclosure costs. A deed of trust is used instead of a mortgage in some states.

mortgage acceleration clause: a provision in a mortgage that gives the lender the right to demand repayment of the entire loan under certain circumstances, such as default, property sale, change of title, or refinance.

mortgage amortization: the repayment of a loan on a scheduled installment basis. As a loan is amortized, the equity in the associated property is increased. In the early years, the bulk of each payment goes toward interest rather than principal.

mortgage-backed security: a certificate that passes through principal and interest payments to investors.

mortgage banker: a company that uses its own money to provide home loans and then usually sells them to institutional investors—such as insurance companies—and *Fannie Mae.*

mortgage banking companies: mortgage companies that originate and service mortgages. In other words, they make loans to consumers. Mortgage companies then typically sell these loans to other lenders and investors. Some mortgage companies may be subsidiaries of depository institutions or their holding companies, but do not receive money from individual depositors.

mortgage bonds: bonds collateralized by real estate. Two kinds of mortgage bonds are senior mortgages (having a first claim on assets and earnings), and junior mortgages (having a subordinate lien). A mortgage bond may have a closed-end provision that prevents the firm from issuing additional bonds of the same priority against the same property, or may be an open-end mortgage that allows the issuance of additional bonds having equal status with the original issue.

mortgage broker: an individual or company that brings borrowers and lenders together for the purpose of loan origination. Mortgage brokers typically require a fee or commission for their services. Mortgage brokers originate more than half of the residential loans in the United States.

mortgage commitment: a written document stating the willingness of a lender to give a mortgage to a mortgagor. The commitment will provide a time period that the mortgage will be given and an indication of the interest rate to be charged. The mortgage will be granted at *closing of title.*

mortgage constant: the ratio of annual mortgage payments divided by the initial principal of the mortgage. Applies only to loans involving constant payment.

mortgage correspondent: an agent of a lender.

mortgage credit certificate: qualified taxpayers who receive a mortgage credit certificate from a state or local government to buy, rehabilitate, or improve their main homes may claim a credit against income tax for a percentage of their home mortgage interest. The percentage is set by the government and ranges from 10 to 50 percent. If the percentage exceeds 20 percent, the maximum credit is $2,000 per year. The itemized deduction for home mortgage interest must be reduced by the amount of the credit. The credit is not refundable, but any portion that is unused because it exceeds tax liability may be carried over to the following three years, where it can be added to any credit for the current year. The credit is computed on Form 8396. Mortgage credit certificates may be subject to a recapture rule if the home is sold within nine years.

mortgage discount: a one-time charge assessed by a bank or other financial institution at the closing of buying real estate. One discount *point* translates to 1 percent of the initial mortgage amount.

mortgagee: the lender in a mortgage agreement.

Mortgage Guarantee Insurance Company (MGIC): a private company established in 1957 in Milwaukee, Wisconsin to provide *private mortgage insurance (PMI)* to mortgage lenders granting mortgages to mortgagors not having at least a 20 percent down payment upon application. MGIC indemnifies the mortgage lending company should the mortgagor go into foreclosure because of a default. The cost of PMI is included in the *closing costs* by the mortgagee.

mortgage instrument: a written mortgage document that states the terms of the mortgage, including the interest rate, length of payments, payment dates, and remedies the bank is entitled to in the event of the mortgagor's failure to pay as required, including late charges.

mortgage insurance: an insurance on some loans that protects lenders from possible default by borrower. Conventional loans with down payments of less than 20 per cent of the home value usually require *private mortgage insurance (PMI)*. *FHA* and *VA* loans have different insurance guidelines.

mortgage insurance premium (MIP): the amount paid by a mortgagor for mortgage insurance, either to a government agency such as the *Federal Housing Administration (FHA)* or to a *private mortgage insurance (PMI)* company

mortgage interest deduction: a tax write-off, allowed by the IRS, where owners may deduct annual interest payments made on real estate loans.

mortgage lien: a mortgage lien secures the loan that funded the purchase of that property.

mortgage life insurance: the specific insurance that will pay off a mortgage if the borrower dies while the debt is still outstanding. Similar in purpose to *PMI;* both insurance products secure repayment to the lender if the borrower dies.

mortgage loan: a loan for the financing of a parcel of real estate for which real estate serves as collateral.

mortgage market: the interest rate and terms competing mortgage lenders are offering to potential mortgagees.

mortgage note: a legal document obligating a borrower to repay a loan at a stated interest rate during a specified period of time. The agreement is secured by a mortgage or deed of trust or other security instrument.

mortgage out: the obtaining of financing at or in excess of the construction or acquisition cost of a project. The acquirer/developer is not required to invest any equity capital.

mortgage payment table: the tables used to compute the monthly mortgage payment that consists of principal repayment and interest. A loan amortization type of formula is used. The tables have monthly payments for any combination of loan size, interest rate, and term.

mortgage pool: a group of mortgages combined for resale to investors on a secondary market.

mortgage REIT: a type of *real estate investment trust (REIT)* that does not own property but gives construction or permanent mortgage loans for major projects.

mortgage-related closing costs: the costs generally associated with a loan application. They vary, but here are some of the most common ones:

- **loan origination fee:** this fee covers the administrative costs of processing the loan. It may be expressed as a percentage of the loan (for example, 1 percent of the mortgage amount).
- **loan discount points:** these points are additional funds a borrower pays the lender at closing to get a lower interest rate on his mortgage. Typically, each point paid for a 30-year loan lowers the interest rate by .125 of a percentage point. If the current interest rate on a no-point, 30-year mortgage were 7.75 percent, paying one point would lower the interest rate to 7.625. Each point is one percent of the mortgage (for example, if the mortgage is $200,000, one point equals $2,000).

- **appraisal fee:** this fee pays for the appraisal, which the lender uses to determine whether the value of the property secures the loan should the borrower default. The homebuyer usually pays this fee. It may appear on the settlement form as "POC," or "paid outside closing."
- **credit report fee:** this covers the cost of the credit report, which the lender uses to determine the borrower's creditworthiness.
- **assumption fee:** this fee is charged if the borrower take over the payments on the seller's existing loan. It may range from hundreds of dollars to one percent of the loan amount.
- **prepaid interest:** at closing, the borrower may be required to pay in advance the interest for the period.
- **escrow accounts:** also called reserves, these accounts are required if the lender will be paying homeowner's insurance and property taxes for the borrower in an escrow account. The lender sets up the escrow account by adding the cost of the insurance and taxes to the monthly mortgage payments. It is kept in reserve until the bills are due. The bills are sent directly to the lender, who makes the payments.

mortgage release price: the amount required to pay off the full balance of the mortgage at a given time. This amount is the principal balance plus any prepayment penalty.

mortgage relief: acquired release from mortgage debt.

mortgage requirement: the amount of a periodic payment, including interest and principal, required for a mortgage payment.

mortgage risk rating: the amount of risk for a mortgagee in granting a mortgage loan. Principle in mortgage risk is that a maximum of 28 percent of the mortgagor's salary is devoted to the mortgage payment and 33 percent to total debt payments (including the mortgage).

mortgage servicing: monitoring and administering a mortgage loan after it has been made. This may include collecting monthly payments, record keeping, tax and insurance records, and foreclosures.

mortgage share (participation) agreement: a written agreement between institutional investors to buy or sell ownership shares in mortgages.

mortgagor: the borrower in a mortgage agreement.

move-in condition: a house that is ready for an occupant.

move-up buyer: an owner of one home who is looking to buy a bigger, more expensive home.

moving expenses: an adjustment to income permitted to employees and self-employed individuals who move for work-related reasons, providing certain requirements are met. Form 3903 is used to compute deductible moving expenses.

mullion: a vertical bar between adjacent window or door units.

mullion windows: two side-by-side windows, separated by a slender vertical divider.

multi-dwelling property: a residential property containing individual units for several households within the same structure.

multidwelling units: properties that provide separate housing units for more than one family, although they secure only a single mortgage.

multifamily mortgage: a residential mortgage on a dwelling that is designed to house more than four families, such as a high-rise apartment complex.

multifamily property: a residential property containing individual units for several households within the same structure.

multiple dwelling: more than one dwelling unit sharing a common wall and roof.

multiple listing: an arrangement where the real estate listings of many local agents are provided.

multiple listing service (MLS): a service combining the listings, in one database, of all the available homes, except those being sold by the owner, in a specific area.

multiple offers: more than one offer to purchase a property, which usually occurs in a seller's market.

multi-ply construction: increasing the fire rating of a structure by using more than one layer of gypsum wallboard.

municipal: having to do with a city or town or its government.

municipal housing inspector: an inspector employed by cities or counties to verify that all contractors are meeting building codes on all construction sites within a specific area.

municipal sewer: also called public sewer, it is the main sewer system, to which private sewers are connected.

muniments of title: documentation of ownership, such as a deed.

muntin: a small vertical or horizontal strip between small panes of glass in a window.

mutual consent: two or more parties agree to something.

mutual funds: a trust or corporation formed to invest the funds it obtains from shareholders in diversified securities.

mutual savings banks: state chartered banks, which are owned by the depositors and operated for their benefit. Many of these banks hold a large portion of their assets in home mortgage loans.

mutual water company: a business entity providing water services in a particular locality.

N

NAHI: see *National Association of Home Inspectors.*

NAR: see *National Association of Realtors.*

NAR code of ethics: a formal code of ethics and standards of practice by which members of the *National Association of Realtors®* must abide.

National Apartment Association (NAA): a group that consists of 60 state and local associations of managers, investors, developers, owners, and builders of apartment houses and other residential rental property. Phone: 703-518-6141, Web: www.naahq.org.

National Association of Exclusive Buyer Agents: a national organization of buyer's brokers, whose members do not accept property listings. Phone: 407-767-7700, Web: www.naeba.org.

National Association of Home Builders (NAHB): founded in 1942 and located in Washington, D.C., with 155,000 members and 824 local groups, this organization of homebuilders provides educational and political information and research services. Its publications include *Builder Magazine, Forecast of Housing Activity, Housing Economics, Housing Market Statistics* and *The Nation's Building News.* Its membership consists of single, multifamily, and commercial builders. Phone: 800-368-5242, Web: www.nahb.org.

National Association of Home Inspectors (NAHI): a professional association of independent home inspectors who meet the group's education and performance requirements. Phone: (952) 928-4641, Web: www.nahi.org.

National Association of Independent Fee Appraisers (NAIFA): an organization of real estate appraisers that offers the following professional designations: IFA–Member; IFAS–Senior Member; IFAC–Appraiser-counselor. Phone: 314-781-6688, Web: www.naifa.com.

National Association of Real Estate Appraisers (NAREA): an organization founded in 1966 whose members adhere to The Code of Ethics and Uniform Standards of Professional Appraisal Practice. Phone: 320-763-7626, Web: www.iami.org.

National Association of Real Estate Investment Trusts (NAREIT): a trade association that serves *REITS*, it collects data on the performance of REITs and prepares definitions to be used. Phone: 202-739-9400, Web: www.nareit.com.

National Association of Realtors® (NAR): a trade organization for real estate agents and brokers who become members by agreeing to abide by the organization's code of ethics. Members may call themselves *realtors*. Phone: 800-874-6500, Web: www.realtor.org.

National Association of Review Appraisers and Mortgage Underwriters: an organization that awards the Certified Review Appraiser (CRA) designation. Phone: 320-763-6870, Web: www.iami.org.

National Council of Real Estate Investment Fiduciaries (NCREIF): an organization that collects historical data on various institutional-grade property types, sorted by geographic areas. Publishes data on income and value changes. Its index, called Russell-NCREIF Real Estate Performance Report, is often cited as the benchmark for institutional real estate performance. Phone: 312-819-5890, Web: www.ncreif.com.

National Council of State Housing Agencies (NCSHA): a nonprofit clearinghouse of information on affordable housing and local and state housing agencies. Phone: 202-624-7710, Web: www.ncsha.org.

National Electric Code: an affiliate of the National Fire Protection Association, sets a minimum standard for electrical installations. Web: www.nfpa.org.

National Flood Insurance: insurance based on the National Flood Insurance Program, enacted by Congress in 1969, provides coverage for those people suffering real property losses as a result of floods. Any real estate located in a flood plain area cannot be financed through a federally regulated lender unless flood insurance is purchased.

National Housing Act: a federal act passed in 1985 to promote the construction of new houses, the repair and modernization of existing houses, and the improvement of housing and living conditions for lower-income Americans.

National Real Estate Index: a data provider for many types of property in more than 50 cities. Web: www.realestateindex.com.

National Society of Real Estate Appraisers (NSREA): an affiliate of the *National Association of Real Estate Brokers*, its purpose is to formulate rules of ethics and professional conduct and enforce these rules to the benefit of its members. Designations given by this organization are Master Real Estate Appraiser, Certified Real Estate Appraiser, and Residential Appraiser, after the completion of a course of study and final exam. Phone: 301-552-5760, Web: www.nsrea.org.

national tenant: a well-known and more substantial *lessee* with a presence in most of the United States.

natural vacancy rate: the average time an apartment in a particular market would be empty if supply and demand were in balance.

NCREIF: see *National Council of Real Estate Investment Fiduciaries*.

necessary: an expense that is appropriate and helpful in furthering the taxpayer's business or income-producing activity. See also *ordinary*.

needs-based pricing: an asking price based on the amount of funds required to pay off the seller's mortgage, the cost of remodeling, or the purchase of another house.

negative amortization: when the outstanding balance of a loan grows larger because each monthly payment is too small to cover both the principal and interest of that loan. This sometimes happens with *adjustable-rate mortgages.*

negative cash flow: when operating expenses exceed income and an owner must make a financial contribution.

negligence: a lack of such reasonable care and caution as would be expected of a prudent person. A penalty may be assessed if any part of an underpayment of tax is due to negligent or intentional disregard of rules and regulations.

negotiable:
  (1) able to be changed through discussions and modifications.
  (2) alternately, something that is legally transferred to another by endorsement or proper delivery.

negotiable instrument: an unconditional promise, in writing, to pay a certain sum of money, payable on demand.

negotiate: to bargain or attempt to reach an agreement between two or more parties through discussion.

negotiation: the process of bargaining that precedes an agreement.

neighborhood: a district or locality with distictive characteristics, often with a major street for shopping or restaurants.

neighborhood life cycle: a pattern that describes the physical and social changes that residential areas experience over time. This life cycle includes the phases of birth, early growth, maturity, and decline. Neighborhoods decline for several reasons, including the physical aging and deterioration of the building structures as well as the aging of the population. Architectural obsolescence makes these neighborhoods less attractive, and the intrusion of business or industrial areas detracts from the overall quality.

net:
  (1) the amount remaining after certain adjustments have been made for debts, deductions, or expenses.
  (2) the proceeds from the sale of an investment minus the purchase price, including commissions and other expenses.
  (3) term on an invoice to indicate that the full amount is payable.

net assets: same as *net worth*.

net capital: a firm's net worth, minus deductions taken for any assets that might not easily be converted into cash at their full value.

net cash flow: the income that remains for an investment property after the monthly operating income is reduced by the monthly housing expense, which includes principal, interest, taxes, and insurance (*PITI*) for the mortgage, homeowners' association dues, leasehold payments, and subordinate financing payments.

net current assets: same as *working capital*.

net earnings: same as *net profit*.

net floor area: the usable floor area after deducting stairs, walls, and similar features.

net income: the amount remaining when expenses are deducted from gross income.

net income multiplier: the price of an asset divided by the net income it generates in a given period of time—for rental property, usually one month.

net interest margin: the dollar difference between interest income and interest expenses, usually expressed as a percentage of average earning assets.

net investment: the level of investment minus equipment depreciation.

net leasable area: the floor space in a building that is actually under lease and able to be rented to tenants. Nonleasable area includes hallways, building foyers, areas devoted to utilities, elevators, etc.

net lease: also referred to as a triple net lease; the *lessee* pays not only a fixed rental charge but also expenses on the rented property, including maintenance.

net listing: a listing agreement where the broker's commission is an amount above a net price set by the owner. If that price is not met, a commission is not earned.

net long-term gain: in taxation, the excess of total long-term gains minus total long-term losses on the sale of real estate. Long-term classification is for real estate held one year or more, and is reported on Schedule D of Form 1040 (for sole proprietors) or Form 1120 (for corporations).

net loss: the excess of total expenses over rental revenue for a real estate business.

net operating income (NOI): the income from property or business after operating expenses have been deducted, but before deducting taxes and financing expenses.

net operating loss (NOL): a net loss for the year attributable to business or casualty losses. In order to mitigate the effect of the annual accounting period concept, the law allows taxpayers to use an excess loss of one year as a deduction for certain past or future years. In this regard, a carryback period of two years (three or five years for certain losses) and a carryforward period of 20 years is allowed.

net present value (NPV): a technique for determining whether the expected performance of a proposed investment promises to be adequate. The difference between the present value of cash inflows generated by real estate and the amount of the initial investment. The present value of future cash flows is computed using the cost of capital (minimum desired rate of return, or hurdle rate) as the discount rate.

net proceeds: the amounts received from the sale or disposal of real property less all relevant deductions (direct costs associated with the sale or disposal).

net profit: gross sales minus taxes, interest, depreciation, and other expenses. Also called net earnings, net income, or bottom line.

net realizable value: the expected selling price of property minus costs to sell. Net amount received upon sale. Gross receivables less allowance for doubtful accounts, representing the expected collectibility of those receivables.

net tangible assets: net worth minus goodwill.

net worth: the total worth of a person or entity once the liabilities are deducted from the assets.
 • **individual:** total assets less total liabilities less estimated taxes describe the person's personal equity, which is normally the basis upon which a loan is given.
 • **corporation:** total assets less total liabilities equal to stockholders' equity.

net yield: the return on an investment after subtracting all expenses.

newel:
 (1) the principal post of the foot of a staircase.
 (2) the central support of a winding flight of stairs.

New England Colonial: inspired by an early-American style, New England Colonials have a central hall with staircase; the living room, dining room, and the kitchen are downstairs. Bedrooms and baths are above. The houses have symmetrical exteriors with a central doorway. They often have porches and garages attached. The traditional exterior material is clapboard siding, and with a gabled roof covered with shingles. *(see Appendix A)*

New England farm house: a simple box-shaped house with clapboard siding and a gable roof.

new town: a mixed-use planned development providing residences, general shopping, services, recreation, and employment. Typically near a metropolitan location, it can enjoy the associated amenities.

NLA: see *net leasable area.*

NNN: see *net lease.*

no bid: a decision by the *Veterans Administration*, when a loan it has guaranteed goes into default, to pay the guarantee amount to the lender instead of acquiring the property in foreclosure. The result is that often the lender obtains the property at the sale.

no-cash out refinance: a situation where a new mortgage will cover the remaining balance of the first loan, closing costs, or any liens, but does not yield more than one percent of the principal in cash.

no deal, no commission clause: a clause placed in a listing agreement stating that no commission will be paid to the broker until the property title has actually been transferred. If this is not in the listing agreement, commission is payable once a ready, willing, and able buyer, who agrees to the terms of the sale, is found.

no-documentation loan: a loan application where verification of income is not required; typically granted in cases of large down payments.

nodular cast iron: commonly used for fittings, valves, pipe, etc., this iron has magnesium or cerium added while in a liquefied state, so that it can be formed into globular nodules. Also called ductile cast iron, it has good corrosion-resistant characteristics and is less brittle than gray cast iron.

NOI: see *net operating income.*

nominal loan rate: the loan rate stated on the face of the loan note, which is different from the effective interest rate. If *points* are charged, the effective rate will be higher.

no money down: real estate acquisition strategies based on seller-provided financing and/or existing loan assumption and minimal use of cash down payments. It is a method using a maximum amount of leverage to achieve maximum profits from real estate investments.

non-alienation clause: a clause in a document forbidding an individual from selling or transferring a subject property to another; normally used in a trust where the grantor of the trust believes the designated beneficiary to be a spendthrift.

non-assumption clause: a statement in a mortgage contract forbidding the assumption of the mortgage by another borrower without the prior approval of the lender.

nonbusiness bad debts: a bad debt loss not incurred in connection with a creditor's trade or business. A nonbusiness bad debt is deductible as a short-term capital loss and is allowed only in the year the debt becomes entirely worthless.

non-cash expense: an income statement expense for which no cash was spent, such as amortization or depreciation.

non-conforming loan: any loan that doesn't meet the qualifications or is too large to be purchased by *Freddie Mac* or *Fannie Mae.*

non-conforming use: property use that is in violation of the current zoning ordinance but had been in use prior to the zoning ordinance's enactment.

noncurrent asset: an asset that is not easily convertible to cash, or not expected to become cash within the next year. Examples include fixed assets, leasehold improvements, and intangible assets.

non-destructive examination: any type of inspection for quality or condition that does not damage the object in question. Visual inspection, X-rays, and ultrasound are examples.

non-disturbance clause: a section of a rental agreement that provides for the continuance of leases if the owner of the building forecloses.

nonexclusive listing: see *open listing*.

non-judicial foreclosure sale: a foreclosure sale enabled in those states permitting the use of a power of sale clause to be inserted into a mortgage or deed of trust empowering the mortgagee to advertise and sell a property at a foreclosure sale upon the mortgagor's payment default. A non-judicial foreclosure sale enables a foreclosure action without a formal judicial action.

non-liquid asset: an asset that cannot easily be converted into cash.

non-loadbearing wall: a wall that does not support the weight of a building or structure. A non-loadbearing wall could, theoretically, be removed without affect to a building's structural soundness.

non-performance: the failure or refusal to perform a specified action; the failure to fulfill contractually agreed upon terms or actions. Non-performance creates a liability, which can enable a judicial damage action.

non-recourse: lacking personal liability.

nonrecovery property: a property that does not qualify for a cost recovery deduction under *ACRS* or *MACRS*, or property the taxpayer elects to exclude from ACRS or MACRS by choosing a depreciation method not based on a number of years.

nonrecurring closing costs: one-time-only fees for items such as loan points, credit report, title insurance, home inspection, appraisal, etc.

non sequitur: *(Latin)* it does not follow. The conclusion of a statement or phrase is illogical.

nontaxable exchange: an exchange on which no gain or loss is recognized in the current tax year.

nontaxable income: income that is by law exempt from tax.

normal wear and tear: the physical damage and depreciation arising from ordinary use and time.

notarize: a Notary Public attests to the genuineness of a signature.

Notary Public: a public officer given the right to authenticate a document, accept a person's oath, administer depositions, and to conduct other activities in commercial business. An official seal is used by the Notary.

note: a legal document that obligates a borrower to repay a mortgage loan at a stated interest rate during a specified period of time. Often called the promissory note, it represents a borrower's promise to pay the lender according to the agreed-upon terms of the loan, including when and where to send the payment. The note lists any penalties that will be assessed if payments aren't made on time, and also warns the borrower that the lender can "call" the loan—demand repayment of the entire loan before the end of the term—if the terms are violated.

note rate: the interest rate specified in a mortgage note.

notes payable: the funds due to a lender.

notes receivable: the funds owed to an individual or entity by a borrower.

notice: a written communication of a legal action or one's intent to take an action.

notice of cancellation clause:
(1) a notice, often in writing, in which an individual or business gives a notice of termination to another, pursuant to a cancellation provision in a contract to forestall future liability.
(2) alternately, a notice given between an insurer and a re-insurer or an insurer and an insured of the termination of a contract or policy at the time of renewal, or in the latter case, for nonpayment of premium payments.

notice of cessation: a notice to one or more individuals to cease and desist from performing a particular action.

notice of default: the initial action taken by a lender when a mortgage falls into arrears and attempts to reconcile the issue out of court have failed. The written notice will normally give the defaulting party the terms necessary to remedy a default and the time period during which is must occur.

notice of nonresponsibility: a clearly stated notice that an owner or operator will not assume responsibility for an inherent risk.

notice of pendency: also called a lis pendens, Latin for "suit pending." Recorded notice of the filing of suit, the outcome of which may affect title to a certain piece of property.

notice to pay rent or quit: also called a three-day notice to quit, this is a notice by a landlord to a tenant to either pay the rent due or vacate the premises. With a long-term lease, the notice may list penalties.

notice to quit: a notice to a tenant to vacate rented property.

notorious possession: an open and active occupancy of a piece of real estate that acknowledges the fact that the borrower is in possession. Notorious possession is one of the important tests when finding for or against a claim of property under adverse possession, which is to acquire land by unauthorized but lengthy occupation.

novation: the substitution of a subsequent borrower in place of the original borrower, who is then released from liability. This must be done with the approval of the lender.

NPV: see *net present value.*

nuisance:
(1) a land use that interferes with surrounding land uses.
(2) an activity by a property owner that annoys or seriously disturbs other property owners, making it discomforting to use their own property.

null and void: invalid.

nuncupative will: an oral will made by a testator/testatrix, before an insufficient number of witnesses, just prior to death. Nuncupative wills depend on the oral testimony of those witnesses present as proof. They are illegal in several states and are enforceable in others only if they meet specific guidelines.

O

OAR: see *overall rate of return.*

obiter dictum: the opinion of a judge having no direct legal or binding effect on the outcome of a pending judicial decision. An obiter dictum is considered to be an incidental judicial remark about some point that may or may not be directly relevant to the matter before the bench.

obligatory: the legal requirement of a debtor, obligor, to pay a debt and the legal right of a creditor, *obligee*, to demand satisfaction of a debt or enforce payment in the event of default.

obligee: the person to whom a debt or obligation is owed.

obligor: the person responsible for paying a debt or obligation.

occupancy: residing in or using real estate.

occupancy agreement, limited: an agreement that allows for occupancy of a premises, for a stated period of time if certain terms are met; most often used to allow a prospective buyer to obtain possession, under a temporary arrangement, usually prior to closing.

occupancy date: a buyer should add a provision to his purchase offer that holds the seller responsible for paying rent should they not move out on or prior to the agreed-upon date. This provides the buyer money to pay for his or her own unexpected housing or lodging expenses if the property isn't ready after closing.

occupancy level: see *occupancy rate.*

occupancy rate: the number of units currently occupied in a facility, neighborhood, or city, stated as a percentage of total capacity.

occupancy ratio: the ratio of rented or leased space to the total amount of space available.

Occupational Safety and Health Administration (OSHA): this government agency oversees safety in most places of work. Web: www.osha.gov.

off-balance-sheet financing: financing from sources other than debt and equity offerings, such as joint ventures, *R&D* partnerships, and operating leases.

offer: indicating a readiness to purchase a property at a specified price; presenting for acceptance a price for a property parcel; the bid price in a real estate or security transaction. Once a prospective buyer has made an offer, the seller has the opportunity to accept, decline, or make a counteroffer. If the offer is accepted, the buyer will receive a ratified sales contract. This contract is the starting point for working with an approved lender to get a mortgage if the buyer is not already *pre-approved*.

offer and acceptance: these two requirements of a contract forming mutual consent combined with valuable consideration are the major elements of a contract.

offeree: one who receives an offer.

offerer: one who makes an offer.

offering statement: a *prospectus.* Document that must accompany a new issue of securities for a real estate company or partnership. It includes the same information in the registration statement, such as a list of directors and officers, financial statements certified by a CPA, underwriters, the purpose and use for funds, and other relevant information that prospective buyers of a security want to know.

offer to purchase: a proposal to buy property at a specified price, whereupon the seller has the options of accepting or rejecting the offer or making a counteroffer.

office building: a structure primarily used for the conduct of business

office condominium: a building in which the units are used as commercial offices. The purchaser of an office condominium owns the title to the individual office unit and not to the property. Maintenance fees are assessed to each owner.

Office of Interstate Land Sales Registration (OILSR): the division of the U.S. Department of Housing and Urban Development that regulates offerings of land for sale across state lines.

Office of Thrift Supervision (OTS): a federal agency that regulates and supervises federally chartered savings and loan associations. This agency is part of the Treasury Department. Phone: 202-906-6000, Web: www.ots.treas.gov.

office park: a large tract of land devoted to development of office buildings.

offset statement: an occupant's expressed interest in property that is being rented.

off-site: not on a construction site proper. In a different location. For example, utility lines are brought into a development from off-site.

off-site costs: the expenditures related to construction but located elsewhere.

off-site improvements: portions of a development required for the use but that are not located there, such as streets, sewers, schools.

off-street parking: parking spaces on private property rather than on the public streets.

off the books: payments for which no formal record is kept.

OILSR: see *Office of Interstate Land Sales Registration*.

omnibus clause:
(1) a provision in a will that stipulates that any assets not enumerated still pass to the heirs.
(2) alternately, a clause in liability insurance policies that extends coverage to unnamed others beyond the insured.

one-time charge: an expense that a company recognizes in a single reporting period, and which the company claims is unlikely to recur in the future.

one-year adjustable-rate mortgage: this *adjustable-rate mortgage (ARM)* offers a low initial interest rate with an interest rate that adjusts annually after the first year. The rate cap per annual adjustment is usually 2 percent; the lifetime adjustment caps can be 5 percent or 6 percent. This type of mortgage may be good for the buyer who anticipates a rapid increase in income over the first few years of the mortgage; it lets the buyer maximize his purchase power immediately. It's also good for homeowners who don't plan to live in a home for more than a few years.

- **advantages:** some one-year ARMs let borrowers convert to a fixed-rate loan at certain adjustment intervals; ask about this option. Generally, conversions to fixed-rate mortgages are allowed at the third, fourth, or fifth interest rate adjustment dates.

- **details:** one-year ARMs come in terms from 10 to 30 years. The most typical ones are 10, 15, or 30 years. The one-year ARM is most often indexed to the weekly average yield of U.S. Treasury securities adjusted to a constant maturity of one year. Can be used to buy one-family principal residences, including condos, and planned unit developments. *Manufactured homes* are also eligible.

- **ongoing costs:** homebuyers should not forget that there are ongoing costs associated with owning a home. They include, but are not limited to:
  - monthly mortgage payment;
  - mortgage insurance;
  - homeowner's insurance;
  - property taxes; and
  - utilities, such as gas, oil, water and electricity.

Another cost homebuyers should consider is how much it will cost to maintain their home. These costs include everything from cleaning and minor repairs to yard work and painting. *Condominium* owners and people living in *planned unit developments* should factor in any *homeowners' association* fees or similar costs.

online real estate listings: properties listed for sale on the Internet.

on-site improvements: directly enhancing the physical nature of the property, such as renovating a building, installing a new driveway and parking lot, and gardening.

on-site management: managing property directly at its location; functions may include showing prospective tenants the facilities, collecting rents, and doing upkeep on the property.

open-end lease: a lease contract providing for a final additional payment on the return of the property to the *lessor*, adjusted for any value change.

open-end loan: a loan where the borrower may add to the principal without renegotiating the terms of the loan. Additional sums borrowed under the terms of an open-end loan will have the same rate of interest and life of loan terms as the original loan. A home equity loan is often open-ended.

open-end mortgage (deed of trust): a mortgage or trust deed that can be increased by the *mortgagee*. The mortgagee may secure additional money from the *mortgagor* though an agreement that typically stipulates a maximum amount that can be borrowed.

open house: a method of showing a home that is for sale. The house is left open at an advertised time for prospective buyers to see. The house may be advertised in the newspaper and/or outside the house.

open housing: housing where purchase or lease is available to everyone regardless of race, ethnic origin, color, or religion.

opening escrow: the deposit given by a buyer of property is delivered to the *escrow* agent, who retains it for the seller.

open listing: a property marketed by a number of brokers simultaneously. This type of agreement permits a real estate agent to sell the property, while allowing the homeowner or other agents to attempt to make the sale.

open listing agreement: a listing agreement given to many brokers and/or agencies. The property owner pays a commission only to the broker who actually produces a buyer for the property.

open mortgage:

(1) a mortgage that is overdue and, therefore, open to foreclosure at any time.

(2) alternately, a mortgage that does not have a prepayment clause and permits the mortgagor to repay the mortgage at any time without paying a penalty.

open occupancy: housing where purchase or lease is available to everyone regardless of race, ethnic origin, color, or religion, and affirmative action is actively pursued.

open space: land that is left undeveloped for use as parks, walking paths, etc.

open space ratio: in a development, the ratio of open space to developed land.

open year: a taxable year for which the statute of limitations has not yet expired.

operating asset: an asset that contributes to the regular income from a company's operations.

operating costs: the day-to-day expenses incurred in running a business, such as sales and administration, as opposed to production. Also called *operating expenses.*

operating expense ratio: a mathematical equation obtained by dividing *operating expenses* by *gross income.*

operating expenses: the amounts paid to maintain property, such as property taxes, utilities, insurance, repairs, maintenance, legal, management fees, etc.

operating income: a measure of a property's or company's earning power from ongoing operations, equal to earnings before deduction of interest payments and income taxes. Also called operating profit or *earnings before interest and taxes (EBIT).*

operating lease: the regular rental of property between the lessee and lessor for a fee.

operating leverage: the idea that you can make more from a property in rent or a related revenue stream if you don't have to increase fixed costs to operate or maintain it over time.

operating statements: financial reports on a property.

opinion of title: a certification, usually from an attorney, as to the validity of title to property being sold, stating that the property is clear and marketable. The opinion of title is essential to obtaining title insurance, or a mortgage, and to the transfer of title.

opportunity cost: when taking one particular action, the cost of forgoing the next best investment.

optimize: to increase the efficiency or effectiveness of a process as much as possible.

option: an agreement to buy or sell property on or before a specified date at an established price. The sale or exchange of an option to buy or sell property results in capital gain or loss if the property is a capital asset.

optionee: one who receives or purchases an option.

option listing: a listing agreement that also gives the listing broker the right to purchase the property.

option listing agreement: a contract, given for a consideration, where an *optionor* gives an option to the *optionee* for the right, but not the obligation, to purchase property within a certain period of time, at a certain price. If the option is not exercised within the specified period of time, it will expire.

optionor: a person or business that gives or sells an option.

option to purchase: a contract that gives one the right, without any obligation, to purchase a property, within a certain period of time and at a certain price, subject to conditions.

oral agreement: arrangements that are not memorialized in writing and are not usually legally binding.

oral contract: a contract not in writing. Some oral contracts are enforceable, but those applicable to the sale of real estate are unenforceable.

ordinance: a law enacted by local authorities to govern the activities of people or things, such as land usage.

ordinary: common and accepted in the general industry or type of activity in which the taxpayer is engaged. It is one of the tests for the deductibility of expenses incurred or paid in connection with a trade or business; for the production of income; for the management, conservation, or maintenance of property held for the production of income; or in connection with the determination, collection, or refund of any tax.

ordinary and necessary business expenses: a tax term describing current and necessary business expenses, which are allowed as deductions. Ordinary and necessary business expenses do not include long-term capital losses.

ordinary annuity: a series of equal payments occurring in equally spaced time periods.

ordinary income: income including salaries, fees, commissions, interest, dividends, and many other items. Taxed at regular tax rates, unlike long-term capital gains.

ordinary interest: interest based on a 360-day year instead of a 365-day year. The former is referred to as simple interest and the latter is termed exact interest. The difference between the two types of interest can be significant when a substantial investment is involved.

ordinary loss: for income tax purposes, a loss that is deductible against ordinary income. Usually more beneficial to a taxpayer than a capital loss.

original cost: the total costs associated with the purchase of an asset, for accounting purposes.

original equity: the initial investment by the underlying real estate owner.

original principal balance: the total amount of principal owed on a mortgage before any payments are made.

origination fee: a fee paid to a lender for processing a loan application. The origination fee is stated in the form of *points*. One point is one percent of the mortgage amount.

origination process: the process by which a loan is funded, including the due diligence process, and lender committee approvals.

OSHA: see *Occupational Safety and Health Administration.*

other buyer costs: there are other costs associated with the *closing* that are typically paid by the buyer. They often include:
* **fees paid to the lender:** loan discount points, loan origination fee, credit report fee, appraisal fee, and assumption fee.
* **advance payments or prepaid fees:** interest, mortgage insurance premium, and hazard insurance premium.
* **escrow accounts or reserves:** state and local law and lenders'

policies vary, but these reserves may have to be set up if the lender will be paying property taxes, mortgage insurance, and hazard insurance.

- **title charges:** closing (or settlement) fee, title insurance premium, title search, document preparation fees, and attorney fees. The fees the buyer pays for a real estate attorney are not part of settlement procedures.

- **recording and transfer fees:** states often impose a tax on the transfer of property. The payment of a fee for recording the pur chasing documents may be required.

- **additional charges:** surveyor's fees, termite and other pet infestation inspection fees, and the cost of other inspections required by the lender.

- **adjustments:** items paid by the seller in advance and items yet to be paid for which the seller is responsible. The most common expense is property taxes, but others may have to be addressed.

other contingencies: a contingency in a contract states that if a certain requirement is not met, the deal can be canceled. Some of the most common contingencies related to home purchases include:

- **professional home inspection:** this states that a sales contract is contingent on a satisfactory report by a professional home inspector. A buyer has the right not to proceed with the purchase of the home, or to re-negotiate the terms of purchase, if any major problems are uncovered.

- **termite inspection:** this states that the property is free of both visible termite infestation and termite damage.

- **asbestos:** it's best to hire a qualified professional to inspect the home, take samples for asbestos, and offer solutions to correct any problems.

- **formaldehyde:** this colorless, gaseous chemical was used in foam insulation for homes until the early 1980s and is emitted by some construction materials. It is suspected of causing cancer, and it can also irritate the throat, nose, and eyes. A qualified inspector can determine if the gas is present in the home.

- **radon:** most homebuyers require that the house be tested for radon, a naturally occurring, odorless gas that can cause health problems.

- **hazardous waste sites:** the Environmental Protection Agency has identified contaminated hazardous waste sites across the country. The local office of the Environmental Protection Agency can supply more information.

- **lead-based paint:** the house should also be inspected for lead-based paint, which can lead to very serious health problems. If the house was built before 1950, it's likely certain lead-based paint was used. For houses built between 1950 and 1978, there is a lesser chance lead-based paint was used. Lead disclosure regulations can vary from state to state.

other financial companies: companies that include credit unions, mortgage brokers, insurance companies, investment bankers, and housing finance agencies.

- **credit unions** are cooperative, not-for-profit institutions organized to promote savings and to provide credit, including mortgage loans, to their members. Credit unions either service the mortgages they originate or sell them to other investors.

- **mortgage brokers** are independent real estate financing professionals who specialize in the origination of residential and/or commercial mortgages. Mortgage brokers originate loans on behalf of other lenders—including banks, thrifts and mortgage banking companies, but do not service loans.

- **insurance companies** and investment bankers are large institutional investors in mortgages that do not receive deposits from consumers. They use premiums from their clients' insurance polices and investment packages to fund their mortgage-lending activities.

- **housing finance agencies** are typically associated with state or local governments. They are generally geared toward assisting first-time and low-to-moderate-income borrowers. They use tax-exempt bonds to fund mortgage lending, and as a result are often able to provide interest rates that are below current market rates.

other people's money (OPM): the use of borrowed funds by people or businesses to increase the return on an investment. The term implies that debt can be used to maximize investment profits or minimize the risk of personal loss.

outbuilding: any structure located on a lot in addition to the house or main building. Outbuildings can be barns, shops, sheds, etc.

outgo: same as *expenses*.

outlay: an expenditure.

outstanding balance: the amount still unpaid and owed on a debt, loan, or other financing agreement.

overage:
(1) in leases for retail sales, amounts to be paid, based on gross sales, over the base rent.
(2) alternately, a selling price received for property in excess of the expected price. An excessive amount; surplus.

overage income: a rental based on a percent of sales or profit that is in addition to the constant rental amount.

overall capitalization rate: see *overall rate of return*.

overall rate of return (OAR): net operating income divided by the purchase price of property. *Net operating income (NOI)* of property relative to its market value. If rental income property worth $1,000,000 results in a NOI of $100,000, the overall return is 10%. NOI compared to the initial cost of the property as distinguished from its market price.

overbuilding: a situation where there is more real estate construction than the market can absorb.

overhead: the fixed costs of doing business, not directly related to a specific job or project. Overhead includes items such as management salaries, office rent, and administrative costs.

overhead ratio: operating expenses divided by the sum of taxable equivalent net interest income and other operating income.

over-improved property: a property whose sale price is not high enough to recoup the costs of its improvements

overimprovement: land improvement that is more extensive than the surrounding neighborhood justifies or that can be economically warranted.

override: a percentage of a commission or a fee paid to someone higher in the organization or above a certain amount.

overriding royalty: a percentage of royalties derived from an oil and gas lease payable to someone other than the property lessor. It is a net royalty interest in the oil and gas recovered at the surface free of all operating expenses.

owner: the person (or entity) to whom a piece of property belongs. In real estate, the person or entity with title to the property.

owner financing: a property purchase transaction in which the property seller provides all or part of the financing.

owner occupant: the owner of a property who lives there.

owner of record: the person or persons who, according to the public records, own a particular property.

owner's equity: net worth minus liens and other encumbrances.

ownership: a person or entity that has title or a right to something, which is typically being held.

ownership form: the methods of owning real estate. Ownership form has important consequences for income tax, estate tax, corporate income tax, and survivorship. Real estate may be owned by one or more persons. Methods of ownership include tenancy in common, joint tenancy, a tenancy by the entirety, tenancy in severalty, partnership, limited partnership, and corporation.

ownership in severalty: the ownership of property by one person or one legal entity (corporate ownership).

ownership rights to realty: the right to possess, exclusively occupy, enjoy, control, and dispose of real estate. Ownership rights to realty are granted by the ownership of a title to real property.

P

package mortgage: a mortgage on both the purchased real estate and personal property of a durable type, with the entire amount financed, is considered one mortgage.

packaging:

(1) the transfer of both real estate and personal property.

(2) alternately, the putting together of a group of properties to be sold together, possibly at a discount price because several items are bought in combination.

pad site: an individual freestanding site for a retailer; pad sites are often adjacent to a larger shopping center or other freestanding retailers.

paper profit: an increase in value that would be realized if the property were sold. Until a sale occurs, the increased value is not recognized in the accounts. Only, when the property is sold, will there be a realized gain (or loss).

paper title: a document of title to property that may not in fact be valid.

parapet: a protective low wall along a roof or edge, or below a terrace.

parcel: a piece of land that is usually a part of a larger acreage.

parol: a statement made verbally.

parol evidence: oral evidence, rather than written.

parol evidence rule: permits oral evidence to augment a written contract in certain cases.

partial interest: the ownership of a part of the ownership rights to a parcel of real estate.

partial payment: a payment that is not sufficient to cover the scheduled monthly payment on a mortgage loan.

partial release: the release of a portion of a property from a mortgage.

partial taking: the purchase of part of the property or property rights when condemnation takes place. The owner must be justly reimbursed.

participation or participating mortgage: an agreement between a mortgagee and a mortgagor that allows the lender to have a percentage of ownership in that particular property. Allows the lender to share in part of the income or resale proceeds.

partition:

(1) the division of real estate between owners, giving each an undivided interest.

(2) alternately, an interior wall dividing an area into two or more rooms or separate areas.

partition action: a court action to order a compulsory sale of real estate owned jointly between two or more owners. A partition action divided the proceeds of a real estate sale among the joint owners rather than physically dividing the real estate into separate undivided interests.

partnership: an agreement between two or more persons to go into lawful business. Either partner may bind the other, within the scope of the partnership. Partners are individually liable for the debts of the partnership. A partnership is not normally subject to taxes, and the various items of partnership income, expenses, gains, and losses flow through to the individual partners and are reported on their personal income tax returns.

party wall: a boundary wall between two properties, built along the line separating the properties, partly on each parcel. Either owner has the right to use the wall and has an easement over that part of the adjoining owner's land covered by the wall.

passive income: generally, income from rents, royalties, dividends, interest, and gains from the sale of securities. A meaning created by the Tax Reform Act of 1986 distinguishes passive income (or loss) from active income and portfolio income. Passive income is income from business activities in which the taxpayer does not materially participate, and all rental activities (except those of qualified real estate professionals). See also *active income* and *portfolio income.*

passive income generator (PIG): a business or investment that produces passive income that can be used to offset passive losses.

passive investor: someone who invests money but does not manage the business or property.

passive loss: a tax term referring to a loss from a passive activity, such as ownership, but not operation, of rental real estate.

pass-through certificates or securities: securities supported by a pool of mortgages. The principal and interest are due monthly on the mortgages, and are passed through to the investors who bought the pool.

patent defect: a visible deficiency in a piece of property such as a sagging porch, etc.

payback period: the amount of time required for cumulative estimated future income from an investment to recover, or pay back, the amount initially invested.

payee: one who receives a payment.

payer: one who makes a payment.

payment bonds: security that a contractor's bills will be paid from the money given by the client, so that the client is not held liable.

payment cap: a consumer safeguard that limits the increase of monthly payments on an *adjustable-rate mortgage*. Since it does not limit the amount of interest the lender is earning, it may cause negative amortization.

payment change date: the date when a new monthly payment amount takes effect on an *adjustable-rate mortgage (ARM)* or a *graduated-payment adjustable-rate mortgage (GPARM)*. Generally, the payment change date occurs in the month immediately after the adjustment date.

pediment: the triangular gable at the top of the front of a classical building; a similar design is also used above doorways and openings.

penalty: the money that will be paid by a person or business for violating a statute or legal court order. Also, may be assessed for violating the provisions of a contract.

penalty clause: a provision in a contract that specifies the dollar amount or rate an individual must pay for not conforming to its terms.

pendente lite: *(Latin)* pending the suit. A lawsuit where the outcome is pending.

penthouse: a luxury-housing unit located on the top floor of a building. Sometimes, it is a unit built on the roof of a high-rise building.

percentage lease: a lease where the rent is based on a percentage of the sales volume made inside the leased premises. It is common in retail leases.

per diem interest: interest calculated per day. Depending on the day of the month on which *closing* takes place, the borrower will have to pay interest from the date of closing to the end of the month. The first mortgage payment will probably be due the first day of the following month.

perfecting title: removing a *cloud* or claim from the title.

periodic payment cap: for an *adjustable-rate mortgage (ARM)*, a limit on the amount that payments can increase or decrease during any one adjustment period.

periodic tenancy: a tenancy arrangement that continues on a week-to-week or month-to-month basis with no clear termination date fixed. This sometimes occurs when a tenant continues to occupy a dwelling after the end of a lease.

permanent mortgage: a mortgage for an extended period of time, 10 to 25 years.

permit: a legal document that allows a specific action to be taken. Permits provide legal permission to undertake a project, and are usually given by local governmental agencies. Some of the most common permits are for general projects or permits that require property owners and builders to meet specific local building codes. With most major home improvement projects, work permits are required. Check with local government to determine if there are building restrictions in historic areas or in environmentally sensitive areas.

per se: *(Latin)* by itself. A matter that is alone and not connected to another matter.

personal assets: personal property and other assets a person has in his estate.

personal financial statement: a document showing the financial health of an individual, which may be requested for a loan application.

personal liability: an individual's responsibility for a debt.

personal property:

(1) in terms of a business, taxable personal property includes machinery, equipment, furniture, supplies, leased equipment, movable machinery, and libraries used in a business. It includes items that have been used in the business

(2) things movable, property that is not real estate.

personal residence: the place that one claims as one's primary home. This dwelling establishes one's legal residence for voting, tax, and legal purposes. *Condominiums, cooperative apartments, townhouses, mobile homes,* and houseboats, as well as houses, can all qualify as residences.

personal-use property: property owned for personal well-being and enjoyment, including a taxpayer's home, vehicles, furniture, clothing, and other property.

per stirpes: *(Latin)* by the roots. A legal way to distribute an estate. Each beneficiary receives an apportioned share of the property.

per-unit allocation: allocating common or central costs to each *unit* of property.

pest-control inspection: a professional inspection to determine whether or not there are insects in a dwelling, which is usually required by a lender.

phased building: portions of construction are completed prior to other portions being started. For example, the exterior of a building, wall, and roof, would be competed prior to interior work being started. Construction is often done in this manner to protect the incomplete parts, and for economic reasons.

physical damage insurance: insurance coverage for any risk that can cause physical damage to the insured item.

physical depreciation or deterioration: the decline in value of property due to all causes: age, effects of the elements, breakage, wear and tear.

picture window: a large window, often single-paned, framing an exterior view.

piggyback loan:
(1) a loan, with participation by two or more lenders, in the financing of a single mortgage.
(2) alternately, a combination of a construction loan with a permanent mortgage.

pilaster: a projecting square column forming part of a wall.

pipefitter: a contractor whose job is to install piping for steam, cooling, hot water, etc.

piping, PVC: polyvinyl chloride, a lightweight, resilient, chemical-resistant, strong, and durable thermoplastics, with a long lifespan, made into piping that is often used for cold-water systems and where chemicals are found. Solvent cement joins the ends of the piping by applying a primer to soften the surface of the material, with the solvent cement applied to the pipe end and the inside of the fitting end, then inserting the pipe into the fitting using a twisting motion to spread the solvent cement. The cement cures rapidly and the joints fuse together.

piping area drawing: a drawing, done by the layout person for the piping system, which shows, to scale, the routing of the piping system, using either elevation views or plan and section views.

piping codes and standards: local and state laws establish *codes* applicable to piping and piping systems. Materials are covered by American Society for Testing and Materials (ASTM) Standards, with other regulations being set by the American Society of Mechanical Engineers (ASME), American Petroleum Institute (API), American Water Works Association (AWWA), American National Standards Institute (ANSI), American Welding Society (AWS), Manufacturers Standardization Society of the Valve and Fitting Industry (MSS), Plastics Pipe Institute (PPI), Copper Development Association

(CDA), and the Uni-Bell PVC Pipe Association.

piping isometric drawing: a three-dimensional drawing that shows the layout, sizes, and dimension of the piping system of a structure.

pitch (of a roof): the slope of a roof; steepness.

PITI: see *principal, interest, taxes and insurance.*

PITI reserves: a cash amount that a borrower must have on hand after making a down payment and paying all closing costs for the purchase of a home. The *principal, interest, taxes, and insurance (PITI)* reserves must equal the amount that the borrower would have to pay for PITI for a predefined number of months.

plaintiff: in a legal action, the party initiating the suit.

planned community: a description of a neighborhood built with certain guidelines in mind.

planned unit development (PUD): a project or subdivision that includes common property that is owned and maintained by a homeowners' association for the benefit and use of the individual PUD unit owners.

planning commission: a governmental body having the responsibility for planning the future development of a jurisdictional area. A planning commission is responsible for developing and managing a zoning ordinance as well as interfacing with a professional planning department.

planning grid: a grid showing the dimensions of a structure to give the builder some choice in locating openings and allowing matching of vertical and horizontal surfaces. Material lists are matched to the grid, so that the use of standard sized materials can minimize waste.

plan view: a floor plan of a structure that is shown from a horizontal plane above the structure.

plat: a plan or map of a specific land area, showing the boundaries of individual properties.

plat book: a public record of maps showing the division of streets, blocks, and lots, and providing the measurements of the individual parcels.

plat map: a map showing land, with township, streets, improvement, lot lines, etc., within a specific area.

pleadings: formal allegations by all of the parties to an action including complaints, answers, and replies to counterclaims.

pledged account mortgage (PAM): a type of graduated-payment loan under which a portion of the borrower's down payment is used to fund an account pledged to the lender. The account is then drawn down during the initial years of the loan to supplement periodic mortgage payments. The effect is to lower the payment amounts in the first years of the loan; payments will then gradually rise.

pledgee: an individual to whom a mortgage or property is pledged.

pledgor: an individual who is responsible for making the payments on a mortgage on property that has been pledged.

plot: a parcel of land or small lot.

plot plan: a scale diagram showing the proposed or existing use of a specific parcel of land and the location of the structure in comparison to the boundaries of the property, utility services, compass directions, etc.

plottage: the combining of two or more contiguous land parcels to make a larger, more useful and valuable piece.

plottage value: the result of combining two or more parcels of land so that the one larger parcel has more value than the sum of the individual parcels.

PMI: see *private mortgage insurance.*

pocket card/pocket license card: a pocket-sized card required for salespersons and brokers in most states. Issued by the state licensing agency, it identifies its holder as a *licensee.*

point: one point is equal to one percent of the amount of the principal of the mortgage. It is a fee charged by the lender.

points: a one-time fee charged by the lender for originating a loan, measured in points, which is the percentage of the amount of the principal. Also called *discount points.*

policy: a real estate owner's rules regarding the use of the property by a tenant. Alternately, a written contract in which one party guarantees to insure another against a specified loss.

population density: the population per square mile of a given area.

porch:
(1) a room attached to the outside of a building.
(2) a shelter over a doorway.

portfolio: holdings of investment assets.

portfolio diversification: choosing alternative investment instruments having different risk-return features.

portfolio income: in the case of real estate, portfolio income is typically rental and lease payment income, and investments in mortgages and other long-term debt instruments that produce interest income, while equity investments generate dividends.

portfolio lender: a lender that makes loans with its own funds and keep the loans on the company's books, inside the institution's portfolio.

positive cash flow: net amounts available to an equity investor after deducting all periodic cash payments from rental income.

positive leverage: profitably using borrowed funds to increase the return on an investment. When the return on the borrowed funds exceed the after-tax interest costs.

possession: the holding, control or custody of property.

possession by adverse possession: a way to acquire title to real estate when an occupant has been in actual, open, exclusive, and continuous occupancy of property for an extended period of time.

possessory action: litigation undertaken to obtain or maintain possession of real property.

potential gross income: the amount of income that a property will generate by the sale or rental of property or rendering of services, without vacancies or interruptions.

potentially responsible parties (PRP): in the case of an EPA-designated *Superfund* site, all owners, operators, transporters, and disposers of hazardous waste are potentially responsible parties.

power of attorney: a legal document that authorizes another person to act on one's behalf. A power of attorney can grant complete authority or can be limited to certain acts and/or certain periods of time.

power of sale: a provision in a mortgage agreement that grants the lender (or trustee) the right to sell the property upon default.

Prairie style: popularized by the residential designs of Frank Lloyd Wright, Prairie style homes feature a long low roofline with a continuous row of windows, a plain exterior and a very open design with long horizontal lines.

preamble: a clause at the beginning of a legal document explaining its purpose; it neither confers or increases powers contained within it and is, therefore, not an essential element of it.

pre-approval: the process of determining how much money a prospective homebuyer or refinancer will be eligible to borrow prior to application for a loan. A pre-approval includes a preliminary screening of a borrower's credit history. Information submitted during pre-approval is subject to verification at application. Being pre-approved for a mortgage can make a buyer more attractive to a seller.

pre-approval letter: a letter from a lender confirming the amount that can be borrowed by a person whose ability to borrow has already been assessed by the lender.

prearranged refinancing agreement: a formal or informal arrangement between a lender and a borrower wherein the lender agrees to offer special terms (such as a reduction in the costs) for a future refinancing of a mortgage, as an inducement for the borrower to enter into the original mortgage transaction.

pre-closing: prior to actual closing, all information is available in order to insure that the appropriate parties properly execute all documents. A pre-closing is used primarily when the closing is expected to be complicated by many extraneous factors.

pre-depreciation profit: the profit before considering noncash expenses.

preemptive right: the right of a current stockholder to maintain the percentage ownership in a real estate company by purchasing new shares on a proportionate basis before they are issued to the public. It allows existing stockholders to keep the value and control they presently enjoy. The new shares may be issued to the current stockholders at a lower price than the going market price. Further, brokerage commissions do not have to be paid.

preexisting use: property use that is in violation of the current zoning ordinance, but had been in use prior to the zoning ordinance's enactment.

prefabricated: constructed in a factory, usually in modules or units, and then assembled where it is to be used.

prefabricated house: a house made using standardized components that are pre-assembled in a factory and then erected on the site. Normally, the prefabricated house is trucked onto the home site, where it is installed on a completed foundation.

preforeclosure sale: a procedure in which the investor allows a mortgagor to avoid foreclosure by selling the property for less than the amount that is owed to the investor.

prelease: the obtaining of lease commitments in a development prior to its being available for occupancy.

premise or premises: land and any existing buildings that are part of a conveyance as noted in a deed.

premium:
(1) the amount paid for real estate over and above the expected prevailing price. The value of a mortgage or bond in excess of its face amount.
(2) alternatively, periodic fee paid for insurance protection.

prepaid expenses: the taxes, insurance, and assessments paid in advance of their due dates. These expenses are included at *closing*.

prepaid interest: the interest that is paid in advance of when it is due. Typically charged to a borrower at *closing* to cover interest on the loan between the closing date and the first payment date.

prepayment: any amount paid to reduce the principal balance of a loan before the due date. Payment in full on a mortgage that may result from a sale of the property, the owner's decision to pay off the loan in full, or a foreclosure. In each case, prepayment means that payment occurs before the loan has been fully amortized.

prepayment clause: a clause in a mortgage that gives a borrower the privilege of paying off the mortgage before it becomes due.

prepayment fee: a charge, often required by the terms of a mortgage, that is assessed on the remaining principal when an obligation is paid off before its full term. See *prepayment penalty.*

prepayment penalty: a fee that a borrower is assessed for the right to make a loan payment before the due date, such as paying a mortgage early. Buyers should make sure they don't have a prepayment penalty attached to their loan, because it limits their chance to save money on their loan.

prepayment privilege: the right of a borrower to retire a loan before maturity.

prequalification:
(1) the process of determining how much money a prospective homebuyer will be eligible to borrow before he or she applies for a loan.
(2) confirmation of the amount to be borrowed by a person whose ability to borrow has already been assessed by the lender.

presale: the sale of proposed properties still in the planning stages and/or before construction is completed.

prescription: a method of obtaining title to property through adverse possession, such as open, notorious, and continuous use of the property for a statutorily prescribed period of time.

prescriptive easement: a legally enforceable passage through the property of another, by long-term usage without objection by the owner, which establishes precedence; common law considers that a right has been established.

present value analysis: a way of valuing real estate that computes the discounted present value of an expected stream of income, including rental income and future capital gains or losses.

present value of annuity: the current value of a future level stream of income to be received for a finite number of periods.

present value of one: the value today of an amount to be received in the future, based on a compound interest rate.

present value tables: tables providing the present values of $1 or an annuity of $1 for different time periods and at different discount rates.

preservation district: similar to a *landmark district*, this is an official city zoning designation covering historic, environmental, parkland, or scenic areas with strict rules about what landowners and renters can do with the space.

pre-sold home: a home that is sold prior to being built.

preterit: the past action(s) of a property owner or tenant.

preventive maintenance: maintenance procedures conducted to prevent later repairs and extending a useful life.

price appreciation: an increase in the value of real estate or personal property. The price may increase because of a number of factors, such as shortage in supply, improved economy, favorable political environment, tax incentives, or increased profitability.

price fixing: an illegal conspiracy by competitors to maintain a uniform price.

price-level adjusted mortgage: an adjustable or variable payment loan which uses the rate of inflation as an index. The interest rate is a rate net of any inflation premium.

price range: the upper and lower limits of what a buyer will pay for a home.

primary beneficiary: the person who will receive the benefits of a trust or insurance policy, when distribution is made.

primary financing: a loan that is paid before all other loans in the event of default.

primary lease: a rental agreement between the owner and a tenant. When the tenant rents to someone else, it is called a sublease.

primary location: real estate located in the most excellent area for its designated use.

Primary Metropolitan Statistical Area (PMSA): if a metropolitan area has a population of over a million, Primary Metropolitan Statistical Areas may be defined within it. PMSAs consist of a large urbanized county or cluster of counties that demonstrate very strong internal economic and social links, in addition to close ties to other portions of the larger area. When PMSAs are established, the larger area of which they are component parts is designated a *Consolidated Metropolitan Statistical Area (CMSA)*.

primary mortgage market: a mortgage market in which original loans are made by lenders. The market is made up with lenders who supply funds directly to borrowers and hold the mortgage until the debt is paid.

prime contractor: see *general contractor*.

prime lending rate: the interest rate that banks charge to their preferred customers. Changes in the prime rate influence changes in other rates, including mortgage interest rates.

prime tenant: a major tenant in an office building or shopping center. The prime tenant occupies more space than the others and will attract customers to the site. They are normally more credit worthy.

principal: the amount borrowed and remaining unpaid. It is also the part of the monthly mortgage payment that reduces the remaining balance of a mortgage.

principal balance: the outstanding amount of principal owed on a mortgage. The principal balance does not include interest or any other charges.

principal broker: the licensed broker responsible for the operations conduced by the firm.

principal, interest, taxes, and insurance (PITI): the payment amount calculated to include the principal, interest, taxes, and insurance on an amortizing loan; represents the borrower's actual monthly mortgage-related expenses.

principal payments: payments received on the contract price.

principal place of business: the main place where work is performed or business is transacted. Taxpayers who engage in more than one business can have more than one principal place of business. For purposes of the home-office deduction, a principal place of business may also be an area of a taxpayer's home that is used for the management and recordkeeping portions of the business, provided there is no other fixed location where the taxpayer performs such functions.

principal residence: the primary residence of an individual; the place where a person lives most of the time. May be a single-family house, condominium, trailer, or houseboat. A principal residence may qualify for a *homestead rebate*.

principle of conformity: the concept that a house will be more likely to appreciate in value if it is similar to other houses in the neighborhood.

principle of progression: an appraisal term stating that the value of lower-end real estate is enhanced by the proximity of higher-end properties.

principle of regression: an appraisal term stating that the value of higher-end real estate can be brought down by the proximity to lower-end properties.

privacy fence: a structure erected between two pieces of property.

private mortgage: a mortgage contract in which the lender is not a registered financial institution but may be a friend, family member, or individual investor.

private mortgage insurance (PMI): an insurance policy required on some loans to protect lenders from possible default by borrower. Conventional loans with down payments of less than 20 percent of the home value usually require private mortgage insurance

private offering: an offering of securities, stock, and/or debt, directly to investors (usually large institutional investors) rather than through the public exchange markets. An advantage of a private placement to a real estate business is that the securities do not have to be registered with the Securities and Exchange Commission.

private property: privately owned property.

private sewer: a sewer that belongs to the building where it is installed but discharges into the public sewer. Also known as a building sewer.

privity: a mutual interest in the same property or rights established by law or legalized by contract.

probate court: a court having the responsibility of performing probate of wills and of administering estates. In certain states, a probate court can appoint guardians for minor children of an estate.

probate or prove: the process of establishing the validity of a will in court. The *probate court* administers the will as directed, or as authorized, to settle financial obligations.

processing fee: a fee charged by most lenders to pay for gathering the information necessary to process the loan.

process time: the time needed for performance of an operation to completion.

production home: a mass-produced homes, i.e., a tract of homes built by one builder.

professional appraiser: an expert in real estate who has an education in real estate appraisal as well as having significant professional experience. A recognized license may be obtained from the Member Appraisal Institute. However, no national requirement exists as to who may do an appraisal. When an appraisal is done by a federally insured agency, the appraiser must be licensed by the state.

profit: the sum remaining after all costs, direct and indirect, are deducted from the income of a business.

profit and loss statement: a financial statement depicting a business entity's operating performance; reports the components of net income, including sales of real estate, rental income, operating rental expenses, income from rental operations, and income before tax. The income statement shows the cash flow for an entire accounting period, usually a quarter. The income statement is included in the annual report of the real estate corporation.

pro forma statement: *(Latin)* according to form. Financial statement with amounts or other information that are completely or partially assumed. The assumptions supporting the amounts are usually provided. The statement may be prepared in determining the possible financial effects of buying or renting property.

progress payments: the payments made to a contractor as the various construction stages are completed. The contractor uses progress payments to pay the various subcontractors and suppliers as construction proceeds.

project budget: an outline of the construction budget and all costs for land, equipment, financing professional services, etc.

projection period: the time duration for estimating future cash flows and the resale proceeds from a proposed real estate investment.

promissory note: see *note*.

property: the ownership rights that one individual has in lands or goods to the exclusion of all others. Property rights include exclusive occupancy, possession, use, and the right of disposition. Individuals, groups, organizations, and governments may own property.

property and casualty policy: an insurance contract providing coverage for risks primarily associated with negligence, and acts of omission associated with third-party injuries or property losses. Property and casualty policies normally exclude losses associated with war, riots, and unreasonable negligence.

property brief: a summarization of the attributes and characteristics of the property, such as that indicated in the legal records (title search).

property damage liability insurance: an insurance policy that promises to pay all the legal obligations of the insured due to negligence in which damage to the property has been caused.

property damage liability losses: losses arising from damage to or destruction of property.

property depreciation insurance: insurance protection for the replacement cost of damaged property. Thus, the accumulated depreciation is not subtracted in determining the amount of reimbursement.

property description: a legally acceptable description of real estate, including metes and bounds, government rectangular survey, or lot numbers of a recorded plat. All property deeds have a legal description.

property insurance: an insurance affording protection against losses due to damage to or destruction of property or contents therein. Insurance protects assets and any future income thereon from loss, such as a fire, etc.

property inventory: a listing of all assets a person or business own, their cost and appraised value.

property line: the official dividing line between two properties. Legal boundary of property.

property management: the operation of property as a business, including rental, rent collection, maintenance, etc.

property report: the Interstate Land Sale Act requires this report for the sale of subdivisions of 50 lots or more. The report is filed with HUD'S *Office of Interstate Land Sales Registration (OILSR)*.

property residual technique: a way for appraisers to value property by estimating its future income.

property tax: the taxes paid on privately owned properties; based on local tax rates and assessed property values.

property tax deduction: the U.S. tax code allowing homeowners to deduct the amount they have paid in property taxes.

property under contract: real estate being offered for sale that has received a contract for sale but has not gone to a closing.

property value: the value of a piece of property based on the amount a buyer will pay.

proposal: a detailed presentation of an offering to perform a job for a specified amount under certain conditions. Often given by a subcontractor to a general contractor.

proprietary lease: a lease in a cooperative apartment building; the lease a corporation provides to the stockholders, which allows them to use a certain apartment unit under specified conditions.

proprietorship: the ownership of a business, including income-producing real estate, by an individual, as contrasted with a partnership or corporation.

prorate: the allocation of expenses to be paid by the buyer and seller at time of closing.

proration of taxes: the proportionate division of taxes at the closing between the buyer and the seller.

prospect: a potential customer or client.

prospect cards: a file of prospective real estate customers, showing their address, telephone number, time and date of last contact, types of properties in which they are interested, and their financial capabilities.

prospectus: a formal statement about a business or investment that is for sale, to invite the interest of prospective investors. The document must accompany a new issue of securities for a real estate company or partnership, and must include the same information in the registration statement, such as a list of directors and officers, financial statements certified by a CPA, underwriters, the purpose and use for funds, and other relevant information.

proximity damage: a decline in value of real estate property because it is near something damaging to its worth.

proxy:
(1) a person who is authorized to exercise another's rights, particularly in some meeting.
(2) also, the document giving to another the authority to so represent.

public auction: a meeting in an announced public location to sell property to repay a mortgage that is in default.

public domain: land owned by the federal, state, or county government that the public might use, as distinguished from property owned privately by individuals and businesses.

public housing: government-owned housing units made available to low-income individuals and families for low rental rates.

public lands: land owned by federal and local governments, including parks and forest preserves.

public offering: an offering of new securities of a real estate company to the investing public, after registration requirements have been filed with the SEC.

public record: the documents located at government entities that are available to anyone making a proper search request. In real estate, such public documents include deeds, subdivision plats, and assessment record cards.

public report: a report published by a governmental unit that is publicly available.

public sale: a public foreclosure sale, where public notice is given and anyone is allowed to participate.

public sewer: see *municipal sewer.*

public syndicate: a group of at least two people or businesses combining to engage in a real estate project that would exceed their individual financial abilities. A syndication allows earning to be proportionately shared.

PUD: see *planned unit development.*

pueblo style: a twentieth century style made of adobe, with a flat roof, stucco wall surfaces, usually earth-colored. Inspired by the adobe structures in the Southwest. (*see Appendix A*)

punch list: a list detailing items to be fixed, which is compiled by a buyer prior to closing on a property.

punitive damages: the damages used to penalize the defendant for bad faith, malice, fraud, violence, or evil intent, and are designed as both punishment and as a deterrent for future actions of the defendant. Punitive damages are in excess of the actual damages.

Also called exemplary damages.

purchase agreement: a document that outlines the purchase price and conditions of the transaction.

purchase and sale agreement: a written contract signed by buyer and seller stating the terms and conditions under which a property will be sold. The purchase and sale agreement is a written contract that is signed by the buyer and seller. It states the terms and conditions under which a property will be sold. It includes: description of property; price offered; down payment; earnest money deposit; financing; personal items to be included; closing date; occupancy date; length of time the offer is valid; special contingencies; and inspection.

purchase contract: a legal document binding a buyer to purchase and a seller to sell a property for a set price.

purchase-money mortgage (PMM): a mortgage obtained by a borrower as partial payment for a property. Type of seller financing that is a mortgage loan from the seller instead of cash for the purchase price of the real estate.

purchase money transaction: the acquisition of property through the payment of money or its equivalent.

purchase order: the authorization, in writing, to perform a service or supply a material, indicating the cost of such.

purchasing power risk: a risk resulting from possible increases or decreases in price levels that can substantially impact real estate values.

purlins: beams that span across a roof to support the roof framing system.

pyramid zoning: a form of zoning regulation permitting all the uses permitted in more restrictive zoning to also apply to less restrictive zoning. The net effect of pyramid zoning is to pyramid only a few uses to more restrictive zoning regulations, while allowing the broader base of uses to be applicable in less restrictive applications.

Q

quadrangle: a rectangular area bordered on all sides by buildings; often grassy with decorative landscaping. A quadrangle can be found in a central business district or on the site of an academic institution.

quadrant: one of four equal parts created when an object or area is divided by lines that intersect at right angles. Alternately, one fourth of a circle.

quadrominium: a four-unit building with four tenants in a condominium type of ownership and management.

qualified opinion: an accountant's or auditor's opinion of a financial statement for which some limitations existed, such as an inability to gather certain information or a significant upcoming event that may or may not occur.

qualified lender: a bank or lending agency qualified under specific local or federal programs that underwrite the loans.

qualifying: the process determining an individual's financial ability to meet the terms of a loan. When selling real estate, the sales broker must qualify the buyer to make certain he/she has the financial ability to purchase the property.

qualifying guidelines: there are two main elements that lenders consider when determining whether a borrower qualifies for a specific mortgage. The first is the monthly mortgage costs: *PITI.* Mortgage costs should not exceed 28 percent of a borrower's gross monthly (pre-tax) income. The second qualifying guideline relates to total monthly housing costs and other debts; these costs should not exceed 36 percent of gross monthly income. Lenders follow these guidelines because they believe these percentages allow homeowners to pay off their mortgages fairly comfortably without the worry of loan defaults and foreclosures. However, these guidelines can be exceeded in certain cases, such as borrowers with a good credit history or with a larger down payment.

qualifying ratio: calculations that are used in determining whether a borrower can qualify for a mortgage. They consist of two separate calculations: housing expense as a percent of income ratio, and total debt obligations as a percent of income ratio.

quantity survey: an estimated itemization of all costs in constructing a structure, including site acquisition and preparation and a detailed cost estimate of all materials, labor, and overhead required to reproduce the structure. Quantity surveys are used by contractors in preparing a project's bid price. Also, an appraisal estimate of the replacement cost of a structure, including current costs of materials and labor.

quantity take-off: an itemization of the entire number of items that are necessary to complete a building project, as it appears on the blueprint.

quasi-contract: legal obligation to do something imposed upon someone by law, which bears the force of a contract and is subject to legal action as a contract. It is basically a legal obligation to pay for a benefit received, as if a contract had actually occurred.

Queen Anne style: a Victorian-era style of home, which is multistory and features steeply-pitched roofs, turrets, high chimneys, and decorative trim. They usually have one-story porches. (*see Appendix A*)

quick ratio: a measure of a company's liquidity, used to evaluate creditworthiness. Relevant in cases of purchasing business property. Equals quick assets divided by current liabilities, and is also called the *acid-test ratio*.

quid pro quo: (*Latin*) this for that. It is used to mean something given in exchange for something else.

quiet title suit: lawsuit filed to ascertain the legal rights of an owner to a parcel of property, to remove a defect, or to remove a *cloud* on the title.

quitclaim deed: deed that conveys only the grantor's rights or interest in real estate, without stating the nature of the rights and with no warranties of ownership. It is often used to remove a *cloud* on a title.

quotation: highest bid to buy and the lowest offer to sell a parcel of real estate in a particular market at a specified time. Sometimes also refers to a proposal to perform certain work for a specified price.

R

R&D: research and development.

racial steering: the illegal practice of directing certain races away from some neighborhoods and into others.

radiant heating: the use of radiation to generate heat, such as with baseboard heating, where the circulating hot water is radiated through conduction by thin metal fins at the bottom of the wall. The room is warmed by air circulating around the heating unit using convection.

radon: a colorless, odorless, naturally forming gas that seeps into some homes from the ground, through sump pumps, cracks in the foundation, etc.; it is a carcinogen (cancer-causing) substance.

rafter: any of the beams that slope from the ridge of a roof to the eaves to serve as support for the roof. (see *Appendix B*)

rafter plate: the top plate of a building's walls. The rafters rest on the rafter plate.

rail:

(1) a horizontal bar placed between upright supports, as in a fence or staircase; a guard or barrier

(2) a horizontal piece in a door or paneling. (see *Appendix B*)

raised ranch: a *bi-level*; a type of house that has the lower floor partially below the ground.

RAM: see *reverse annuity mortgage*.

ranch house: a long, one story style of home with all of the rooms on one floor. This style was originated in mid-twentieth century California. (see *Appendix A*)

range capacity: the total number of range grasslands acres that are needed to support one animal unit for a certain time period.

range lines: lines which run parallel to the principal meridian six miles apart to create "ranges" of land. From the Government Surveying Method.

ratable: an estimated insurance risk to calculate a reasonable premi-

um that would provide sufficient resources, while still being affordable, in the event that the company is required to pay a claim.

rate cap: the maximum interest rate charge allowed on the monthly payment of an *adjustable-rate mortgage*, either during an adjustment period, or over the life of the loan.

rate-improvement mortgage: a loan that entitles a borrower to a
one-time interest-rate cut without refinancing.

rate lock: the lender's commitment to the borrower to guarantee a
specific interest rate for a certain period of time. Also called a rate
commitment.

rate of return: *yield.* The return on an investment.

rate of return on investment (ROI): income divided by the total
amount invested.

rate type: rate type determines how payments adjust over the loan
term. Rate types include fixed-rate (does not change), balloon,
and adjustable-rate.

ratification: approval of a prior act or contract, which gives it the
confirmation to make it binding.

rating: a value quantifying the capabilities or endurance of an item
or substance.

ratio: a proportion of one value to another, related value. For example, defective units to operational units.

rational motive: a determination proving that the motivation of a
testator was rational when making the devises of a will.

raw land: property that has not been developed or improved; without added improvement such as sewers, utilities, streets, or structures.

raze: to demolish.

ready, willing, and able buyer: in real estate, one who is capable of
action and planning to do so. For example, having the financial
ability and being agreeable to the terms of a contract.

real asset: an asset that is intrinsically valuable because of its utility,
such as real estate or physical equipment.

real capital: capital, such as equipment and machinery, that is used to produce goods. Distinguished from *financial capital*, which are funds available to acquire real capital.

real estate: land and anything permanently affixed to it, such as buildings.

real estate agent: a person licensed by a state to represent a buyer or seller in a real estate transaction in exchange for a commission. Agents must work in association with a *real estate broker* or brokerage company.

real estate board: a local group of *real estate brokers* who are members of the state and national board of realtors. They meet regularly to help determine licensing requirements, as well as managing the multiple listing service of their area.

real estate broker: a person, corporation, or partnership licensed by a state to represent a buyer or seller in a real estate transaction, in exchange for a commission. Brokers supervise licensed real estate agents, who act for the broker, who is legally the principal agent in any transaction.

real estate calculators: calculators that have additional financial functions that includes present value, purchase price, property appreciation, lease costs, and loan and mortgage amortization.

real estate commission:
(1) the amount received by a real estate salesperson and agency upon sale of a property.
(2) alternately, the agency that enforces real estate license laws.

real estate counselor: a person who is paid to provide advice about real estate.

Real Estate Educators Association: a professional organization composed of teachers of real estate in colleges and proprietary license preparation schools. Address: Real Estate Educators Association, 740 Florida Central Parkway, Suite 1020, Longwood, FL 32750; Web: www.reea.org.

real estate investment trust (REIT): a publicly traded company that owns, develops, or operates commercial properties.

real estate market: the current transaction activity by buyers and sellers, including markets for various properties, such as housing, condominium, land, and office markets.

real estate mortgage investment conduit (REMIC): REMICs may be partnerships, corporations, trusts, etc., and are used to hold a fixed pool of mortgages, which are then marketed as tax exempt mortgage-backed securities (MBS) for investors. By redirecting the cash flow from the underlying standard MBS, the issue can create a security having several classes, also called tranches, that may carry different coupon rates, average lives, prepayment sensitivities, and final maturities. Investors with different investment horizons have the opportunity to own a tranche that satisfies their investment criteria and portfolio needs.

real estate owned (REO): property acquired by a lender, through foreclosure, which is held as inventory.

real estate property tax: local government taxes assessed on real estate.

Real Estate Settlement Procedures Act (RESPA): a federal law designed to make sellers and buyers aware of settlement fees and other transaction-related costs. It also outlaws kickbacks in the real estate business.

real estate syndicate: a pool of investor money, which is used to purchase real estate.

real estate valuation: professional opinion of the market value of a home or property.

real income: income, adjusted for inflation.

real interest rate: the interest rate adjusted for inflation.

realized gain: a gain that has occurred financially but isn't necessary taxable due to a tax-free exchange.

realized gain or loss: the difference between the amount received upon the sale or other disposition of property and the adjusted basis of the property.

realized profit or loss: reported in the income statement for tax purposes, it's the taxable profit or loss resulting from a sale.

real property: land and anything permanently affixed to it, such as buildings and their structural components.

real return on investment: return on an investment after adjustment for inflation.

realtor: the designation for an agent or broker who is a member of the *National Association of Realtors®* and subscribes to a strict code of ethics.

realtor-associate: a licensed salesperson, not a broker, who is a member of the *National Association of Realtors®*.

Realtors National Marketing Institute (RNMI): an affiliate of the *National Association of Realtors®*, which produces educational programs and literature for its member. Publications include *Real Estate Today* and *Real Estate Perspectives*. Web: www.rscouncil.com.

realty: land and anything permanently affixed to it, such as buildings.

reappraisal lease: a lease that has a rental, based on a percentage of the appraised value, that is periodically reviewed and adjusted by independent appraisers.

reassessment: the revision or reappraisal of the value estimate of property, which may be for tax purposes or contract negotiations.

rebate:

(1) a refund that resulted from an overpayment of tax or purchase price.

(2) alternately, an amount given as an incentive to buy.

recapture:

(1) a contract clause that may allow the prior owner to recover the property under certain circumstances.

(2) alternately, return of an owner's investment through, among other things, depreciation allowance.

recapture clause: a clause in a lease that would allow the landlord a percentage of the tenant's profits over the original fixed amount of rent or, alternately, allow the landlord to cancel the lease if the profits of the tenant fall below a specific level.

recapture of depreciation or cost recovery: each year that a depreciable business asset is owned, depreciation is claimed that theoretically corresponds with the using-up of the property through normal wear, obsolescence, etc. Thus, the property should be worth approximately its adjusted basis. If the property is sold for more than its adjusted basis, section 1245 of the U.S. tax code requires that the gain on personal property and certain nonresidential real property (to the extent of depreciation claimed) be recaptured; that is, included as ordinary income on the tax return. The purpose of this recapture is to prevent capital gain treatment of gain resulting from claiming depreciation. The recapture of depreciation or cost recovery rules doesn't apply when the property is disposed of at a loss.

recapture rate: the annual return rate of the capital of a *wasting asset* that is returned from the depreciating asset's earned income.

recasting: a loan term revision that is often made when a borrower is having difficulty making the payments, such as extending the loan for additional years or modifying the interest rate.

receipt: the receiving of something or a written acknowledge that something, such as cash or documents, has been received.

receivables: money owed to a business by customers.

receiver: a court-appointed manager of the affairs of a business or piece of property during a bankruptcy or foreclosure. The responsibility for managing the affairs prudently (collecting funds, paying bill, etc.) is carried out under court direction, and may either result in a return to a solvent state or a recommendation for liquidation.

recession: specifically defined as two consecutive quarters with negative economic growth. A recession is the business cycle phase of a deteriorating economy, which results in less business and consumer spending; usually, it will lead to the depression of real estate prices.

reciprocity: a situation where individuals or entities give certain rights to each other in return for the rights being given to them.

recission of contract: a contract cancellation that is done for certain reasons, such as illegality of the deal.

reclaim: to convert property from an unusable state (e.g., contaminated, flooded, etc.) to a useful condition. To secure the return of property or rights.

reclamation: the conversion of property from unusable to usable condition.

recognized gain: taxable income portion of the money received from the sale of real estate.

reconciliation: in an appraisal, the process of adjusting comparables for an estimated value of a subject by using cost, market comparison, and income approaches.

reconstructed operating statement: a statement of income, which is either revised due to new information, or reconstructed from information or records if the original is lost.

reconveyance: the conveying of a property, by a lender, back to the borrower once he has completely paid off his mortgage.

reconveyance deed: a deed that is issued to convey the property to the original owner, once the mortgage is repaid.

recordation: the recording of deeds and other instruments in a public registry to give notice of ownership or legal and financial claims to the public.

recorded map: also known as a *plat*, it is a plan or map of a specific land area, showing the boundaries of individual properties.

recorded plat: the map, which is filed in the office of the county recorder, of a specific land area showing the boundaries of individual properties.

recorder: a public official who is responsible for keeping records of all real estate transactions.

recording: the filing of property-related documents in the public record.

recording fee: the fee charged for conveying the sale of a piece of property into the public record.

recourse loan: a loan that gives the lender access to additional capital beyond the pledge collateral that secures the loan. If the borrower defaults on the loan, the lender may pursue other assets to recover the loan in full.

recovery fund: in those states that have recovery funds, a charge is assessed as part of the registration fee for licensed real estate brokers as a contribution to the fund, which is used to compensate individuals who have sustained losses in a transaction with a broker or agent. If a settlement is awarded by the state's real estate commission, the fund's assets will be debited if the broker or agent fails to provide a recovery.

recovery period: the period of time, determined by each individual state, in which a person can seek financial recovery from a broker or agent.

recovery property: tangible depreciable property that is not excluded from ACRS (*Accelerated Cost Recovery System*) or MACRS (*Modified Accelerated Cost Recovery System*). Generally, this property, acquired for use in a trade or business or property, is held for the production of income.

rectangular survey: a rectangular system of land survey, also called a government rectangular survey, used to subdivide public land, that divides a district into 24-square-mile quadrangles from the meridian (north-south line) and the baseline (east-west line). The tracts are divided into six-mile-square parts called *townships*, which are in turn divided into 36 tracts, each one mile square, called *sections*.

redemption period: the period of time during which a property owner can pay all defaulted payments and charges and redeem a defaulted mortgage or land contract. The time period varies state-by-state.

redevelop: the rebuilding of an area with new structures after demolition and removal of the existing structures.

red herring: a preliminary prospectus aiming to obtain financial backing without details.

red lining: the illegal practice of refusing to finance home loans in specific neighborhoods.

reduction certificate: certification in writing, by the lender, of the remaining balance, date of maturity, and interest rate on a mortgage.

refinance: modification of existing debts, including mortgages, typically by replacing one or more existing obligations with new loans. Usually done when interest rates are more favorable or when the borrower wants to take money out of the home's equity.

refinancing: replacing an older mortgage with a new mortgage at better terms. See *refinance*.

reformation: the correction of a contractual error that did not reflect the intent of both parties to the deal. Fault needs to extend to both parties unless the error of one person was due to fraud by the other.

regional shopping center: a larger shopping center, often enclosed, that contains 300,000 to 900,000 square feet of shopping space, including at least one major department store.

register: to formally record a transaction or event.

registrar: an individual who maintains official records, such as mortgages, deeds, etc.

registration statement: documented relevant information about a new securities issue of a company, limited partnership, or publicly traded *real estate investment trust (REIT)*, which must be filed with the SEC. This lengthy document contains financial, historical, and administrative details about the issue—such as which properties the REIT owns—and allows investors to make educated decisions.

rehabilitate: the restoration of a building or structure to a good condition.

rehabilitating tax credit: the Tax Reform Act of 1986 provides incentive for the use and rehabilitation of old structures or historical building. This credit, which is based on a percentage of the cost incurred in the rehabilitation, is given in an effort to arrest urban decay.

rehabilitation mortgage: a mortgage that provides for the costs of repairing and improving a resale home or building.

reinstatement clause: an insurance policy clause that states that policies that lapse because of nonpayment of premiums can only be reinstated if all unpaid premiums are paid, and other requirements are fulfilled.

REIT: see *real estate investment trust*.

release:
(1) the freeing of real estate from a lien once the mortgage is paid in full and the debt is retired or forgive debt by the creditor.
(2) alternately, the voluntary abandonment of a legal right against another.

release clause: a provision in a purchase contract that allows a seller to continue marketing the home and accepting other offers.

release of lien: to free a piece of real estate from a mortgage.

relocation: the movement of a person or business from one region or location to another.

relocation clause: a clause in a lease allowing the landlord to move a tenant within the same building.

relocation company or service: a firm that administers all aspects of relocating new employees from one location to another.

remainder: an interest or estate that remains after all costs have been deducted or when the original life tenant has died.

remaining term: the original loan term minus the term when payments were already made.

remediation: a cleanup of an environmentally contaminated site.

REMIC: see *real estate mortgage investment conduit*.

remodel: updating or altering the appearance and functional utility of a building.

renegotiate: legally revising the provisions, terms, or conditions of a contract.

renegotiated rate mortgage (RRM): this mortgage expires at preestablished times, which allows for renegotiation of the terms of the mortgage. Also referred to as a *rollover mortgage*, this mortgage comes due in a *balloon payment,* which may be paid or refinanced at current rates.

renewal option: the right, without any obligation, of a tenant to continue a lease at a specified term and rent.

renovate: a general term to cover changes and upgrading of an existing property.

renovation cost: the amount spent to change or upgrade an existing property.

rent: the amount paid from a tenant to a landlord for the use of property.

rentable area: see *net leasable area.*

rental agency: a business that aids a tenant in finding the rental property or a landlord in finding a tenant.

rental concession: the discounts and reduction in rental charges to attract new tenants or to keep present ones. Concessions may also be in the form of some free rental or a large allowance to adapt the space to the needs of the tenant. High occupancy will induce a large retailer to relocate or a bank to offer better financing.

rental contract: a lease. A contract providing for the payment of rent by the *lessee* to the *lessor,* for the use of real property for a stated time period.

rental income: income received by the taxpayer for allowing another person's use of the taxpayer's property. Rental income includes advance rental payments, late payments, and current payments. Payments received for lease cancellation and forfeited security deposits are rental income the year received or forfeited. Rental income is considered passive income for purposes of the passive loss rules, except that of qualified real estate professionals.

rental rate: the charge for each rental unit for a specified period of time.

rental value: the valuation of the worth of a rental property by considering the net income derived from the property and a capitalization rate.

rent bid model: the model based on an assumption that space should be controlled by the activity that offers the highest bid. Maximizes usefulness.

rent control: governmental policy that governs the rate that may be charged to tenants for space rented.

renter's insurance: a policy for renters, which covers their personal possessions.

rent escalator: a lease provision that allows the landlord to raise the rental rate to account for inflation or higher interest rates.

rent-free period: that portion of the term of a lease where no rent is required, usually as part of a concession.

rent loss insurance: policy covering any loss of rent or rental value in the event that damage renders the property uninhabitable.

rent multiplier: method used to compute the price of an income-producing property by dividing the asking or market price of the property by the current gross rental income. If the current gross rental income is $30,000 and the asking price is $300,000, the gross income multiplier is 10. Also referred to as gross rent multiplier.

rent roll: list of tenants, including the lease rent and lease expiration date.

rent-up period: amount of time needed to fully rent newly constructed properties.

REO: see *real estate owned.*

reorientation: changing the market appeal of a property.

replacement cost: the amount it would cost to replace an asset at current prices.

replacement cost accounting: an accounting method that allows for additional depreciation on some part of the difference between a depreciable asset's original cost and its replacement cost.

replacement value: the value of an asset as determined by the estimated cost of replacing it.

reserve price: see *upset price*.

RESPA: see *Real Estate Settlement Procedures Act*.

restoration: refurbishing a building to its original condition.

retail gravitation: the ability of a shopping center to draw business away from other shopping areas. Usually, the larger the center, the greater its power.

retail land developer: an individual or corporation that takes a raw piece of land through the approval process with the town and then installs the necessary utilities to turn the property into individual lots, ready for construction.

retail lot sales: the sale of the developed lots for building homes, office buildings, industrial buildings, shopping centers, etc.

retail property: property to be used by a retail business for the sale of merchandise or services.

retainage: a construction contract term for the funds that are earned by the contractor but not paid until some agreed-upon date, such as the completion of the job. This is supposed to be an incentive to complete the job in a timely manner.

retention clause: a provision in a contract that allows the client to hold back a portion of payments until the project is complete.

return on assets (ROA): a measure of profitability for a company or a real estate partnership, equal to a fiscal year's earnings divided by its total assets, expressed as a percentage.

return on equity (ROE): an indicator of profitability. ROE is calculated by taking a year's worth of earnings and dividing them by the average shareholder's equity for that year.

return on invested capital (ROIC): a measure of how effectively a company uses the money (borrowed or owned) invested in its operations. Calculated by net income after taxes, divided by total assets, less excess cash, minus non-interest-bearing liabilities.

return on investment (ROI): the profit generated by a property, such as rents, etc. Usually stated with the profit as a percentage of the total amount invested.

reuse appraisal: an appraisal to determine the resale value of a vacant or improved property in an urban area that is now or will be under development, done in accordance with the *National Housing Act*.

revaluation: the reconsideration of the value or worth of a property.

revaluation clause: a clause in a reappraisal lease (a rental in which the payment is a percentage of the appraised value) that is periodically adjusted after being reviewed by independent appraisers.

revenue sharing: the splitting of operating profits and losses between the general partner and limited partners in a limited partnership. More generally, the practice of sharing operating profits with a company's employees, or of sharing the revenues resulting between companies in an alliance.

reverse annuity mortgage: see *reverse mortgage.*

reverse leverage: when the interest on borrowing exceeds the return on investment of the funds that were borrowed.

reverse mortgage: a loan available to older owners who have equity in their homes but need cash. Monthly payments are made to the owners (instead of by them), and the loan does not have to be repaid until the property is sold.

reversion:
(1) an interest or estate in which an individual has a fixed interest in the future, such as the remaining part left after obligations are paid, which would revert for distribution.
(2) the right of a lessor, upon termination of a lease, to possess leased property.

reversionary factor: the mathematical factor used to determine the current worth of future *cash flow.*

reversionary interest: the interest a person has in property that is now held by another. Upon termination of that possession, the property will revert back to the grantor.

reversionary lease: the rental agreement that will only begin after the expiration of the current rental agreement.

reversionary value: estimated value of a property at the expiration of a certain time period.

rezoning: the modification of the designation of a parcel or group of parcels on the zoning map, which changes the permitted usage of the area. Changes in zoning are usually requested by individuals or businesses and then approved by the zoning commission of a town. Normally, these changes are only granted if there is no adverse affect on other properties within the area.

rider: an amendment or attachment to a contract or a modification to an insurance policy.

right:
(1) a just claim to power or privilege or something that belongs to a person by law, nature, or tradition, etc.
(2) alternately, the claim of a person or entity to property by exercising an option.

right of access: the right of a property owner to go to and return from an adjoining street without interference.

right of courtesy: the legal right of a spouse to a life estate in all lands owned by a deceased spouse.

right of dower: the right of a wife whose husband died intestate (without a will) to the use of all his lands and possessions for the support of herself and her children. The widow is entitled to one-third of all of the assets of the estate of her deceased husband. This right is established in most states, but significantly altered in others.

right of entry: the right to begin usage, for living purposes or construction, of property in the process of being purchased.

right of first refusal: the right to buy or rent a piece of property before it is placed on the open market, which is given to a person by the owner of the property.

right of redemption: a borrower's right to redeem property to be taken in foreclosure by immediately paying off the loan balance and any related costs. The right of a bankruptcy debtor to recover personal property under lien by making restitution to the creditor.

right to rescind: the option to cancel a contract that was previously agreed upon.

right of rescission: the right to cancel, within three business days, a contract that uses the home of a person as collateral, except in the case of a first mortgage loan.

right of subrogation: the substitution of one entity or person for another if both have the same rights and obligations.

right of survivorship: the right of an individual to acquire an interest in another person's property after his or her death if the property is held jointly.

right of way: a right of easement that is established when the property owner lets others use or pass through his property.

riparian: on the bank of a body of water.

riparian owner: an owner who has rights to water on or bordering his land and a reasonable right to water that flows through his property from an adjacent site.

riparian rights: the right of an owner to use a river, stream, or lake that is on or borders his or her property.

risk: uncertainty or variability. A chance of loss. In real estate, the fluctuation in sales or profits and the likelihood of declining value.

risk-adjusted return: a measure of how much an investment returned in relation to the amount of risk it took on. Often used to compare a high-risk, potentially high-return investment with a low-risk, lower-return investment.

risk-free rate: the interest rate on the safest investments, such as federal government obligations.

ROA: see *return on assets.*

roadbed: the base over which a road's paving is installed. The roadbed is usually topped with graded crushed stone.

rod: a unit of linear measurement. One rod is 16.5 feet, or 5.029 meters.

ROE: see *return on equity.*

ROI: see *return on investment.*

ROIC: see *return on invested capital*.

rollover loan:

(1) a long-term loan with a guaranteed interest rate for a shorter period with interest renegotiated periodically, at current market rates, or the extension of a mature loan at current rates.

(2) Alternately, delay allowed for repayment of principal by a bank to a debtor with financial difficulties.

rollover mortgage: a mortgage with a constant rate of interest but the loan is renegotiated or rolled over after a certain period of time. See *renegotiated rate mortgage*.

row house: a dwelling that is attached to, and shares common walls with its neighbors.

royalty: a payment made for the use of property, especially a patent, a copyrighted work, a franchise, or a natural resource. The amount is usually a percentage of revenues obtained through its use.

rule against assignments: the legal concept that a borrower may not give away or reassign the obligation to pay a debt without the lender's permission.

Rule of 69: similar to the *Rule of 72*; a set amount of money invested at a certain percent per certain time period will double in approximately three years.

Rule of 72: an approximation of the time it would take to double an investment when earning compound interest by dividing the percentage rate into 72 to derive the number of years required to double the principal. For example: an investment that yields an annual return of 20 percent will double in less than three years.

Rule of 78: a commonly used accounting method used by banks to formulate a loan amortization schedule. It is often referred to as The Rule of the Sum of the Digits. This method of computing unearned interest is used on installment loans with add-on interest. The number 78 is based on the sum of the digits from 1 to 12. This causes a borrower to pay more interest at the beginning of the loan when there is more money owed, and less interest as the obligation is reduced.

run rate: the revenues that a company would have in the next 12 months if the current revenue rate remained unchanged. Usually calculated by multiplying the latest quarter's revenues by four.

run with the land: an expression that indicates a right or a restriction that will affect all current and future owners.

Rural Housing Service (RHS): a division of the U.S. Department of Agriculture that helps rural communities and individuals by providing loans and grants for housing and community facilities. RHS provides funding for single family homes, apartments for low-income persons or the elderly, housing for farm laborers, childcare centers, fire and police stations, hospitals, libraries, nursing homes, schools, and much more. Web: www.rurdev.usda.gov/rhs.

R value: a measurement of the resistance of a material to the passage of heat. The number of minutes (seconds) required for 1 Btu (joule) to penetrate one square foot (square meter) of a material for each degree of temperature difference between the two sides of the material.

S

sale-leaseback: a technique in which a seller deeds property to a buyer for a consideration, and the buyer simultaneously leases the property back to the seller. This type of transaction is frequently done by retailers for their store properties.

sales-assessment ratio: the selling price of a property divided by its appraisal value. If real estate has a selling price of $400,000 but its assessed value is $380,000, the ratio is 1.053.

sales commission: the percentage of the selling price that is paid to a real estate broker for his or her services in obtaining a purchaser.

sales comparison approach: a method of appraising real estate based on a market comparison of neighboring properties having similar characteristics, to ascertain what is the value of the property.

sales concession: an instance where the seller will pay a cost that is normally paid by the buyer. Usually done to ensure that the sale will go through.

sales contract: an agreement outlining the terms of a purchase, which is signed by the buyer and the seller.

sales deposit receipt: the receipt given for a partial payment made on the sale of the property.

sales expenses: the cost incurred during the sale of real estate, such as real estate commission, attorney fees, etc.

sales incentive: extra compensation given to a real estate broker who has surpassed his sales quota, which may be a flat fee or a percentage of the extra sales dollars over the quota.

sales kit: literature, samples, and other useful information used by brokers or agents for demonstration purposes to prospective purchasers.

salesperson: an individual employed in selling a product or service.

sales price: the amount of money that is paid by a purchaser to a seller for property that is bought.

sales price list: a written list of the prices being asked for homes for sale.

sales ratio analysis: the evaluation of the cause of the difference between the desired selling price of a property and its appraisal value. Reasons could include unexpected deterioration of conditions in the area, quick sale needed, poor appraisal, etc.

sales value: the price a property would bring on the open market.

saltbox style: an early-American, 2 or 2½-story style from the Colonial period. The house is rectangular, and has a steep gable roof that extends down to the first floor in the rear of the building. (*see Appendix A*)

salvage value: the value that an asset will have at the end of its useful life.

SAM: see *shared appreciation mortgage.*

S&L: see *Savings and Loan Association.*

sandwich lease: a leasing arrangement in which an entity leases property from one party and leases it to another party. In this arrangement, the entity is both a *lessee* and a *lessor*, so it both pays and collects rent on the same property.

sanitary sewer: a house drain that carries waste away from the house to a septic system or a municipal sewer system.

sash: the framework which holds the glass in a window. (see *Appendix B*)

satellite cities: subordinate neighborhoods that are tied to an urban area economically.

satisfaction: discharge of an obligation through payment or rendering of service.

satisfaction of lien: the release and discharge of a lien on property after the terms of the lien have been met.

satisfaction of mortgage: a written statement of the lender that the buyer of real estate has paid off the entire mortgage.

satisfaction piece: same as *satisfaction of mortgage.*

Savings and Loan Association (S&L): financial institution that specializes in originating, servicing, and holding mortgage loans, primarily on owner-occupied, residential property. S&Ls also make home-improvement loans and loans to investors for apartments, industrial property, and commercial real estate. Approximately 40 percent of S&Ls are federally chartered, the rest are state chartered. Federal charters are members of the *Federal Home Loan Bank System (FHLBS)*. All federally chartered S& Ls are owned by depositors and the word "federal" must appear in their title. State chartered S&L's can be either mutually owed or stock associations. They have optional membership in both the FHLBS and the FSLIC. Also known as *thrift institutions,* or thrifts.

SBA: see *Small Business Administration.*

Schedule E: part of Form 1040, shows income or loss from real estate transactions, including net rental income.

schematic: a diagram showing a specific design or functional element of a home, such as electrical or plumbing.

schematic designs: renderings of housing plans, both floor and exterior.

seasoned loan: a loan where the borrower has proven his creditworthiness by having consistently made payments.

secondary financing: loan that is subordinate to the primary loan and cannot be satisfied until the primary loan is paid.

secondary mortgage market: a market that trades previously created mortgages with mortgage bankers acting as intermediaries. The market exists because some mortgage investors want to cash in their investment before the actual mortgages occur.

second deed of trust: a deed of trust or mortgage in which the lender subordinates her loan to another lender whose priority is first if there is nonpayment by the borrower.

second home: a residence that is not one's primary residence. A taxpayer may deduct interest and taxes on two personal residences.

second lien: a lien in addition to a first lien and subordinate to that first lien. It can be satisfied only after the first lien has been satisfied.

second mortgage: a second loan that uses an already mortgaged house as collateral. The first mortgage has priority over the second loan. *Home equity lines of credit* represent second mortgages, or second liens, on a property.

Section I and II (Homeowner's Insurance Policy): Section I relates to the home, contents, and accompanying structures. Section II provides comprehensive coverage for personal liability and the medical payments and property damage incurred by those other than the insured.

Section 8 Housing: created by the 1974 amendments to Section 8 of the 1937 Housing Act, it is a federal program in which the government subsidizes much of the rent, in privately owned apartments, on behalf of qualified low-income tenants.

Section 167: the section of the Internal Revenue Code that deals with depreciation. Capital improvements made to real property are depreciable.

Section 1031 (Tax Free Exchange): this section of the Internal Revenue Code deals with tax-deferred exchanges of certain property. General rules for tax-deferred exchange of real estate state that the properties must be like-kind property (real estate for real estate), exchanged and held for use in a trade or business or held as an investment.

Section 1034: the section of the Internal Revenue Code that applied to the sale of a principal residence before May 7, 1997. It allowed the deferment of gain on a house when a more expensive house was purchased. Section 1034 was replaced by Section 121 for sales after May 6, 1997.

Section 1221: the section of the Internal Revenue Code explaining what a capital asset is and is not. Capital assets include real estate such as buildings and raw land. It excludes from the definition receivables, inventory, and intangibles.

Section 1231: Section 1231 assets are depreciable assets and real estate used in a trade or business and held for more than one year.

Under certain circumstances, the classification also includes timber, coal, domestic iron ore, livestock (held for draft, breeding, dairy, or sporting purposes), and unharvested crops.

Section 1245: the section of the Internal Revenue Code applying to gains from the sale of personal property subject to depreciation. In most cases, the gains are at capital gains tax rate limited to the amount of accumulated depreciation taken.

Section 1250: the section of the Internal Revenue Code that applies to capital gains from selling real estate that has been depreciated for tax purposes. Most buildings must be depreciated using the straight-line method.

Section 179 Expense Deduction: an election to treat the cost of certain qualified property as a currently deductible expense rather than as a capital expenditure. A maximum deduction of $20,000 may be claimed for qualified assets placed in service in 2001. This is also referred to as expensing.

sections: one square mile of land broken into 36 tracts for residential development.

secured loan: a loan backed by collateral.

secured note: a written obligation of a borrower that is backed by collateral in the event of default.

secured party: the lender who possesses the collateral of the borrower if the loan is defaulted upon.

Securities and Exchange Commission (SEC): the federal agency created in 1934 by the provisions of the Securities Exchange Act. The SEC administers the federal laws applying to securities; the SEC is empowered to protect the investing public by preventing fraud, manipulation, and other abuses in the securities market. Phone 800-732-0330, Web: www.sec.gov.

securitization: the process of the borrower giving the lender security to obtain the loan.

security: the property that will be pledged as collateral for a loan.

security agreement: legal contract in which the lender controls the pledged property being financed. This agreement describes the property and its location. In the event of default, the lender may sell the collateral.

security deposit: prepayment to a landlord to offset any damage that might occur beyond normal wear and tear. It is considered a damage deposit. Laws in most states require landlords to hold the deposit in a separate account and refund the amount, if no damage is done, within a specified time after termination of the lease.

security instrument: also known as security deed, a *mortgage,* or *trust deed.*

security interest: the claim the lender has against the borrower's property, which is serving as collateral.

seed money: funds, often put up by venture capitalists, needed to finance a new business.

see-through building: a building without tenants where observers can literally see through its windows from one side to the other.

self-amortizing mortgage: a mortgage that will retire itself through regular principal and interest payments.

self-contained appraisal report: a written appraisal report that contains all the information required by *USPAP*, with extensive detail.

seller financing: an agreement where the seller provides the financing for a purchase. Similar to *seller take-back.*

seller's market: a very strong real estate market where sellers have the advantage because there are more buyers than properties for sale.

seller take-back: an agreement in which the owner of a property provides financing, often in combination with an assumable mortgage. See *owner financing.*

seller vs. buyer closing costs: buyers and sellers often negotiate who will pay certain closing costs, and the results vary depending on the negotiated deal. It's not uncommon for a sales agreement to state that either the buyer or seller pays all closing costs. The agreement that a buyer and seller reach must be specified in the sales contract. Negotiations could depend on a variety of factors, including the quality of the home, how long the home has been on the market, whether there are any other interested buyers, and how motivated the seller is to sell the home.

selling agent: a broker or salesperson who writes the contract for a buyer in a real estate transaction.

semiannual: twice yearly.

semi-custom home: a home where the basic structure cannot be changed but changes can be made to some design aspects of the home during construction.

senior mortgage: the primary mortgage on a property, which takes priority over any other liens and is satisfied before any secondary liens.

Senior Residential Appraiser (SRA): a designation granted by the *Appraisal Institute for Residential Appraisers.*

sensitivity analysis: a technique of investment analysis that enables investors to determine variations in the rate of return on an investment property in accordance with changes in a critical factor, such as how much the rate of return will change if expenses rise five percent or rental income drops ten percent. It's an experiment with decision alternatives using a what-if approach.

sentimental value: the emotional value of property to a particular person.

separable or separate property: a property wholly owned by either spouse that was acquired prior to marriage or was received as a gift or inheritance. This property legally belongs to that spouse and cannot be taken away to satisfy a debt against the other spouse or for estate valuation.

septic system: an underground, usually concrete, tank in which organic sewage is decomposed by anaerobic bacteria.

service contract: an agreement bought by a homeowner for servicing of household items.

servicer: an organization that collects principal and interest payments from borrowers and manages borrower's escrow accounts. The servicer also services mortgages that have been purchased by an investor in the secondary mortgage market.

servicing: the collection of mortgage payments from borrowers, and the related responsibilities of a loan *servicer*.

servient estate: land subjected to an *easement*.

setback ordinance: local zoning law or private limitation on how far, in feet, a structure might be situated from the curb or other appropriate marker.

settlement: the final step before a borrower get the keys to a new home; also called the *closing*. The meeting is typically attended by the buyer(s), the seller(s), their attorneys if they have them, both real estate sales professionals, a representative of the lender, and the closing agent. The purpose is to make sure the property is physically and legally ready to be transferred to the buyer. Final closing costs will be paid at this meeting. They generally include a loan origination fee, attorney's fees, taxes, an amount placed in escrow, and charges for obtaining title insurance and a survey. Closing costs vary according to the area of the country.

Settlement Cost (HUD guide): a *HUD*-published booklet that provides an overview of the lending process, and that is given to consumers after completing a loan application.

settlement document: a document detailing what has been paid and by whom.

settlement fees: also known as "closing fees," they are paid to the escrow agent, who may be an attorney or a title insurance company, for carrying out the written terms of the agreement between the borrower and the seller and the lender, if there is one.

settlement statement: the document detailing the final financial settlement and costs paid by both the buyer and the seller of a property. See *HUD-1 Settlement Statement*.

settlement sheet: see *HUD-1 Settlement Statement*.

severalty: ownership of real estate by only one person; it is often called sole ownership.

severance damages: the monetary award given by the government to a person whose property has been subjected to condemnation.

sewage tax: the levy placed on those who benefit from a sewer system.

sewer: a municipal system of pipes and treatment facilities for the disposal of plumbing wastes.

sewer line easement: an *easement* to build, maintain and operate a disposal line for sewage.

shakeout: refers to the decline in real estate values that occurs during an economic hardship such as a depression or a recession. When this occurs, there is normally huge loss, with some real estate owners declaring bankruptcy.

shakes: a type of shingle, split from a piece of log.

shared appreciation mortgage (SAM): a mortgage where a borrower receives a below-market interest rate in exchange for letting the lender receive a portion of future appreciation in the property.

shared equity mortgage: a mortgage that allows people who have trouble coming up with a down payment to afford property. Essentially, it gives the lender title to a portion of the property in exchange for help with the down payment. For example, if a home costs $100,000, an individual can buy it for $80,000 with an agreement to let the lender hold 20 percent or $20,000 worth of ownership. If the home appreciates in value, the lender gets the same percentage share (20% in this example) of the proceeds at sale. The borrower typically pays all costs of insurance, property taxes, and maintenance.

shared equity transaction: a situation where two buyers purchase a property, with one as the resident co-owner and the other as an investor co-owner.

shingle: used in siding and roofs, a thin piece of material, usually wood, laid in overlapping rows. (see *Appendix B*)

shingle style: a uniquely American style of architecture, shingle style houses can be relatively plain on the exterior, often with porches set into the façade. The houses are covered in wood shingles stained a single color, suggesting the rustic homes of the New England settlers. (see *Appendix A*)

shopping center: a group of retail stores with a common parking area; most shopping centers have one or more anchor stores—usually a department, discount, or food store. The center may or may not be enclosed in a mall.

short form: a document, condensed into a page or two, that is used in lieu of the longer, more cumbersome document.

short-term capital gain: the profit resulting from the sale of an investment that is held for one year or less. Short-term gains are ordinary income and do not qualify for any special tax treatment.

short-term capital loss: the loss resulting from the sale of an investment that is held for one year or less. Short-term losses are deducted from current income and do not qualify for any special tax treatment.

shutter: a hinged wooden/metal cover which covers a window, usually fitted with louvers. (see *Appendix B*)

sidelight: a window or opening at the side of a door. (see *Appendix B*)

siding: the exposed surface of exterior walls of a building.

silent partner: a partner who remains anonymous but has legal rights and obligations.

sill: the support forming the lower side of an opening, as a door sill or a window sill. (see *Appendix B*)

simple assumption: a loan that keeps the original borrower liable in the event that the new borrower defaults on the loan.

simple interest: interest computations that are calculated only on the original principal amount.

simple rate of return: an unadjusted rate of return. The return computed by dividing the anticipated future annual net income by the required investment in real estate.

single-family dwelling: a home designed for use by one family. Even if other dwellings are attached, as in a townhouse, they would have separate plumbing, heating, and electrical systems, etc. They may be detached houses, town houses, condominiums, or co-operatives.

single-family properties: one- to four-unit properties, including detached homes, town homes, condominiums, and cooperatives.

single-property syndicate: equity investors involved in the purchase of one property only, with the total amount of money raised being used for that purpose.

single-purpose agricultural building: an agricultural structure used for only one purpose. Examples are milking sheds and greenhouses. Such buildings may be contrasted with, for example, barns; barns are generally used for a variety of farming purposes.

sinking fund: the fund set aside for periodic payments, aimed at reducing a financial obligation taken out to buy real estate, or to accumulate enough funds to buy property or for plant expansion. The principal deposited into the sinking fund earns interest. The total amount accumulated is then used for the desired purpose.

SIOR: see *Society of Industrial and Office Realtors*®.

site: a piece of land or property where development will take place.

site analysis: the evaluation of an area to determine its appropriateness for designated objectives.

site assessment (environmental): an evaluation of a site, prior to acquisition of title to the property, for the existence of hazardous waste.

site-built home: a home that is constructed on a piece of property chosen by the potential homeowner.

site development costs: the total expenses required to make a property suitable for its designated purpose.

site plan: the document that states how a particular parcel of land will be improved; all structures and site improvements, such as driveways, parking lots, landscaping, and utility connections, are included.

site survey: the determination of the measurements of a specific location.

situs: a term used to refer to the economic location of a particular parcel of land. Economic location is an important factor in determining the success or failure of real estate since investors need specific types of land for specific uses at specific places.

six-month adjustable-rate mortgage: this *adjustable-rate mortgage* (*ARM*) offers a low initial interest rate for the first six months, with an interest rate that adjusts every six months thereafter. The rate caps per adjustment can be 1 or 2 percent; the lifetime adjustment caps can be 4, 5, or 6 percent. This type of mortgage may be right for a borrower who anticipates a rapid increase in income over the first few years of the mortgage. That's because it lets the borrower maximize his purchasing power immediately. It may also be the right mortgage for someone who plans to live in a home for only a few years. The interest rate is tied to a published financial index. When comparing ARMs that have different indexes, look at how the index has performed recently. An approved lender can provide information on how to track a specific index and how to review a 15-year history of the index.

- **advantages:** maximizes a borrower's buying power immediately, especially if he expects his income to rise quickly in the next few years. Lets the borrower select an index that meets his financial needs. These shorter-term ARMs are easier to qualify for, due to a low interest rate and a 1 or 2 percent annual rate cap. Some six-month ARMs let a borrower convert to a fixed-rate loan at certain adjustment intervals.

- **details:** six-month *ARMs* are available with terms of 10 to 30 years. Can be used to buy one- to four-family, owner-occupied principal residences, including second homes, investment properties, and condos, co-ops, and planned unit developments. Manufactured homes are also eligible.

slum area: depressed part of a city or town that might be a high crime area.

Small Business Administration (SBA): federal government agency in Washington, D.C., that makes low-interest loans to qualified small businesses. Phone: 800-827-5722, Web: www.sba.gov.

small claims court: the special court for the purpose of providing fast, inexpensive, and informal settlement of small financial claims between a plaintiff and a defendant, with the parties representing themselves.

Society of Industrial and Office Realtors® (SIOR): an organization, affiliated with the *National Association of Realtors*, whose members are mainly concerned with the sale of warehouses, factories, and other industrial property. Address: 1201 New York Ave., NW, Ste. 350, Washington, D.C. 20005. Phone: 202-449-8200, Web: www.sior.com.

soffit: the underside of an overhang of a building. (see *Appendix B*)

soft market: a market which is better for buyers than sellers. Demand has decreased, or supply has grown too quickly. A buyer's market.

soft money:
(1) in a development or investment, it is money that is tax deductible.
(2) alternately, it is used to describe costs that do not physically go into construction, such as interest, architectural fees, legal fees, etc.

sole ownership/sole proprietorship: a business owned by one person, who has all the rights and obligations.

Southern Colonial: an early-American architectural style, elaborately built, symmetrical, with columns and a colonnade extending across the front of the house. This home typically has three floors and a gabled roof. (*see Appendix A*)

spec house: see *speculation home.*

special agent: a person who is retained to act for another, with limited authority.

special assessment: the charge levied against property owners to finance an improvement benefiting the homeowners or commercial businesses. Special assessments may be made by private management boards or local government bodies.

special deposit account: an account that is established for rehabilitation mortgages to hold the funds needed as portions of the work are completed.

Specialist in Real Estate Securities (SRS): an individual who by his or her expertise, education and experience prepares syndication reports.

special purpose property: a building with limited uses and marketability, such as a church, theater, school, or public utility.

special use permit: the right granted by a local zoning authority to conduct certain activities within a zoning district. Also called a conditional use permit.

special warranty deed: a property deed in which the grantor limits the title warranty to the grantee. A grantor does not warrant a title defect to the property occurring from a happening before the time of his ownership.

specific lien: the lien on a given property, such as a person's house, as collateral for a loan.

specific performance: a legal action in which the court requires a party to a contract to perform the terms of the contract, when he has refused to fulfill his obligations.

specifications: often called *specs*, these are the written requirements for construction, such as for materials, equipment, etc.

specs: short for *specifications*.

speculation: high-risk, often-high return, business transaction undertaken, with no guarantee of success.

speculation home: also called a *spec house*, it is a house that is built without a buyer. The dwelling is constructed prior to being sold. The builder "speculates" that a buyer will be found, thus the term *spec house*.

speculative value: the value that a speculator believes an investment will reach at some point in the future.

speculator: an investor who is willing to take a risk to make a financial gain.

spendable income: the cash flow from income-producing property.

split-level home: a post-World War Two type of house with floor levels staggered so that each level is about one-half story above or below the adjacent one. (*see Appendix A*)

spread: the difference between the price offered by a buyer and the price asked for by the seller of real estate.

springing power of attorney: to obtain the right through authorization to act as a legal representative and agent for another.

sprinkler system: there are two types of sprinkler systems:
• timer-controlled in-ground system that waters the grass and shrubbery of a property; and
• interior fire-protection system that dispenses water from over head sprinklers in reaction to heat.

square footage: the standard unit of area that is used to measure a parcel of real estate. The amount of square feet of livable space in a building or house.

square foot cost: the cost of the standard unit of area that is used to measure a parcel of real estate. Commercial property rentals are generally quoted on the basis of square foot cost.

square foot method: a means of appraising a building by simply multiplying its *square foot cost* by the total amount of square feet in the structure being evaluated. Two or more buildings may then be compared by analyzing their total square foot costs.

squatter's rights: the legal allowance to occupy the property of another in absence of an attempt by the owner to force eviction. If recognized by state law, this right may eventually be converted to title to the property by *adverse possession*

SRA: see *Senior Residential Appraiser*.

stabilization: economic policies designed to reduce the fluctuation in the business cycle, such as those used by the Federal Reserve. Alternately, the control over rental property exercised by the government, in some areas, that places restrictions on amounts able to be charged.

stagflation: increasing prices during a stagnation in the economy.

stair riser: the vertical surface of a step in a staircase. (see *Appendix B*)

stair tread: the horizontal surface of a step in a staircase. (see *Appendix B*)

standard payment calculation: the method used to determine the monthly payment required to repay the remaining balance of a mortgage in substantially equal installments over the remaining term of the mortgage at the current interest rate.

standby commitment: a commitment by a lender to loan a sum of money at specified terms for the financing of a project. The borrower pays a fee for the privilege of either executing the loan or allowing the commitment to lapse.

standby fee: the amount required by a lender to provide a *standby commitment*. The fee is forfeited if the loan is not closed within a specific period of time.

standby loan: a short-term loan that is made to bridge the term between the end of one loan and the beginning of another. Also called a *bridge loan* or *gap loan*.

starker transaction: generally refers to a tax-free exchange. See *1031* and *like-kind exchanges.*

start rate: referred to as a *teaser rate*, it's the starting interest rate of an adjustable-rate loan. This rate usually lasts between one and twelve months, and then the rate increases based on prearranged criteria.

starter home: a house that is generally of lower than average price and is often purchased as a first home.

State Housing Act: the law of the state that establishes guidelines and requirements for construction of buildings. The standards may differ from state to state.

statement of consideration: enumeration of the consideration given by each party to a contract, which, in some cases, must be in written form to be enforceable. The statute of fraud requires that all contracts for the sale of real estate be in writing.

statute: the law established by an act of legislature; civil or criminal.

statute of frauds: a state law that requires certain kinds of contracts be in writing in order to be enforceable. With respect to real estate, negotiations and preliminary agreements may be oral, but the final agreement must be in writing.

statute of limitations: a specified period of time in which prosecution or suit must be brought against a person, after which any action will be barred.

statutory dedication: the owners of a subdivision or other property file a *plat* that results in a grant of public property, such as the streets in a development.

statutory foreclosure: a foreclosure proceeding not conducted under court supervision, as contrasted with *judicial foreclosure*, which is.

statutory liens: charges resulting in involuntary encumbrances against real estate, derived from legislated law rather than from debts owed to organizations or individuals.

statutory redemption period: the limited period of time for a borrower facing foreclosure and sale to attempt to reclaim the property.

statutory right of redemption: the legal right of a mortgagor to redeem the property after it has been sold at a foreclosure sale. State law grants the right for a limited period of time, depending on the state.

step loan: a type of *adjustable-rate mortgage (ARM)* for which the interest rate is adjusted only once during the term of the loan. Therefore, the loan shares some of the features of both fixed rate and adjustable loans.

stepped-up basis: an increase in the income tax basis of a property that is a result of a tax-free exchange. As a result of an inheritance, for example, the basis of the inherited property was stepped up to its current market value.

step-up lease: a lease that incorporates increases in agreed-on payments over the term of the lease contract. For example, a particular step-up lease may require that the lessee pay a 10 percent increase each year over the five-year term of the lease.

step-rate mortgage: a mortgage that allows for the interest rate to increase according to a specified schedule—seven years, for example—resulting in increased payments. At the end of the specified period, the rate and payments will remain constant for the remainder of the loan.

stigmatized property: a property with an undesirable reputation, which can be due to problems on the site or nearby.

stile: the vertical framing piece in a panel door.

stipulations: requirements or items specified in a legal instrument.

stock of housing: the number of housing units of a particular category that are available.

stop clause: a provision in a lease agreement that indicates the maximum amount of operating expenditures that must be incurred by the landlord in a given year. Any amount incurred in excess of this amount must be paid by the *lessee.*

stop work order: a written statement from a *building inspector* to halt work on a project until stated corrections are made.

straight lease: a lease that requires periodic equal rental payments that will not change for the term of the lease. Also known as a *flat lease.*

straight-line depreciation: the most commonly used method of depreciation prior to 198, assuming that an asset would lose an equal amount of value each year during its useful life.

straight-line recapture rate: the capitalization rate used to convert the expected income derived from a property into its estimated asset value (capitalized value). The estimated asset value may be computed by dividing the annual income generated by a property by its capitalization rate. The capitalization rate that is used is generally viewed as having two components:

- rate of return on investment; and
- straight-line recapture rate that represents the percentage of cost that the investor believes that he or she must recover each year in order to recoup the entire cost of the asset over its useful life.

straight mortgage: see *deed of trust*.

straight note: a loan agreement requiring only interest payments over the term of the loan, with a *balloon payment*, of the entire debt balance, due at the end of the term.

straw man: an individual who purchases property for another individual for the purpose of concealing the identity of the true acquirer from the seller and any other interested parties.

street improvement: repairing the street for safety and attractiveness. In some localities, the homeowner is responsible for properly maintaining the street adjacent to his or her home.

strict foreclosure: a legal premise in some states where the lender owns the property and may simply evict the borrower for nonpayment and gain full and complete title simply by waiting for a borrower's right to redeem to end.

strip development: commercial land use in which each establishment, usually a retail store, has frontage on a major thoroughfare; generally, there is no *anchor tenant*.

structural analysis: an evaluation of the dimensions of a building to determine its ability to meet the needs of the occupant.

structure: something that is constructed; a building.

stud: a vertical wall framing piece, made of wood or steel, to which plasterboard or siding are attached. (see *Appendix B*)

subagent: an agent who assists another agent in representing a principal in a transaction.

subdivision: a housing development that is created by dividing a tract of land into individual lots for sale or lease.

Subchapter S corporation: a corporation with a limited number of stockholders that elects not to be taxed as a regular corporation. Income is taxed as direct income to the shareholders. Shareholders include, in their personal tax returns, their pro-rata share of capital gains, ordinary income, tax preference items, etc.

subcontract: work done for the general contractor or owner by specialists in certain fields, such as plumbing, roofing, electrical, etc.

subcontract bids: bids that are given in an effort to obtain a job doing work for the general contractor or owner by specialists in certain fields, such as plumbing, roofing, electrical, etc.

subcontractor: specialists in the construction business who are hired by the general contractor. These would include roofers, plumbers, electricians, etc.

subdivider: one who partitions a tract of land for the purpose of selling the individual plots. If the land is improved in any way, the subdivider becomes a *developer.*

subdividing: the act of dividing a tract of land into smaller tracts.

subdivision: property that is divided, from a large parcel, into smaller pieces.

sub-floor: a wood floor, often made of plywood, which is laid over the floor joists and on which the finished floor is laid. (see *Appendix B*)

subject property: a term for the property that is being appraised.

subject to: property that is purchased with conditions to be met, such as "subject to being allowed to subdivided into a certain amount of lots."

subject to mortgage: a situation when a buyer takes title to mortgaged property but is not personally liable for the payment of the amount due. In case of default, the buyer loses only his or her equity in the property.

sublease: a lease agreement between the *lessee* of an original lease and a new Lessee. The new lessee is the subtenant, because he is renting from the original tenant rather than the owner.

sublessor: the initial *lessee* of rented property, who then leases it to a subtenant.

subletting: the process by which a lessee leases the property to another lessee.

submarket: the accumulation of housing units deemed substitutable by homogeneous households, such as those having comparable attractiveness and usefulness.

subordinate: to reduce the priority of payment of a debt or lien.

subordinate financing: any mortgage or other lien that has a priority that is lower than that of the first mortgage.

subordinate ground lease: a lease where the mortgage has priority over the ground lease.

subordinate loan: a second or third mortgage on a piece of property that already has a first mortgage.

subordinate mortgage: a mortgage that is inferior to another. The subordinate mortgage has a claim in foreclosure only after satisfaction of mortgages with more priority.

subordination: moving to an inferior position, as a lien would if it changes from a first mortgage to a second mortgage.

subordination clause: a clause that permits a mortgage recorded at a later date to take priority over an existing mortgage.

subpoena: writ issued by the court requiring a person to appear as a witness or to provide written information in a case. Failure to observe the subpoena may result in a contempt of court citation.

subpoena duces tecum: legal order for a person to present at a deposition or trial documents in his possession, such as related to a real estate transaction.

subrent: see *sublet*.

subrogate: the substitution of one person for another with the substituted person acquiring all rights.

subrogation rights: rights allowing an insurer to act against a negligent third party (including its insurance company) to receive reimbursement for payments made to an insured.

subsequent: something which occurs at a later date. It follows a prior occurrence.

subsequent rate adjustments: the period for rate adjustment on an *adjustable-rate mortgage (ARM)* after the initial adjustment period. It could differ in time from the original duration period.

subsequent rate cap: the specific limit for the maximum amount the interest rate may increase at each regularly scheduled rate adjustment date, which could differ from the original rate cap.

subsidiary: being in an inferior or subordinate relationship. Of lesser importance.

subsidized housing: housing whose rental payments are reduced because of aid granted by the government, private enterprises, or individuals.

subsidy: a grant of money made by the government to private enterprise or another government.

substitution: in valuing real estate, substitution is the principle that the market value of a property can be relatively accurately estimated by determining the market value of similar properties in the general vicinity. By substitution, an appraiser can ascertain the market value of a piece of real estate by analyzing the sales prices of comparable units in the neighborhood sold in the recent past.

subsurface easement: an owner of land allowing another to use space under the ground, such as to install a sewer or gas line.

subsurface exploration: engineering tests performed on soils to determine conditions and ground stability prior to building.

subsurface rights: the owner of real estate generally has exclusive rights to the soil and minerals underneath the land. Significant limitations on subsurface rights have to be disclosed in the title deed at the time of acquisition. If no restrictions are indicated, the buyer can expect to exercise full rights to the property. In many areas subsurface rights can be extremely valuable because of the existence of oil, natural gas, and minerals, and those must be acquired separately.

suburb: a smaller residential community within commuting distance to a city.

succession: the transfer of real estate by legal means, such as through inheritance.

successor: an individual coming later in a sequence.

suitability standards: the financial characteristics or standards that a potential investor is evaluated on to judge his or her suitability for a particular investment program.

sum-of-the-years'-digits method (SYD): a method of calculating depreciation of an asset that assumes higher depreciation charges and greater tax benefits in the early years of an asset's life.

summary appraisal report: a written appraisal report that contains a moderate amount of detail.

summary possession: eviction. The act of removing, dispossessing, or expulsion of an individual from a residence or commercial space for late payments or violation of other covenants.

summary proceeding: a way to obtain a faster decision in a legal case than going to a trial. Procedural rules are followed so there is less time involved in gathering the facts of the dispute and in questioning.

summons: notice sent from a plaintiff to a defendant requiring the defendant to appear before a court or judge.

sump: a drainage system in one's basement to collect excess moisture.

superadequacy: an expensive addition not present in more typical cost-efficient properties, such as a glassed-in atrium at the entrance.

Superfund: the commonly used name for the *Comprehensive Environmental Response, Compensation, and Liability Act (CERCLA),* the federal environmental cleanup law. A site on the Superfund list must be cleaned up by any and all previous owners, operators, transporters, and disposers of waste to the site. The federal government will clean such sites as long as the responsible parties pay for the job. Owners who fail to pay such costs risk prosecution.

super regional center: a shopping center larger than a typical regional mall.

surety: one who guarantees the performance of another, such as agreeing to pay the debts of another if that person does not.

surface rights: the right to use and modify the surface area of real estate.

survey: a drawing or map showing the precise legal boundaries of a property, the location of improvements, easements, rights of way, encroachments, and other physical features. A lender may require a borrower to have a survey of the property performed. This process confirms that the property's boundaries are correctly described in the purchase and sale agreement. Also called a *plot plan*, the survey may show that a neighbor's fence is located on the seller's property, or more serious violations may be discovered. These violations must be addressed before the lender will proceed. The buyer usually pays to have the survey done, but some cost savings may be found by requesting an update from the company that previously surveyed the property.

surveyor: one who is trained in the measurement of land for the purpose of determining its perimeter boundaries, contours, and area.

survivorship: a situation where a joint tenant is entitled to retain property ownership rights after another joint tenant dies. This keeps heirs, business partners, or other associates of the deceased from making claims against the property.

sweat equity: value added to a piece of property by virtue of the work done by the owner, such as in a do-it-yourself improvement.

sweat equity loan: a loan given on the premise that the purchaser personally does some work on the property.

sweetener: a feature added to a purchase to make it more attractive.

swing loan: a short-term loan that allows a homeowner to purchase a home before selling the former residence. Also called a *bridge loan* or *gap loan*.

Swiss Chalet: a 1½ to 2-story house, with a gable roof and decorative woodwork in the Swiss style. (*see Appendix A*)

SYD: see *sum-of-years digits*.

symbol schedule: the legend that defines the symbols on a construction drawing, with their meanings.

syndicate:

(1) a group of investment bankers underwriting and distributing a new or outstanding issue of securities of a real estate business.

(2) alternately, a professionally managed limited partnership investing in different types of real estate.

syndication: a method of selling property whereby a sponsor, or syndicator, sells interests to investors. It may take the form of a *partnership, limited partnership, tenancy in common,* corporation or *Subchapter S corporation.*

syndicator: the sponsor of a *syndicate* involving people or companies buying an interest in a real estate investment or unit. The group of investors are in effect engaged in a joint venture for profit.

T

table funding: originating mortgage loans with internal capital until a group of loans can be packaged for sale in the *secondary mortgage market*.

takeout loan or financing: an agreement by a lender to provide permanent financing after construction of a planned project. The financing usually contains specific conditions for occupancy and income, such as a certificate of occupancy and/or a certain percentage of unit sales or leases in place and paying rent. Most construction lenders require takeout financing prior to beginning construction.

taking: the act of obtaining land through condemnation. Usually, the government will exercise its right to take only after it is determined that the owners of the acquired property are unwilling to settle for a reasonable price.

tandem plan: a government program of providing low–interest-rate mortgages to low-income qualified buyers. In the tandem program, the *Federal National Mortgage Association (FNMA)* purchases low-interest-rate mortgages at a discount from the *Government National Mortgage Association (GNMA)*. In doing this, GNMA subsidizes the low-income homebuyer and incurs a loss on the transaction.

tangible asset: assets having a physical existence, such as cash, equipment, and real estate. Accounts receivable are also usually considered tangible assets for accounting purposes.

tangible property: items of real estate and personal property that have a physical existence; they usually have a long life, for example, housing and other real estate.

tap fees: fees charged for hooking up utilities.

tax and insurance escrow: when a mortgage loan is provided to a borrower, the lender establishes a fund called a tax and insurance escrow to accumulate the debtor's monthly payments for property taxes and insurance premiums for the mortgaged property.

tax assessor: a government official who sets values on real estate property for tax purposes and ascertains the annual property tax assessments that must be collected.

tax avoidance: reduction of one's taxes by using legal tax-planning opportunities, such as estate planning.

tax base: the collective value of property, income, or other assets subject to a tax. For property taxation, the tax base is the total assessed value of all taxable property, less exemptions.

tax basis: the cost basis of an asset, such as a property owned for tax purposes.

tax benefit rule: a rule that limits the recognition of income from the recovery of an expense or loss properly deducted in a prior tax year to the amount of the deduction that reduced taxable income.

tax book: compilation of all *tax maps* of a given tax district that are bound together and kept at the local tax office. The tax book is a public record that an individual can review upon request.

tax court: the U.S. Tax Court is one of three trial courts of original jurisdiction that decide litigation involving federal income, death, and gift taxes.

tax credit: a dollar-for-dollar reduction of income tax liability.

tax deduction: a tax break used to reduce taxable income. Items include mortgage interest, loan *points* that are paid, and property taxes.

tax deed: the document given to a grantee by a government that had claimed a property that is delinquent in taxes. Tax deed sales deal with the selling of property that has arrears of taxes.

tax district: a region or locality that assesses real estate taxes on the properties located within its borders. Frequently, the local county or city is the property-taxing jurisdiction that is empowered, by law, to assess taxes on real estate.

tax evasion: failure to pay taxes legally due the government, often by failure to report some income received or by claiming false deductions.

tax-exempt: tax-free status given to certain nonprofit organizations and governmental entities.

tax-exempt bond: a bond whose interest is free of federal, state, or local tax in the state of the issuer; typically a municipal bond of a state or county agency.

tax-exempt property: real estate that is not subject, in whole or part, to *ad valorem* property taxes. Churches, charities, and government buildings do not pay property tax, because of their tax-free status.

tax flaw: a defect in the tax law that may either provide a loophole to minimize the tax payment or result in higher taxes than there should be.

tax foreclosure: property taken over by the government because the owner has failed to pay taxes on it. The property may revert back to the owner when the taxes are paid. If not, the government may sell the property to collect the amount due.

tax-free exchange: transfers of property specifically exempt from federal income tax consequences in the current year. Examples are a transfer of property to a controlled corporation and a like-kind exchange. See *like-kind exchange* and *Section 1031.*

tax home: the business location, post, or station of the taxpayer. If an employee is temporarily reassigned to a new post for a period of one year or less, the taxpayer's tax home is his personal residence and the travel expenses are deductible.

tax impound: money paid to and held by a lender for annual tax payments.

tax liability: the amount of total tax due the IRS after any credits and before taking into account any advance payments—withholding, estimated payments, etc.—made by the taxpayer.

tax lien: a legal claim placed on a property for nonpayment of taxes.

tax map: a map that documents the area, perimeter location, dimensions, and other data relating to land, for purposes of assessing real estate taxes.

tax participation: the standard portion of a lease that indicates that in the event of an increase in annual assessed real estate taxes during the lease term, the *lessee* will be responsible for higher monthly payments to cover the increase.

tax planning: an evaluation of different tax options of investing in real estate with the purpose of reducing the tax liability in current and future years.

tax preference item: an item falling under Section 57 of the Internal Revenue Code that may result in the imposition of the *alternative minimum tax (AMT)*. These items of otherwise exempt income or deductions or special tax benefit were targeted to ensure that taxpayers who benefit should pay the minimum amount of tax.

tax rate: the ratio of a tax assessment to the amount being taxed. Amount of tax to be paid based on taxable income. The tax rate usually changes as the unit of the tax base changes.

tax refund: the amount the taxpayer gets back when he/she files the income tax return at the end of the reporting year because taxes were overpaid for that year. The tax overpayment equals the tax payments remitted less the tax actually due.

tax return: the generic name of the form used to file taxes payable to a federal, state or local government. The tax return includes items such as gross income, deductions, tax credits and tax due. Individual taxpayers file on a calendar year basis using Form 1040, which is due 3 1/2 months after the tax year. Corporations prepare Form 1120 on a calendar year or fiscal year basis. It is due 2 1/2 months after the tax year. The partnership tax return is Form 1065.

tax roll: the list of all properties subject to a tax in a property-taxing jurisdiction. It indicates the assessed values of all properties in the jurisdiction.

tax sale: a public sale of property, by the government, for nonpayment of taxes.

tax shelter: a term that refers to various tax-advantaged investments and transactions. Real estate is considered a good way to shelter income from taxes.

tax shield: deductions that result in a reduction of tax payments. The tax shield equals the amount of the deduction times the tax rate.

tax stop: a clause in a lease that sets a maximum limit on the amount of property taxes that a *lessor* will pay. The *lessee* is required to pay any taxes in excess of that limit.

taxable income: for the individual, adjusted gross income less itemized deductions and personal exemptions. After taxable income is computed, the tax to be paid can be determined by looking at the tax rate schedules. For corporations, taxable income is gross income less allowable business deductions.

taxes and insurance: the tax and insurance components of a mortgage payment are generally held by the lender in an *escrow account*. The lender pays any property tax and homeowner's insurance bills as they are due, ensuring they are paid on time. These bills may be paid separately by the owner, or paid through an escrow fund set up by the bank or lending agency.

teardown: a building in such poor condition that it cannot be repaired and must be completely rebuilt.

teaser rate: an enticingly attractive initial rate below the market offered in an *adjustable-rate mortgage*. In general, the interest rate reverts to the fully indexed rate at the first adjustment date.

1031 exchanges: also known as *like-kind exchanges*. 1031 exchanges (named for their place in the U.S. Tax Code) allow capital gains taxes on a transaction to be deferred if the proceeds from the sale of an asset are invested in a similar asset. For example, a 1031 real estate exchange could involve the sale of a six-unit apartment property and the purchase of a warehouse or strip mall, as long as both properties had similar value. Real estate is probably the No. 1 asset used in these exchanges, though people apply them to other big-ticket assets.

tenancy: the right of possession of real estate whether by ownership or rental. The period for which a tenant has the right of possession.

tenancy at sufferance: a holdover tenant; a tenancy established when a lawful tenant wrongfully remains in possession of property after expiration of a lease.

tenancy at will: a lease to use or occupy lands and buildings for a not- predetermined length of time, at the will of the owner. Either party may terminate the agreement upon proper notice. The agreement may be written or oral.

tenancy by the entirety: a tenancy in which parties jointly own property. After the death of one, the survivor takes the whole estate. Tenancy by the entirety can be terminated during their lifetime only by joint action of the parties.

tenancy for life: a freehold equity in an estate, restricted to the duration of the life of the grantee or other stipulated individual.

tenancy for years: a form of tenancy created by a lease for a specified period of time.

tenancy from year to year: a lease arrangement by which either party may terminate a tenancy from year to year by giving notice, in writing, of his intention to terminate the lease.

tenancy in common: two or more individuals jointly owning property. Each owns an undivided share of the whole. The shares remain separate even if one party dies.

tenancy in severalty: ownership of property by one person or one legal entity (corporate ownership).

tenant: an individual or corporation leasing a residential or office unit.

tenant changes: changes made by a *lessee* to property during the term of the lease.

tenant fixtures: fixtures added to leased real estate by a *lessee* that, by contract or by law, may be removed by the lessee upon expiration of the lease.

tenant improvements: changes made to accommodate specific needs of a tenant. Includes interior walls, carpeting, paint, lighting, shelves, windows, toilets, etc. that suit a particular tenant's needs.

tenant-stockholder: a tenant in a cooperative share loan who is both a stockholder in a cooperative corporation and a tenant of the unit under a proprietary lease or occupancy agreement.

tenants' union: a group of rental occupants acting together.

tender: to present something of value for another's acceptance.

tenement: a city apartment building that is overcrowded, poorly constructed or maintained, and generally part of a *slum area*.

tenure: the length of time or condition under which something, such as a piece of property, is held. The nature of an occupant's ownership rights; an indication of whether one is an owner or a tenant.

tenure in land: the length of time or condition under which something, such as a piece of property, is held. Classification of one's ownership rights in land. One may either buy the land and own all rights to it, or lease it, where one's rights are described in and limited by the lease agreement.

tenure property: the right and duties of using and holding property.

term: the period of time during which something is in effect. A stated number of years. A condition specified in an agreement.

term, amortization: see *amortization term*.

termination clause: a provision in a contract that, upon a certain occurrence or event, the contract is cancelled.

term loan: a loan requiring only interest payments until the last day of its term, at which time the full payment is due.

termite: a destructive light-colored insect that feeds on wood.

termite clause: a sales contract provision that allows the buyer to have his property inspected for termite or other wood-destroying insects before the deal goes through. This clause can allow cancellation of a deal if such insects are found.

termite shield: an aluminum or metal-treated barrier that is placed between the concrete and wood of the foundation of a newly constructed building to prevent termites from infesting the wood. Many experts say that such a shield is ineffective because the termites simply go around the shield to get to the wood in the foundation.

testament: Also called a last will and testament. See *will*.

testamentary capacity: having the intellect to comprehend the terms and conditions of a *will* and their impact. A *testator* must understand his or her estate and its eventual disposition and effects in order to validate the will.

testamentary intention: interpreting the objective of a *testator* in his or her *will*. The disposition of the testator's estate must be understandable or it could be legally challenged.

testamentary trust: a trust created by a *will* that comes into effect only after the death of the testator. It empowers a trust administrator to implement the terms of the trust.

testate: a person who dies leaving a *will* specifying the distribution of the estate.

testator: a man who makes a *will*.

testatrix: a woman who makes a *will*.

testimonium: a clause that cites the act and date in a deed or other conveyance.

thin market: a market in which there are comparatively few bids to buy or offers to sell real estate. The term relates to a single investment or to a particular investment market, such as the real estate market. In a thin market, buying or selling a few homes can impact disproportionately. Price volatility is generally wider than *liquid markets*.

third party: one who is not directly involved in a transaction or contract but may be involved or affected by it.

third-party origination: a process by which a lender uses another party to completely or partially originate, process, underwrite, close, fund, or package the mortgages it plans to deliver to the *secondary mortgage market*.

threat of condemnation: when a property owner is informed, either orally or in writing, by a representative of a governmental body or by a public official authorized to acquire property for public use, that a decision has been made to acquire his property, and it is reasonable to believe that the property will be taken, a threat of condemnation exists.

thrift institution: depository institutions that primarily serve consumers, and include both savings banks and *savings and loan (S&L) institutions*. These institutions originate and service mortgage loans. A thrift may choose to hold a loan in its own portfolio or to sell the loan to an investor.

tie beam: a horizontal beam, serving as a tie, holding components together.

tight market: market in which the spreads between the asking and offer price of real estate are small. The property may be in abundant supply and actively traded.

time and materials contract: a contract providing for the *contractor* to be paid for time spent on the job plus the cost of materials.

time-shares: a form of property ownership under which a property is held by a number of people, each with the right of possession for a specified time interval. Time-sharing is most commonly applied to resort and vacation properties.

time value of money: a concept that money available now is worth more than the same amount in the future, because of its potential earning capacity. It is the rationale behind compounding for future value or discounting for present value.

time with materials furnished contract: a contract providing for the *contractor* to be paid for time spent on the job, with all materials supplied by the owner.

title: a legal document that establishes ownership of a piece of real estate.

title block: markings on a *blueprint* containing design and revision information.

title company: a firm that provides insurance of a clear title once it completes its search for *liens*.

title defect: a circumstance or an unresolved claim that challenges property ownership. Such claims may arise from current liens against the property, the failure of a former partner to sign a deed, or an interruption in the title records to a property.

title examination: the check of the public record, by the title company, to determine the legal ownership and that there are no claims or *liens* affecting the property.

title insurance: insurance that protects the lender and the buyer against loss arising from disputes over ownership of property. A lender will require the purchase of title insurance to ensure that the borrower is receiving a clear, marketable title. There are two types of title insurance policies:

• **lender's policy** (mandatory): this protects the lender should a flaw in the title be detected after the property has been purchased.

• **owner's policy** (optional, but recommended): this protects the borrower exclusively if a flaw in the title is detected after the property has been purchased.

Generally, the buyer pays the cost of both policies.

title insurance binder: a written commitment, issued by the title company, agreeing to insure title to a property, subject to conditions or exclusion shown.

title report: a document indicating the current state of the title to a property, such as *easements*, *covenants*, *liens*, and any defects.

title risk: possible impediments to the transfer of title of a property.

title search: a review by a licensed title company of the title records on a particular property to ensure that the seller is the legal owner of the property and that there are no *liens* or other *claims* outstanding, before the property passes to a new owner. It attempts to uncover any *encumbrances* on the title, and makes sure the seller is the actual owner of the property. Encumbrances include any liens. Liens can also be filed by the Internal Revenue Service for nonpayment of taxes. Any such claims must be paid by the seller; this often occurs either before or at the closing.

title sheet: the first page of set of construction drawings. Information on the title sheet typically includes the name and address of the architect, as well as an index to the plans.

title theory states: states in which the law splits the title of mortgaged property into legal title, held by the lender, and equitable title, held by the borrower. This is based on the legal assumption that the mortgagee is a partial owner of the real estate securing the mortgage and remains so until the debt is fully paid. The borrower gains full title to the property upon retiring the mortgage debt. The lender is granted more immediate cure to a default than in *lien theory states*.

to have and to hold clause: also known as the *habendum clause*, it defines or limits the quantity of the estate granted in the deed. Declares whether the type of ownership conveyed is *fee simple*, a *life estate*, or something different.

topographic map: a map with contours showing changes in elevation.

topographic symbols: symbols and markings used to represent terrain features on a *topographic map*.

topography: the art of mapping the physical features of a region. Topography describes the elevations and features of an area, such as its flatness, hills, mountains, ravines, etc.

top producer: a term used in the real estate community that refers to agents and brokers who sell a high volume of properties.

Torrens system: a title registration system used in some states. Named after Sir Robert Torrens, a British administrator of Australia, this system allows the condition of the title to be discovered without resorting to a title search.

tort: a civil wrong (not a criminal act) that occurs as a result of a breach of legal duty owed to someone, e.g., negligence. A tort does not arise from a breach of contract.

tortfeasor: one who has committed a *tort*.

tort liability: a legal obligation stemming from a civil wrong or injury for which a court remedy is justified. A tort liability arises because of a combination of a direct violation of a person's rights, the transgression of a public obligation causing damage, or a private wrongdoing.

total debt payment: what a consumer or business pays each month in mortgage, auto loans, credit card debt, and other lending obligations.

total expense ratio: total obligations as a percentage of a buyer's gross monthly income. The total expense ratio includes monthly housing expenses plus other monthly debts.

total lender fees: fees charged by the lender to obtain a loan.

total loan amount: the amount of money borrowed plus any financed closing costs.

total monthly housing costs: total monthly costs made up of principal, interest, property taxes, and insurance.

total paid at closing: all *closing costs*, which also include the down payment and any prepaid fees.

total return: the return earned on an investment over a given time period. It includes two basic components: the current yield, such as rental income and capital gains; and losses in property values. It is typically stated as an annual percentage.

townhouse: a home, generally having two or more floors, often with a garage; it shares walls with other similar units. Modern townhouses are typically found in condominiums and cooperatives, or as part of a planned unit development. In a townhome development, owners are likely to share assessments for common area maintenance and various amenities. (*see Appendix A*)

township: a six-mile by six-mile square area of land delineated by *Government Rectangular Survey.*

township lines: lines determined by a government rectangular survey laying out a standard six-mile square area of land.

tract: a parcel of land, generally held for subdividing and development into residential units.

tract home: a mass-produced house constructed within a project by the same builder, with similar style and floor plan as the other homes in the development.

tract index: a system for listing recorded documents affecting a particular tract of land.

trade equity: other assets, which could include real estate, which are given by a buyer to a seller as part of the down payment.

trade fixture: articles of personal property installed in rented buildings by the tenant. Trade fixtures are removable by the tenant before the lease expires, and are not true *fixtures*. If the tenant fails to remove the fixtures, they become the property of the landlord.

trading down: buying a less expensive home than the one owned currently.

trading on equity: also called *financial leverage*. Borrowed funds are used to magnify returns. Trading profitably on the equity, also called favorable financial leverage, means that the borrowed funds generate a higher rate of return than the interest rate paid for the use of the money. The excess accrues to the benefit of the owner because it magnifies, or increases, his or her leverage.

trading up: buying a more expensive home than the one owned currently.

traffic circle: a circular intersection allowing for continuous movement of traffic at the meeting of major roadways.

transaction: an agreement between a buyer and a seller to exchange an asset for payment. Or in accounting, any event or condition recorded in the books of account.

transaction broker: a real estate professional who does not represent the buyer or the seller, but is hired to help them reach an agreement.

transaction costs: the costs associated with buying and selling real estate.

transfer: to convey something from one entity or person to another.

transferable development rights: a legal designation where the development potential of a site is severed from its title and made available for transfer to another location. The owner of a site within a transfer area retains property ownership, but not approval to develop. The owner of a site within a receiving area may purchase transferable development rights, allowing a receptor site to be developed at a greater density.

transfer development rights: a type of zoning ordinance that allows owners of property zoned for low-density development to sell development rights to other property owners. The landowners purchasing the development rights are able to develop their parcels at higher densities than otherwise permitted. The practice assures that low-density uses, such as historic preservation, are continued.

transfer fee: the fee charged by a mortgage lender to a buyer, a seller, or both for transferring a mortgage when the mortgage property is sold.

transfer of ownership: any means by which the ownership of a property changes hands. Lenders consider the following situations to be a transfer of ownership:
- the purchase of a property subject to the mortgage;
- the assumption of the mortgage debt by the property purchaser; or
- any exchange of possession of the property under a land sales contract or any other land trust device.

transfer tax: the state and/or local tax payable when title passes from one owner to another.

transom:
(1) a cross beam in a window or over a door.
(2) a horizontal window above a door or other window. (see *Appendix B*)

Treasury Bills: securities, which have the full backing of the U.S. Government, that are issued by the Treasury Department.

Treasury Index: the index used to determine interest rate changes for adjustable-rate mortgages.

tri-level: a popular style of home, best suited for side-to-side slopes, in which a one-story wing is attached between the levels of a two-story wing. It is also called a *split- level* house.

triple net leases: a lease requiring tenants to pay all utilities, insurance, taxes, and maintenance costs—in other words, all operating expenses of a property.

triplex: a freestanding building having three separate housing units, all under one roof.

trophy building: a landmark property that is well known by the public and highly sought by institutional investors and pension funds and insurance companies. Generally one-of-a-kind architectural designs, with the highest quality of materials and finish, and expensive trim.

trust: a tax entity created by a trust agreement. This entity distributes all or part of its income to beneficiaries as instructed by the trust agreement. This entity is required to pay taxes on undistributed income.

trust account: a special account, which is used to safeguard the funds of a buyer or seller.

trust deed: a conveyance of real estate to a third party to be held for the benefit of another. Commonly used in some states in place of mortgages that conditionally convey title to the lender.

trustee: a fiduciary who holds or controls property for the benefit of another.

trustee in bankruptcy: a person selected by a judge or the creditors of a bankrupt individual to handle matters, including the sale of the bankrupt person's assets, management of the funds from the sale of those assets, payment of expenses, and distribution of the balance to creditors. The trustee is usually compensated with a specified percentage of the liquidation sale.

trustee's deed: a deed given by a trustee at a deed of trust foreclosure sale.

trustee's sale: a foreclosure sale conduced by a trustee under the stipulations of a deed of trust.

trustor: the individual creating a trust.

Truth in Lending Act: a federal law that requires lenders to fully disclose, in writing, the terms and conditions of a mortgage, including the *annual percentage rate (APR)* and other charges. A lender should provide the borrower a Truth-in-Lending (TIL) Statement within three business days of a loan application. This document outlines the costs of the loan, and it's given to the borrower so he can compare the costs with those of other lenders. Among the costs listed: the annual percentage rate (APR), which is the cost of the mortgage compiled as a yearly rate. It may be higher than the interest rate stated in the mortgage because it includes points and other costs of credit; the finance charge; the amount financed; the payment amount; and the total payments required. The lender is required to give the borrower the final version of his TIL Statement at or prior to the *closing meeting* because it's possible that the APR calculated at the time of the loan application could change by closing.

Tudor: an English-style house with the defining characteristics of half-timbering on the upper floors, and one or more steeply pitched cross gables. Stone or patterned brick walls are common, as are rounded doorways, multipaned windows, and a large stone or brick chimney. *(see Appendix A)*

turnaround property: a deteriorated property that can be restored and sold for a gain.

turnkey project: a development in which a developer completes the entire project on behalf of a buyer, then turns over the keys. All the new tenant or owner has to do is turn the key to the apartment or office in a newly constructed building, because everything is completed and ready for occupancy.

turnover: movement for change of people, such as *tenants*. The sale of one average real estate inventory item within a specified time.

two-step mortgage: an adjustable mortgage with one interest rate for the first five or seven years of the loan and another for the remainder of the loan term.

two-to-four-family property: a piece of property that may be owned by only one person but provides housing for up to four households.

type of use: a stipulation in a contract on how property can or cannot be used.

U

UCC: see *Uniform Commercial Code.*

ULI: see *Urban Land Institute.*

unadjusted basis: the basis of property for purposes of figuring depreciation under *ACRS* or *MACRS.* The unadjusted basis is the original cost or other basis without regard to salvage value.

unaudited opinion: an opinion by a *Certified Public Accountant* who has not audited the relevant financial statements.

underground service: electrical power lines that are run underground in the street and to the building. Underground service has largely replaced the use of aboveground power lines in new housing developments.

underimprovement: property improvements that are below the usual standard expectations.

underlying mortgage: the first mortgage on a property when other mortgages exist on the same property.

undersupply: when demand exceeds the amount of real estate property available, causing the prices to rise.

Underwriter's Laboratories (UL): the independent testing group that assesses the safety and quality of various electrical components. Once a product is approved, the manufacturer can place a "UL" label on the item.

underwriting: how a lender determines the risk of a loan. Underwriting involves an analysis of the borrower's creditworthiness and the quality of the property itself.

underwriting fee: the fee charged by the lender to do the work to verify information, necessary to make a decision as to whether or not to approve a loan. Is typically included in the borrower's *application fee.*

undisclosed heir: one who claims, after the death of an owner lacking a will, a right to a piece of that property.

undisclosed principal: when a major party to a transaction remains anonymous, or when one party is not informed that there is a principal.

undisclosed spouse: a marital partner who is not mentioned in a will but can claim a right to a piece of property.

undivided interest: ownership by two or more persons, which entitles each to the right to use the entire property.

undue influence: when a person is forced to perform in a certain manner due to excessive influence, pressure, or fear brought by another party; this may be used to void a contract.

unearned income: taxable income other than that received for services performed (earned income). Unearned income includes money received for the investment of money or other property, such as interest, dividends, and royalties. It also includes pensions, alimony, unemployment compensation, and other income that is not earned.

unearned increment: an increase in the value of a property that is not due to any effort on the part of the owner.

unencumbered property: real estate that is free and clear of *liens* and obligations, such as a house without a mortgage.

unenforceable: a contract that cannot be legally enforced by the courts, such as contracts with minors and those containing fraud.

Uniform Commercial Code (UCC): the set of statutes that standardize the states' commercial laws.

Uniform Residential Appraisal Report (URAR): the standard form used for the appraisal of a dwelling; it provides numerous checklists, definitions, and certifications.

Uniform Residential Landlord and Tenant Act: legislation dealing with landlord-tenant contracts and relationships; provides protection to renters in 15 states: Alaska, Arizona, Florida, Hawaii, Iowa, Kansas, Kentucky, Montana, Nebraska, New Mexico, Oregon, Rhode Island, South Carolina, Tennessee, and Virginia.

Uniform Settlement Statement: a document that provides an itemized listing of the funds that are payable at *closing*. Items that appear on the statement include real estate commissions, loan fees, points, and initial escrow amounts. Each item on the statement is represented by a separate number within a standardized numbering system. The totals at the bottom of the HUD-1 statement define the seller's net proceeds and the buyer's net payment at closing. The HUD-1 statement is also known as the *closing statement* or *settlement sheet*. The *HUD-1 Settlement Statement* itemizes the amounts to be paid by the buyer and the seller at closing. The (blank) form is published by the U.S. Department of Housing and Urban Development (HUD). Items on the statement include: real estate commissions; loan fees; points; and escrow amounts.

Uniform Standards of Professional Appraisal Practices (USPAP): the set of requirements formulated and adhered to by the members of the Appraisal Foundation.

unilateral contract: a one-sided contract where, even if one party makes a promise, the second party is not legally required to perform, but may do so, thus obligating the first party.

unilateral listing: a listing of property that is open and has no one real estate agent who has the sole right to sell the property.

unimproved land: raw land in its natural state, with no installed improvements or structures.

unincorporated group: an association of persons not treated as a corporation, such as a limited partnership.

unit: a segregated part of a structure, e.g., one apartment in an apartment building or an office in a commercial building.

unit cost: the cost of a single item on a construction budget, for example one 2x4x8' stud. The unit cost is multiplied by the number of units required for the job to determine the total cost.

unities: unity of interest, possession, time, and title that must be necessary to form a *joint tenancy*.

unit in place method: valuation of property based on its replacement cost. Cost of major elements per square foot multiplied by amount of square feet is the estimate of building cost.

unity: the legal dictate necessary for property to be owned as joint tenants.

unity of interest: joint tenants must acquire their interest by the same conveyance and with the same interest.

unity of possession: joint tenants must have equal rights to possession of the entire property.

unity of time: joint tenants must acquire their title simultaneously.

unity of title: joint tenants must acquire their interest from the same deed or will.

unlawful detainer: illegally holding on to or keeping the property of another.

unleveraged: operating without the use of borrowed money.

unlike properties: properties that are used for different purposes and/or are of different types.

unrealized gain: an increase in the value of property while it is being held. Gain is only realized upon sale.

unrecorded deed: a deed transferring ownership from one person to another but that is not officially recorded.

unqualified audit: a complete *audit*.

unqualified opinion: an auditor's opinion of a financial statement, given without any reservations.

unsecured loan: a loan that is not backed by collateral.

unsecured note: a credit note with only the borrower's financial situation and credit history as security.

unsolicited listing: a real estate listing obtained without any effort on the part of the real estate broker.

up-front fee: a fee received immediately when a contract is signed or an investment made.

upgrades: options offered to buyers that go beyond the standard. Usually in a new home, they often include more lighting, better carpeting, etc.

upset date: a contract provision allowing a purchaser the right to cancel a contract if the occupancy requirements are not satisfied by a certain date.

upset price: an established amount, in a bidding procedure or auction, below which the seller is not obligated to accept the bid. Also referred to as a *reserve price.*

upside potential: an approximation of the potential appreciation of value in real estate by considering location, amenities, or increase in rental income.

upzoning: rezoning of property from a lower to a higher use.

URAR: see *Uniform Residential Appraisal Report.*

Urban Development Action Grant: grant intended to stimulate private investment in distress cities and urban areas by providing federal *seed money*, thereby attracting private funds for revitalization. *HUD* funds are transferred directly to cities and states for urban renewal projects.

Urban Land Institute (ULI): nonprofit entity from which you can obtain data and advice on the best utilization of land. Phone: 202-624-7000, Web: www.uli.org.

urban property: real estate located in a heavily populated city area.

urban renewal: older property purchased by a governmental agency and improved or modernized or demolished and replaced.

urban space: land availability in an urban area.

urban sprawl: an unplanned and unexpected expansion of development in an area.

U.S. Department of Agriculture (USDA) Rural Development: formerly Farmers Home Administration, a division of the USDA that provides loan, loan guarantee, and grant programs to improve the quality of life in rural America. Web: www.rurdev.usda.gov.

U.S. Department of Housing and Urban Development (HUD): the federal agency overseeing the *Federal Housing Administration*, in addition to a number of housing and community development programs. Phone 202-708-1112, Web: www.hud.gov.

use tax: a levy charged for use of things such as town water, etc.

useful life: the usual operating service life of property, used for depreciation accounting, which does not necessarily coincide with the actual physical life.

USPAP: see *Uniform Standards of Professional Appraisal Practices.*

usufructuary right: one individual's right to utilize the property of another, such as the privileges given under an *easement.*

usury: excessive and illegal interest charged on a loan.

usury laws: state laws that limit the interest rate charged to persons borrowing money in that state.

utilities: services provided to land or houses by public utility companies, such as water, gas, electricity, sewers, etc.

utility easement: a passage through property that is granted by the owner to a public utility.

utility room: a room that contains the appliances necessary for the maintenance of that establishment.

V

VA: see *Veterans Administration*.

vacancy and credit losses: losses incurred by owner due to tenant failure to pay rent or because property is unoccupied.

vacancy factor: the estimated percentage of rental that won't be made because of actual and anticipated vacancies.

vacancy rate: the percentage of unoccupied rental property. Idle space causes significant cash drain when cash inflows are not received to offset the cash outflows of maintenance. Most properties have a minimum occupancy rate to break even.

vacant land: unoccupied property; not currently being used. It may have utilities and off-site improvements, as contrasted with *raw land* with no improvements or structures.

vacate: to leave a property. If the legally agreed upon term is not fulfilled, vacating a property does not relieve the occupant of liability.

vacation home: a home owned in addition to a person's primary residence. Interest and real estate taxes are tax deductible with the IRS, though certain conditions apply.

VA guarantee: the *Veterans Administration* will guarantee up to 50 percent of a home loan up to $45,000. For loans between $45,000 and $144,000, the minimum guaranty amount is $22,500, with a maximum guaranty of up to 40 percent of the loan up to $36,000, subject to the amount of entitlement a veteran has available. For loans of more than $144,000 made for the purchase or construction of a home or to purchase a residential unit in a condominium or to refinance an existing VA guaranteed loan for interest rate reduction, the maximum guaranty is 25 percent up to $60,000. Web: www. homeloans.va.gov.

VA loan: a loan made through the *Department of Veteran Affairs*.

VA mortgage: a mortgage that is guaranteed by the *Department of Veterans Affairs*. Also known as a *government mortgage*.

valid: factual information. Representations made by a realtor to a prospective purchaser fall into this category.

valid contract: an agreement that is legally binding because it is in conformity with all legal requirements and conditions.

valid deed: a legally proper instrument that transfers title of real estate from seller to buyer.

valuable consideration: value is exchanged in accordance with an agreement involving performance, currently or in the future, by the parties. Without reasonable consideration for performance, a contract may not be valid.

valuation: the estimated worth of a property as valued through an *appraisal*.

value: an expression of monetary worth of a particular piece of real estate.

value after the taking: any value left of a property after it's been condemned.

value before the taking: the market price of all the property prior to a *condemnation* proceeding.

value in exchange: the giving of money, goods, or services in exchange for goods or services provided by another party.

value in use: the discounted value of net cash to be obtained from a property, calculated by consideration of annual cash inflows plus the disposal value.

vapor barrier: a layer of material that obstructs the passage of water vapor.

variable interest rate: a loan rate that changes, usually based on fluctuations in the rate paid on Treasury bills or bank certificates of deposit.

variable maturity mortgage: a long-term mortgage loan where the interest rate may be adjusted periodically by the lender. Payment levels may remain the same, but the loan maturity is lengthened or shortened to achieve the adjustment.

variable rate: an interest rate that changes periodically in relation to an index.

variable-rate mortgage (VRM): a loan with an interest rate that adjusts with the changes in rates paid on Treasury bills or bank certificates of deposit. Also see *adjustable-rate mortgage (ARM)*.

variance: an allowable deviation from the land use prescribed by the existing zoning ordinances.

vendee: a buyer of real property.

vendee's lien: the legal right of a purchaser of a piece of real estate to the paid purchase price plus direct costs of acquisition, if the seller fails to render the deed to the property.

vendor: a seller of real estate or other products.

vendor's lien: the seller's claim to property held by a buyer as collateral for a debt, also called a *purchase-money mortgage*.

venture capital: a financing source for new businesses or turn-around ventures with high-risk/high reward possible. Venture capital can be anything from *seed money* to full financing; sources include wealthy individuals, *limited partnerships*, and business investment companies.

venue: the geographic location of a court action, which occur in the place where jurisdiction applies.

verification: a sworn statement made before a qualified officer that the contents of a document are correct.

verification of deposit: a document signed by the borrower's bank or other financial institution verifying the borrower's account balance and history.

verification of employment (VOE): a statement by borrower's employer to confirm the borrower's salary and position and is part of the loan process.

verify: to collect supporting evidence. To prove.

Veterans Administration (VA): an agency of the federal government. A program of the *Department of Veteran Affairs* allows many qualified veterans to purchase a house without a down payment based on certain conditions. Moreover, the qualification guidelines for VA loans are more flexible than those for either the *Federal Housing Administration (FHA)* or conventional loans. Web: www.homeloans.va.gov.

vicarious liability: the responsibility of one person for the acts of another.

Victorian style: an architectural style of the mid-19th Century, characterized by front porches with spindlework detailing. Many Victorians are known for their heavy ornamentation and bold colors. (*see Appendix A*)

violation: an act or condition contrary to the permitted use of a property.

visual right: an occupant's right to see out of a window without being hindered.

voidable contract: a contract that may be rejected by either of the parties.

volatile market: sudden and unpredictable short-term price movements in real estate.

voluntary alienation: the conveyance of title between two parties or businesses by use of a deed.

voluntary bankruptcy: the declaration of bankruptcy by an insolvent person or business.

voluntary conveyance: a deed given by a mortgagor to the mortgagee to satisfy a debt and avoid foreclosure. Also known as *deed in lieu of foreclosure.*

voluntary lien: a lien that a homeowner gives willingly to a lender, such as a mortgage.

VRM: see *variable-rate mortgage.*

W

wainscot/wainscoting: the lower part of an interior wall when it is finished differently from the upper part.

waiver: the voluntary surrender of a right, privilege, or claim, usually in writing.

waiver of lien: voluntarily relinquishing the right of a *lien*, usually temporarily. This waiver may be explicitly stated, or implied.

waiver of tax lien: a form signed by a taxing jurisdiction certifying it will not file a *lien* against a property owner for back taxes. This form comes into play when real estate is being sold by an estate after the owner's death.

walkaway risk: the risk that occurs when a buyer or seller decides not to go through with the transaction. If property is not sold at the offered price, that price may not be realized at a later date. The buyer faces the same risk.

walk-out basement: a type of basement that allows a door to open into the yard because the basement is at ground level.

walkup: a building of two or more floors with no way to be accessed except through stairs. This type of building is usually in cities.

warehouse fee: the lender's cost of holding a borrower's loan temporarily before it is sold on the *secondary market*. It usually involves a closing cost fee.

warehouse property: a commercial structure used to hold products and goods for a fee; a storage facility. Usually located in a non-residential area.

warehousing: loans made by banks to other lenders for their underwritten stocks or bonds. These stocks and bonds are issued to both household and institutional investors for their portfolios. Also, when lenders store up loans before packaging them for sale in the secondary market.

warranted price: the amount considered fair for a real estate transaction, justified by the conditions involved in the exchange.

warranty: an agreement between a buyer and a seller of goods or services, detailing the conditions under which the seller will make repairs or fix problems without cost to the buyer. Many homes, both old and new, carry warranties as a sales incentive.

warranty deed: a deed that assures that the title to a property is free of any legal *claims* or *encumbrances;* includes covenants of seizing, express warranties of title, right to quiet enjoyment, and freedom from encumbrances.

warranty insurance: insurance on a property, covering repair and/or replacement costs in the event of damage or loss. Warranties vary considerably as to what is covered and the duration of the policy.

warranty of habitability: implied assurance, from the landlord to the tenant, that an apartment is safe and free from any hazard.

wasting asset: natural resources are typically considered wasting assets because they are extracted at a faster pace than nature can replace them.

waterfront property: a structure adjacent to a lake or other type of water, which has a higher sale value due to greater demand.

water right: the legal right of a landowner to the water found on or adjacent to his property. See *riparian.*

watershed:
(1) a land area where water collects.
(2) also, a dividing point that sends water runoff flowing into different drainage areas.

water table: the natural level of water below the ground.

weak market: low volume of real estate transactions; also referred to as a depressed market.

wear and tear: the decline in the value of a property due to physical damage, old age, or environmental factors.

weather-stripping: thin strips of a resilient material used to cover the joints of doors and windows, so as to keep out heat, cold, and rain.

well:
(1) a deep hole or shaft sunk into the earth to tap and remove an

underground supply of water or natural gas.

(2) also, a shaft in a building or between buildings that is open to allow access for light and air.

wellhold: the space that holds the staircase and the space around it.

Western framing: house framing that has the wall framing resting on top of the subfloor, with each story built up as a separate unit. Balloon framing, another type, has the studs running from the bottom of the first floor to the top of the second floor. Also called platform framing.

Western row house: a nineteenth-century-style house usually built to cover an entire street or block.

wetlands: land, situated near water, that meets various criteria regarding water level, soils, and plant growth. They may include swamps, marshes, and floodplains. Wetlands are subject to extreme levels of government regulation regarding building activity.

what-if analysis: an affordability analysis based on predictions. A what-if scenario can include changes to monthly income, debts, or down payment funds or to the qualifying ratios or down payment expenses that are used in the analysis. A what-if scenario can be used to explore different ways to improve a borrower's ability to afford a house. Many lending and personal finance websites offer ways to run this analysis.

white elephant: a property considered undesirable in the marketplace: too expensive to maintain or unable to generate enough rent to pay for itself.

wild deed: an improperly recorded deed.

will: a legal document that outlines the disposition of a deceased person's estate.

Williamsburg Georgian: an English-style house representative of the early Colonial houses built in America during the early 1700s. Williamsburg designs were two- and three-story rectangular houses with plain exteriors and two large chimneys rising high above the roof at either end of the house. See *Georgian*.

winterize: adapting property or machinery for operation or storage during the cold-weather months.

without recourse: words used to endorse a note or bill that indicate that the holder can't look to the debtor personally for compensation if the loan isn't paid. The holder's only recourse is to go after debtor's property.

witness: an individual who provides evidence under penalty of perjury, under oath in a trial. It is also the observance of an event or transaction or contract.

workers' compensation insurance: government-mandated insurance that covers job-related injuries to employees, and is paid for by employers.

working capital: the ability of any business to meet financial obligations, expand and take advantage of new opportunities. As a formula, it is cash plus accounts receivable plus inventory minus the sum of accounts payable plus accrued liabilities and short-term loans.

working drawing: a drawing made to scale, with details and markings to facilitate use by builders and engineers during construction.

workout: when a lender loosens some terms for overdue payment when a borrower runs into trouble paying back a loan. The lender may lower an interest rate or lengthen the time of repayment so the borrower can work out the problems paying the debt.

workshop: an area set aside for working with materials or machinery.

wraparound mortgage: a mortgage that includes the remaining balance on an existing first mortgage plus an additional amount requested by the mortgagor. Full payments on both mortgages are made to the wraparound mortgagee, who then forwards the payments on the first mortgage to the first mortgagee.

writ: a court order requiring a person or business to react in a specific manner.

write-down: when an owner makes a downward adjustment in the accounting value of an asset.

write off: to charge an asset amount to expense or loss, in order to reduce the value of that asset and one's earnings.

writ of ejectment: a court order allowing a landlord to evict a tenant because of nonpayment of rent or damaging property. The writ contains needed instructions and directs an officer of the court to execute it.

writ of execution: a court order allowing the seizure and sale of property due to nonpayment of taxes or foreclosure of property.

writ of mandamus: a court order that stops or directs a judicial directive.

wrongful foreclosure: a foreclosure that is legally improper and caused a borrower to suffer damages.

Y

yard: a tract of ground on the property, adjacent to the building or buildings.

year-over-year: compared to the same time period in the previous year.

year-to-date (YTD): so far this year; for the period starting January 1 of the current year and ending today.

yield: the return on an investment. Volume or amount produced. Alternately, a permanent deformation in a material caused by its being bent or stretched.

yield curve: a graph that shows current interest rates of similar obligations ranked by maturity.

yield to maturity (YTM): the average rate of return on a bond with a maturity of at least one year if it is held to its maturity date and if all cash flows are reinvested at the same rate of interest. It includes an adjustment for any premium paid or discount received. Yield to maturity is used to compare the relative values of different types of investments, including bonds and real estate.

Z

zero lot line: a lot where a home is set to the lot boundary, leaving very little space between the houses.

zero rate loan: a loan with large down payment and the balance being paid in equal periodic payments over a short period of time, with no interest charged. Usually offered by an eager seller.

zero net: when there is no money left for the seller, from the sale of a property, after all outstanding expenses are paid.

zone: to set off an area of land by ordinance for a specific purpose. Changing that purpose typically requires application to a *zoning board of appeals.*

zoning: rules and regulations controlling the use of land, determining how private property is to be used or what construction is allowed. Zoning may be either commercial, residential, industrial, or agricultural. Zoning also restricts height limitations, noise, parking, and open space. Residential zoning may consist of single-family house, two-family houses, or apartments.

zoning board of appeals: a local government board that is used to resolve zoning disputes.

zoning laws: ordinances created by local government to cover real estate development, including structural and esthetic points. They usually define usage classifications from agricultural to industry, and also building restrictions such as minimum and maximum square footage requirements and violations penalties and procedures.

zoning map: a map that shows a locality divided into districts, shows the status and usage of each district, and is kept current.

zoning ordinances: regulations determined by each municipality to establish different zoning restrictions and classifications, for example, building height, type of buildings, etc. Penalties are assessed for violation of zoning ordinances. Though, after appeal, some changes to zoning ordinances are allowed, called *zoning variances.*

zoning records: a compilation of zoning requirements and any changes made to them.

zoning variance: a modification of an existing zoning law, which can be made in certain instances; for example, to build a taller building than allowed, or a different type of housing than allowed.

Appendices

APPENDIX A
HOUSING STYLES

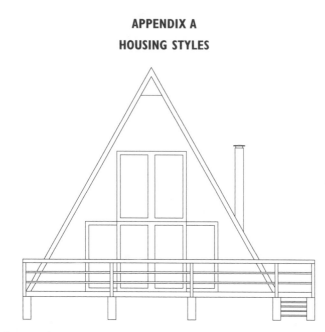

A-frame: the outer shape of a structure that has steeply sloped roofs and is in the shape of an "A," hence the name.

bi-level: a home that is built on two levels, with an entrance on a level between the two; it often has the garage and storage or recreation room in the lower level and the balance of the home in the upper level.

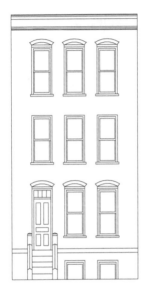

brownstone: a nineteenth-century-style row house, usually having four to five stories with a front staircase from the street leading to the first floor.

bungalow: a small one-story house or cottage, often with a front porch. The bungalow became the most common building style in the United States between the world wars.

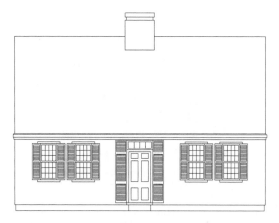

Cape Cod: a style of wood-frame house with a central entrance and a steep roof. Cape Cods have one or two stories, often with dormer windows on the second floor.

Craftsman style: an architectural style that evolved near the turn of the century, characterized by low-pitched, gabled roofs, large, overhanging eaves, usually with exposed roof rafters.

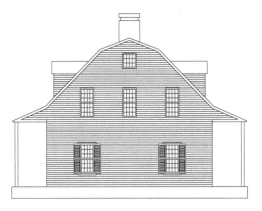

Dutch Colonial: a design that features a barnlike gambrel roof, over-hanging eaves, and a ground-level front porch. And, if it has more than one story, it will have dormers.

Eastlake house: a nineteenth-century-style house with plenty of distinctive three-dimensional ornamentation, an open front porch, and a turret.

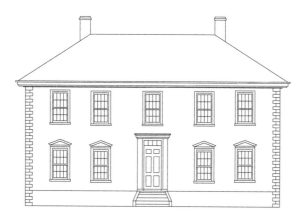

Georgian style: a large, English-style home, usually two to three stories, characterized by paneled front doors, double hung windows, and a simple exterior.

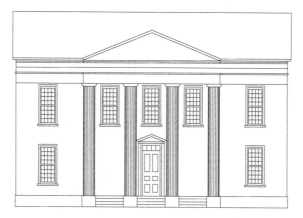

Greek Revival style: a nineteenth century style whose most prominent feature is a pillar-anchored pediment forming a portico in front of the house.

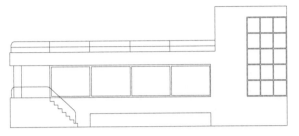

International style: a type of architecture characterized by very functional design, with buildings constructed of steel, reinforced concrete, and large walls of glass.

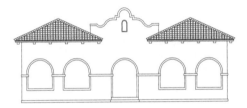

Mission house: a style of housing that resembles the old mission churches of Southern California. It has a tile roof, widely overhanging eaves, arch-shaped windows and doors, stucco walls, and a pyramid roof.

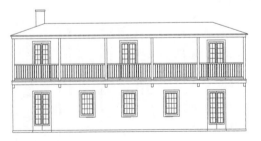

Monterey style: a two-story house with a balcony design adopted from the early California Spanish period; the railed balcony runs across the front of the house at the second-floor level. Roofs are low pitched or gabled, and exterior walls are constructed in stucco, brick, or wood.

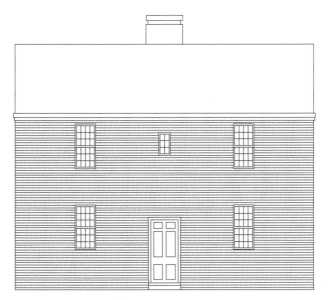

New England Colonial: an early American style home that has a symmetrical exterior with a central doorway; the living room, dining room, and the kitchen are downstairs; a central hall has a staircase leading to the bedrooms and baths on the second floor.

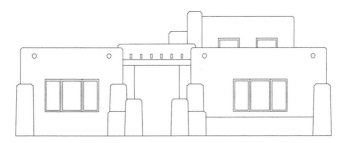

Pueblo style: a twentieth century style made of adobe, with a flat roof, stucco wall surfaces; usually earth-colored.

Queen Anne style: a Victorian-era style of home, it is multistory and features steeply pitched roofs, turrets, high chimneys, and decorative trim. This style usually has one-story porches.

ranch house: a long, one story style of home with all of the rooms on one floor. This style was originated in mid-twentieth century California.

saltbox style: an early American, 2 or 2-1/2-story style from the Colonial period. The house is rectangular with a steep gable roof that extends down to the second floor in the front, and to the first floor in the rear of the building.

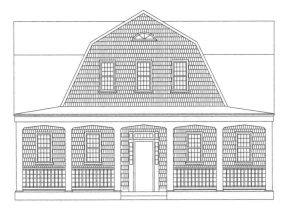

shingle style: a uniquely American style of architecture, shingle style houses can be relatively plain on the exterior, often with porches set into the façade. The houses are covered in wood shingles stained a single color, suggesting the rustic homes of the New England settlers.

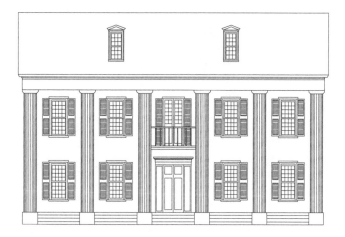

Southern Colonial: an early-American architectural style, elaborately built, symmetrical, with columns and a colonnade extending across the front of the house. This home typically has three floors and a gabled roof.

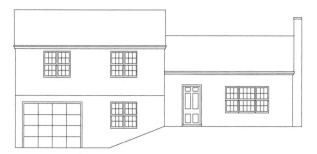

split-level home: a type of house with floor levels staggered so that each level is about one-half story above or below the adjacent one.

Swiss Chalet: a one and one-half or two-story house with a gable roof and decorative woodwork in the Swiss style.

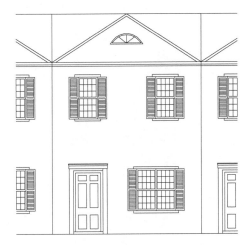

townhouse: a home, generally having two or more floors, often with a garage; it is shares walls with other similar units. Modern town-houses are typically found in condominiums and cooperatives, or as part of a planned unit development.

Tudor: an English-style house with the defining characteristics of half-timbering on the upper floors, steeply pitched cross gables, stone or patterned brick walls, multipaned windows, and a large chimney.

Victorian style: an architectural style of the mid-nineteenth century, characterized by front porches with spindlework detailing. Many Victorians are known for their heavy ornamentation and bold colors.

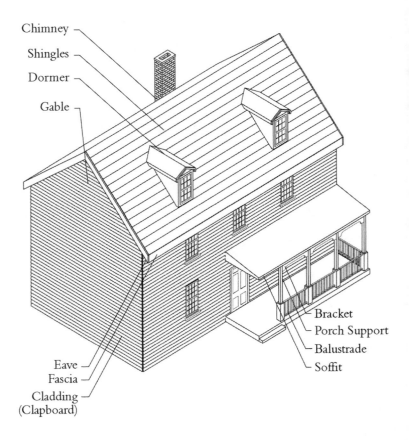

Chimney

Shingles

Dormer

Gable

Bracket

Porch Support

Balustrade

Soffit

Eave

Fascia

Cladding
(Clapboard)

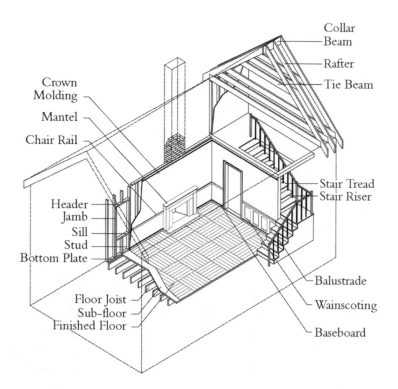

Collar Beam

Rafter

Tie Beam

Crown Molding

Mantel

Chair Rail

Stair Tread
Stair Riser

Header
Jamb
Sill
Stud
Bottom Plate

Balustrade

Wainscoting

Floor Joist
Sub-floor
Finished Floor

Baseboard

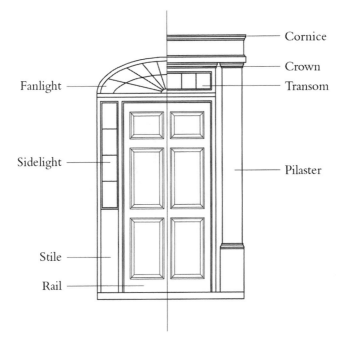

Cornice

Crown

Fanlight

Transom

Sidelight

Pilaster

Stile

Rail

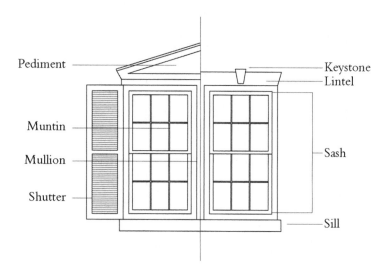

Pediment

Keystone
Lintel

Muntin

Mullion

Sash

Shutter

Sill

Illustrations by Maureen Slattery

APPENDIX C

MEASUREMENTS

UNITS OF MEASUREMENT
US standard units

Basic units are the foot (ft), pound (lb), and second (sec).

Linear:

12 inches (in)   . .= 1 foot (ft)
3 feet (ft) . . . . . .= 1 yard (yd)
5½ yards (yd)   . .= 1 pole
22 yards (yd) . . .= 1 chain (= 4 poles)
220 yards (yd) . .= 1 furlong (= 10 chains)
1,760 yards (yd) .= 1 mile (= 8 furlongs = 5,280 feet)

Square:

144 square inches (sq in) . = 1 square foot (sq ft)
9 square feet (sq ft). . . . . . = 1 square yard (sq yd)
30G square yards (sq yd). . = 1 perch
40 perches . . . . = 1 rood
4 roods . . . . = 1 acre (= 4,840 sq yd)
640 acres . . . . = 1 square mile (sq mile)

Volume:

1,728 cubic inches (cu in) = 1 cubic foot (cu ft)
27 cubic feet (cu ft) . . . . . = 1 cubic yard (cu yd)

Capacity:

4 gills . . . . . .= 1 pint (= 16 fluid ounces)
2 pints . . . . .= 1 quart (= 32 fl oz)
4 quarts . . . .= 1 gallon (= 128 fl oz)
2 gallons . . . .= 1 peck
8 gallons . . . .= 1 bushel (= 4 pecks)
8 bushels . . . .= 1 quarter (= 64 gallons)
1 barrel (oil) .= 42 gallons

LENGTH, AREA, AND VOLUME
Conversion factors
Standard to metric:

To convert		Multiply by
Length:		
inches	to millimeters	25.4
inches	to centimeters	2.54
inches	to meters	0.254
feet	to centimeters	30.48
feet	to meters	0.3048
yards	to meters	0.9144
miles	to kilometers	1.6093
Area:		
square inches	to square centimeters	6.4516
square feet	to square meters	0.0929
square yards	to square meters	0.8361
square miles	to square kilometers	2.5898
acres	to hectares	0.4047
acres	to square kilometers	0.00405
Volume:		
cubic inches	to cubic centimeters	16.3871
cubic feet	to cubic meters	0.0283
cubic yards	to cubic meters	0.7646
cubic miles	to cubic kilometers	4.1682
Liquid:		
fluid ounces	to milliliters	28.5
pints	to milliliters	473.00
pints	to liters	0.473
gallons	to liters	3.785
Length:		
millimeters	to inches	0.03937
centimeters	to inches	0.3937
meters	to inches	39.37
meters	to feet	3.2808

To convert		Multiply by
meters	to yards	1.0936
kilometers	to miles	0.6214

Area:

square centimeters	to square inches	0.1552
square meters	to square feet	10.7639
square meters	to square yards	1.196
square kilometers	to square miles	0.3860
square kilometers	to acres	247.10
hectares	to acres	2.4710

Volume:

cubic centimeters	to cubic inches	0.0610
cubic meters	to cubic feet	35.315
cubic meters	to cubic yards	1.308
cubic kilometers	to cubic miles	0.2399

Capacity:

milliliters	to fluid ounces	0.0352
milliliters	to pints	0.002114
liters	to pints	2.114
liters	to gallons	0.2642

OTHER UNIT CONVERSIONS

To convert			Multiply by
acres	to	hectares	x 0.405
	to	square chains	x 10
	to	square feet	x 43,560
	to	square kilometers	x 4.047×10^{-3}
	to	square yards	x 4840

GEOMETRICAL SHAPES AND FORMULAE

Figure	Dimensions	Area	Perimeter
circle	radius r	πr^2	$2\pi r$
rectangle	sides a and b	$a \times b$	$2(a+b)$
square	side a	a^2	$4a$
triangle	base a, height h (other sides b and c)	$\frac{1}{2}ah$	$a+b+c$

APPENDIX D
MORTGAGE INTEREST RATE FACTOR CHART

To calculate your monthly principal and interest payments for both fixed and adjustable loans, find the appropriate interest rate, then look at the column for the desired term of the loan (the interest rate factor). To calculate your principal and interest payment, multiply the interest rate factor by the total loan amount in 1,000's.

Factors per $1000

Interest Rate	Term 15 Years	Term 30 Years
3	6.91	4.22
3.125	6.97	4.28
3.25	7.03	4.35
3.375	7.09	4.42
3.5	7.15	4.49
3.625	7.21	4.56
3.75	7.27	4.63
3.875	7.34	4.70
4	7.40	4.77
4.125	7.46	4.85
4.25	7.52	4.92
4.375	7.59	4.99
4.5	7.65	5.07
4.625	7.71	5.14
4.75	7.78	5.22
4.875	7.84	5.29
5	7.91	5.37
5.125	7.97	5.44
5.25	8.04	5.52
5.375	8.10	5.60

Interest Rate	Term 15 Years	Term 30 Years
5.5	8.17	5.68
5.625	8.24	5.76
5.75	8.30	5.84
5.875	8.37	5.92
6	8.44	6.00
6.125	8.51	6.08
6.25	8.57	6.16
6.375	8.64	6.24
6.5	8.71	6.32
6.625	8.78	6.40
6.75	8.85	6.48
6.875	8.92	6.57
7	8.99	6.65
7.125	9.06	6.74
7.25	9.13	6.82
7.375	9.20	6.91
7.5	9.27	6.99
7.625	9.34	7.08
7.75	9.41	7.16
7.875	9.48	7.25
8	9.56	7.34
8.125	9.63	7.42
8.25	9.70	7.51
8.375	9.77	7.60
8.5	9.85	7.69
8.625	9.92	7.78
8.75	9.99	7.87
8.875	10.07	7.96

Interest Rate	Term 15 Years	Term 30 Years
9	10.14	8.05
9.125	10.22	8.14
9.25	10.29	8.23
9.375	10.37	8.32
9.5	10.44	8.41
9.625	10.52	8.50
9.75	10.59	8.59
9.875	10.67	8.68
10	10.75	8.77
10.125	10.82	8.87
10.25	10.90	8.96
10.375	10.98	9.05
10.5	11.05	9.15
10.625	11.13	9.24
10.75	11.21	9.33
10.875	11.29	9.43
11	11.36	9.52
11.125	11.44	9.62
11.25	11.52	9.71
11.375	11.60	9.81
11.5	11.68	9.90
11.625	11.76	10.00
11.75	11.84	10.09
11.875	11.92	10.19
12.00	12.00	10.29

APPENDIX E
HOME BUYER'S CHECKLIST

General Considerations

Type of House _____

Location _____

Lot size/acreage _____

Pre-Qualified Loan Amount _____

Price Range _____

New Construction or Resale _____

Condition of House (move-in/fixer-upper) _____

Tax Affordability _____

Important phone numbers

Real Estate Agent(s) _____

_____

_____

Mortgage broker/bank _____

_____

Attorney _____

_____

Home Insurance _____

_____

Home Feature/Interior	Important	Preferred	Not Important
Number of bedrooms			
Number of bathrooms			
Living room			
Family room			
Dining room			
New or updated kitchen			
Appliances included			
Condition of appliances			
Washer/dryer			
Type of heating system			
Central air conditioning			
Plumbing updated			
Electric updated			
Ample closet space			
Attic			
Finished basement			
Fireplace			
Mother-in-law room			
Mud room			
Upstairs laundry			
Cable/broadband ready			

Home Feature/Exterior	Important	Preferred	Not Important
Size of property			
Fenced-in yard			
Patio/Deck			
Garage (attached)			
Garage (detached)			
Landscaping			
Garden			
Swimming pool			

Location Requirements	Important	Preferred	Not Important
Neighborhood			
School system			
Proximity to work			
Proximity to church/ place of worship			
Proximity to shopping			
Proximity to parks			
Public transportation			
Crime rate			
Flood plain